The Perils and Prospects of
Southern Black Leadership

Gordon Blaine Hancock, 1952

The Perils and Prospects of
Southern Black Leadership:
Gordon Blaine Hancock, 1884–
1970 · *by* Raymond Gavins
Duke University Press
Durham, N.C. · 1977

© 1977, Duke University Press
L.C.C. card no. 76-44090
I.S.B.N. 0-8223-0381-7
Printed in the United
States of America

Contents

Preface

According to the late Nobel Peace Prize winner Ralph J. Bunche, in a memorandum for the Carnegie-Myrdal Study, black leadership consists of individual and collective contributions to black uplift, including black spokesmen, community organizations, protest movements, and race relations. A fundamental part of the Negro experience, it is an essential area of research and writing in Afro-American history. Careful inquiry into its dynamics richly illuminates our understanding of the programs, philosophies, and tactics black leaders advocated in the past and, to a great extent, promote in the present. For the New South, particularly during the age of segregation and its stormy aftermath, black leadership is one window through which historians can view black responses to oppression.

Traditionally, biographers of Negro leaders have singled out men and women of undisputed national reputation, a few heroes and heroines esteemed the most outstanding representatives of their race. Frederick Douglass, Booker T. Washington, W. E. B. Du Bois, Mary McLeod Bethune, and more recently, Martin Luther King, Jr. and Malcolm X, have been perennial subjects, while many lesser known members of the black vanguard remain undeservedly obscure. To achieve broader perspective, it is imperative that we pay more attention to the latter, who have waited perhaps too long in the shadows of the former—the Great Negro Leaders.

Among noted black educators, clergymen, editors, and organizers in the South between the death of Washington and the rise of King, for example, one finds a number of interesting prospects. Studies of such significant minor figures will provide new names and faces and close-up data for a larger portfolio, one which specialists and students alike might use with profit. By documenting what influential blacks of varying persuasions, at a given time and place, were feeling, thinking, saying, and doing, these accounts should permit a fuller interpretation of the Negro's struggle for equality. At the same time, they should make an important contribution to Afro-American intellectual history.

This book seeks to study the motivations, roles, strengths, and shortcomings of black leadership by focusing in depth upon one black leader, Gordon Blaine Hancock, who was probably the most articulate and popular champion of his race in Virginia for over a quarter century preceding the *Brown* decision of 1954. Contemporaries of Hancock, whether warm admirers or cold critics, acknowledged his conspicuous achievements as educator, minister, journalist, ideologue, and interracialist. But today only a handful of people have heard of Hancock, and little has been written about him.

A professor of sociology, economics, and religion at Virginia Union University in Richmond and pastor of that city's Moore Street Baptist Church, Hancock worked for improvement in race relations and contributed substantially to Negro thought and action. In forceful speeches before hundreds of black and white audiences nationally, and in his weekly press release that appeared in 114 Negro newspapers, he preached the dual gospel of interracial cooperation and black self-help. Much of what he said concerning prejudice, urbanization, economic status, and black solidarity foreshadowed our own times. During World War II, moreover, he convened the historic Durham Conference of Southern black leaders. Challenged by the conferees' forthright demands, white liberals abandoned the old Commission on Interracial Cooperation and joined them in founding the Southern Regional Council. Although dwarfed by and increasingly isolated from the civil rights avant-garde in his later years, Hancock retained a penchant for bread-and-butter issues and called for black-white detente.

Hancock's importance lies in his instructive pronouncements, some of which were original. Major emphasis is therefore given to his racial ideology. Yet, by tracing his intellectual odyssey in Virginia and the South, it is possible to present the man, brilliant, sensitive, introspective, and dignified, though occasionally pompous and opportunistic. An effort is made to disclose how national and regional currents and black and white associates affected Hancock, and conversely, to assess his influence on them. To look through his eyes and to see the times as he did sheds much light upon the kaleidoscopic interactions of blacks with the ubiquitous color problem: the racial milieu of late nineteenth- and early twentieth-century South Carolina, Richmond Negroes in the 1920's, Negro responses to the Great Depression and New Deal, Southern white liberals and the Negro during World War II, and the perils of desegregation since 1954. Hancock lived through those com-
viii

plex events and tumultuous decades, and he mirrored the fears, dilemmas, and hopes of his generation.

The central problem confronting Hancock's generation was how to end segregation and achieve integration without sacrificing black identity or abandoning ideals of self-help and racial solidarity. Launching a relentless if moderate assault on bigotry and caste, braving the criticisms of Northern blacks, seeking support from white liberals, men like Hancock moved within an orbit of conflicting and changing expectations. With the coming of *Brown*, as younger and more militant voices called for direct action and mass demonstrations, they lost both visibility and status, overshadowed by the changes that they had helped to create. Gordon Blaine Hancock, as a man and as a type of black leader, symbolized the fate of this older leadership group.

Many people helped to bring the present study to fruition, but it is not possible to mention all of them here. Professors Paul M. Gaston, of the University of Virginia, and Willie L. Rose, now of Johns Hopkins University, guided it in its infancy. As a graduate student I benefited immensely from their encouragement and wisdom. For moral and spiritual support I am grateful to Hancock's widow, Marie D. Hancock. Also, special thanks are due to all the persons listed in the bibliography under interviews, letters responding to inquiries, and individual evaluation forms. Invaluable assistance came from the research director of the Southern Regional Council and the library staffs of Atlanta University, Benedict College, Columbia University, Duke University, University of North Carolina, University of Virginia, Virginia State College, and Virginia Union University.

Professors James E. Blackwell and John W. Blassingame read the entire manuscript and offered insightful criticism, as did Mary F. Berry, John Hope Franklin, and August Meier. Two of my colleagues in the Duke history department, John W. Cell and Sydney Nathans, went over various chapters and corrected factual errors. Robert F. Durden, our chairman, worked with me long hours on the index at a time when I was at my lowest ebb, while Richard L. Watson, a most sympathetic coworker, cheered me on. I wish to express special appreciation to Dorothy Sapp for typing the manuscript, and to Vivian Jackson and Grace Guyer for typing the index.

The students who took American and Afro-American history under me challenged and crystallized my thinking; I trust they will not be too disappointed with the results. Fellowships from the National Endowment for the Humanities and the Whitney M. Young, Jr., Memorial Foundation provided me with a year's leave of absence to complete the writing of this work, and I am proud to acknowledge their grants. The Duke University Research Council, upon the recommendation of outside readers, awarded me a publication subsidy. I gladly thank the Council for its backing, as well as Ashbel G. Brice, John Menapace, Barbara Williams, and Reynolds Smith of Duke University Press for being uniformly cordial and helpful.

Although the lengthy hours of research and writing were mine to bear, my wife, Kathryne, and children, Marva and Raymond, were painfully aware of my absence. To them, for their forbearance, tolerance, and endurance, I wish to dedicate this book.

Hillsborough, North Carolina
May, 1977

The Perils and Prospects of
Southern Black Leadership

I. Formative Years and After

People who talked with Hancock during the 1960's found him to be a nostalgic old man. Like the proverbial African griot, he never tired of recounting past Negro strivings in the South, almost as though he had withdrawn to an earlier era. Hancock's sense of history, of roots, embraced not only his childhood, development and training, but frequently revealed an assertive, altruistic personality. It is in the context of those recollections, together with other evidence and parallel testimony, that one finds the sources of his subsequent thought.

Although prejudice and discrimination in rural South Carolina affected Hancock, the black community, particularly growing up in a family which idealized education and Christian service, made lasting impressions on him. Formal study at Benedict, work as a preacher and a principal, increasing personal dissatisfaction, and the broadening social and intellectual influence of Colgate and Harvard were also very important in the shaping of his racial philosophy.

An early awareness of black deprivation and a strong sense of racial responsibility motivated Gordon Blaine Hancock to become a champion of the Negro's cause. Born June 23, 1884, in Ninety-Six township, Greenwood County, South Carolina,[1] he grew up in an era when the Palmetto State maintained "the subordination of the Negro by a caste system based on race under which black and white seldom came into personal contact except in the relationship of employer and laborer."[2] A visitor to Ninety-Six in Gordon's boyhood days would

1. G. James Fleming and Christian E. Burckel, eds., *Who's Who in Colored America* (Yonkers-on-Hudson, N. Y.: Christian E. Burckel and Associates, 1950), pp. 236–237; U. S., Post Office, Postal Route Map of South Carolina, September 1, 1944. Ninety-Six commonly appeared in contemporary documents as 96. Originally in Abbeville County, it later became a part of Greenwood County, which was organized from sections of Abbeville and Edgefield Counties in 1897. See U.S., Bureau of the Census, *Twelfth Census of the United States: 1900. Population*, I (Washington, D. C.: United States Census Office, 1901), 353.

2. George B. Tindall, *South Carolina Negroes 1877–1900* (Baton Rouge: Louisiana State University Press, 1952), p. 302. C. Vann Woodward, *The Strange Career of Jim Crow* (New York: Oxford University Press, 1955), demonstrates how the system worked.

have found no signs of a New South trend toward industrial and commercial development. The worn-out post office and train stop were its most important contacts with the outside world, and served as favorite gathering places for local cronies. The small grocery store of William Pressley and Company, "the first and only colored enterprise of the kind ever started in 96," lent some dignity to the otherwise demoralized Negro quarters. Besides a few churches and schools, all strictly segregated, there were no other places of public assembly, recreation, or culture. A moderate contrast to Greenwood, the county seat about fourteen miles west, which had mills, stores and a newspaper, the town remained rural to the core, backward, and a bastion of white supremacy.[3]

The economic status of blacks in Ninety-Six and its environs was deplorable. A cotton and subsistence farm area, it could have easily been a microcosm of the Old South. In 1900 it had 2,395 residents, of whom 1,545, or 65 per cent, were Negroes. Greenwood County, reporting a comparable ratio, had a population of 28,343, of whom 18,906, or 66.7 per cent, were Negroes.[4] The county's total population rose to 34,225 in 1910, including 12,923 whites and 21,302 Negroes, with Negroes comprising 62.2 per cent of the population. Although blacks far outnumbered whites, the whites owned over 95 per cent of the 288,949 acres of farm land in 1910. Of the 2,932 Negro farmers in 1910, only 112 owned their farms free of debt. There were 95 who operated mortgaged farms, 68 part owners, 2,568 tenants, and 89 not specifically designated. A similar pattern prevailed in Negro home ownership. Negroes had 4,438 farm and other homes in 1910, 439 debt free, 192 mortgaged, 3,609 rented, and 198 unclassified.[5] Outside of farming or sharecropping most black men worked as wage

3. "Autobiographical Reflections," n.d., Gordon Blaine Hancock Papers, Richmond, Virginia, hereinafter cited as "Reflections"; "Biographical Sketch of Reverend Robert Wiley Hancock, 1862–1902," Greensboro, North Carolina, in the possession of Mrs. Mae Hancock Garner, a half-sister of Gordon B. Hancock and the only surviving sibling; interview with Gordon B. Hancock, September 25, 1968, Richmond, Virginia.

4. *Twelfth Census of the United States: 1900*, I, 350.

5. U.S., Bureau of the Census, *Thirteenth Census of the United States: 1910. Agriculture*, VII (Washington, D. C.: Government Printing Office, 1913), 510–514.

hands, while black women were primarily domestics.[6] Clearly, they lived within the shadow of the plantation.

Besides economic captivity, blacks suffered political and social isolation as well. After 1877 they strove to overcome the heritage of slavery and protect their gains, particularly the rights of suffrage and officeholding, but reactionary elements thwarted the effort and made white domination absolute. Indeed, if fraud and chicanery failed, intimidation and violence were used to control blacks. Proscriptions were rampant. An act of 1879 prohibited interracial marriage, while the Eight Ballot Box Law of 1882 neutralized the black vote by, in effect, imposing a literacy test. Other statutes in 1889 repealed the civil rights and public accommodations laws enacted during Radical Reconstruction and virtually legalized black economic serfdom. In 1890, when Ben Tillman captured the governorship with strident appeals to agrarian discontent and Negrophobia, the movement to eliminate Negroes from South Carolina politics reached flood tide. The Tillmanite constitutional convention of 1895, over the futile protest of six lone Negro delegates, disfranchised blacks and paved the way for rigid segregation. Greenwood County, like the other forty-three counties where blacks constituted a numerical majority, became a crucible of racial conflict and fear.[7]

Denied equal citizenship and excluded from politics, blacks turned to their own churches, schools, lodges, burial and secret societies for a meaningful existence. Having antecedents in Africanisms, which scholars have found in even greater abundance among Sea Island blacks,[8] these institutions nurtured pride and solidarity. Baptists and African Methodists, schoolmarms and masters, the Independent

---

6. U.S., Bureau of the Census, *Negro Population in the United States 1790–1915* (Washington, D.C.: Government Printing Office, 1918), p. 746; Benjamin E. Mays, *Born to Rebel: An Autobiography* (New York: Charles Scribner's Sons, 1971), pp. 1–21.

7. I. A. Newby, *Black Carolinians: A History of Blacks in South Carolina from 1895 to 1968* (Columbia: University of South Carolina Press, 1973), pp. 31–37; Tindall, *South Carolina Negroes 1877–1900*, pp. 73–91.

8. See Mason Crum, *Gullah: Negro Life in the Carolina Sea Islands* (Durham: Duke University Press, 1940); Willie Lee Rose, *Rehearsal for Reconstruction: The Port Royal Experiment* (Indianapolis: Bobbs-Merrill, 1964); and Okon E. Uya, *From Slavery to Public Service: Robert Smalls, 1839–1915* (New York: Oxford University Press, 1971).

Order of Odd Fellows, the Colored Knights of Pythias, the Future Progress Society, and the Brothers and Sisters of Charity, among others, were integral parts of this infrastructure. Their projects in mutual aid, singing bees, public orations, picnics, banquets, excursions, parades and ceremonies involved every stratum within this small Negro world. Despite poverty, black families were generally stable. A network of supportive relationships, knotted in the churches and fraternal clubs, kept desertions, illegitimacy, and crime low. Unlike the cities of Charleston and Columbia, the county did not have a burgeoning black intellectual and professional elite. Leadership usually came from a handful of ministers and teachers, at times poorly trained, who rejected class distinctions and identified with the masses.[9]

If blacks knew their place, they did not always stay in it. Nor did they accept injustice without complaint. Race relations were invariably paternalistic and strained by an endemic violence. According to Tuskegee Institute, for years a national clearinghouse on Negro statistics, 142 black Carolinians died at the hands of lynch mobs between 1882 and 1920.[10] The most diabolical local lynchings occurred in the 1890's. For example, an undetermined number of blacks died in the infamous Phoenix Riot of November 8–11, 1898, resulting from a dispute between Democrats and Republicans over black voting rights. For several days an armed white mob, allegedly searching for "niggers" who had signed an affidavit to vote and murdered a white man, moved through black neighborhoods, butchering all who resisted. One group of blacks with guns ambushed the whites, seriously wounding several of the mobsters, but they soon fled. The terror subsided when eleven black men were captured and taken to the grounds of Rehoboth Church in Phoenix, near Ninety-Six, for "trial." Forced to make "confessions," four of the eleven were killed and the others permitted to escape. The whites brought another Negro to the scene the next day and riddled his body with bullets, and the bloodshed finally ended. There were rumors that over thirty-five Negroes lost their lives. However, because of insufficient and conflicting reports

9. Interview with Hancock, September 25, 1968; Mays, *Born to Rebel*, pp. 22–34; Tindall, *South Carolina Negroes 1877–1900*. pp. 282–290.
10. Newby, *Black Carolinians*, p. 60.

and the wide area over which the mob ranged, no one ever knew the precise number of victims.[11] But the fear born of this ordeal smothered the open political aspirations of the black community.

This repressive, closed society had a powerful shaping influence on Hancock. As he recalled in an interview, at least three childhood incidents sparked his consciousness of color—hearing white ruffians in a country store voice "their low opinion of niggers," having his parents rebuke him for playing with a white boy, and trudging "down the same dusty road" with white children to a separate school.[12] He was fourteen years old when the Phoenix Riot broke out; later he noted in an autobiographical sketch that "it caused great travail and trembling among the Negroes." One black man was "shot to death on the main road, and no Negro in Ninety-Six went to town for weeks." He once told his wife, "Negroes were taken into the woods and chained to logs, the white men beat them, and many died."[13] Benjamin E. Mays, former president of Morehouse College in Atlanta, at the time lived in Epworth, ten miles from Ninety-Six. He described the Phoenix episode as his earliest memory, recollecting that a crowd of white men carrying rifles "cursed my father, drew their guns and . . . made him take off his hat and bow down to them several times."[14] For Hancock and Mays, then two precocious youths, the shock of mob violence had a lasting effect. Their eloquent appeals for nonviolence more than a generation later, no doubt, stemmed from that fateful November in 1898.

Close family ties, a protective medium against the hostile environment, gave Hancock positive direction. Anna Mark, his mother, came up from slavery. Born in 1863, one of twelve children, she attended freedmen's schools after the Civil War and at age sixteen, encouraged by her Yankee mentor, passed the county examination to become "the first colored teacher in Ninety-Six." A personable, attractive woman, she married Robert Wiley Hancock in 1881 and bore him two

11. Tindall, *South Carolina Negroes 1877–1900*, pp. 256–259; Columbia *State*, November 9, 1898; Charleston *News and Courier*, November 11, 12, 28, 1898.

12. Reported in Richard Bardolph, *The Negro Vanguard* (New York: Vintage Books, 1959), p. 171.

13. Interview with Mrs. Marie D. Hancock, August 16, 1973, Richmond, Virginia.

14. Mays, *Born to Rebel*, p. 1.

children, Edith and Gordon. She worked in the colored school, "was active in Bethlehem Baptist Church at 96, and helped out in the fields." At the age of twenty-three in 1886 she died suddenly, probably from hypertension. Only two when this happened, Gordon never really knew his mother. Yet, under the careful tutelage of a loving father, he came to know her will to achieve and her "great desire to help her people."[15]

With Anna gone, Robert Wiley Hancock became the paramount influence on his son. The elder Hancock was born September 10, 1862, in nearby Abbeville County. His slave "mother died when he was quite young," and his father, believed to be a white man, did not claim him. His maternal grandmother, Annie, "cared for him . . . the best she could." He attended school in Jamaica Plains, Massachusetts, where she lived. After graduating in 1876, he worked in Pressley's store in Ninety-Six and took a night course in bookkeeping "under the Honorable W. J. Brodie of Charleston who . . . was the public teacher at 96." He went to Alabama in January 1880, "having secured a job weighing ore in the woodstock furnace in Anniston." He returned within nine months, began farming, married, and started a family. Bethlehem Baptist of Ninety-Six licensed and ordained him for the ministry, but Anna's sudden death made his itinerary quite lonesome.

Between 1888 and 1901 the Reverend Robert Hancock held pastorates in Mills Way, Flint Hill, Phoenix, Parksville, Laurens, and Newberry. Because he recognized "the great need for education and charity among his entire people," schools and missionary circles were established in all of his churches. In 1890, determined to better himself, he attended Benedict College at Columbia, which enhanced his reputation as a preacher.[16] He also wed his second wife, Georgia Anna Scott, the daughter of a sharecropper. A fine stepmother to Edith and Gordon, she bore him four girls and two boys.[17] In 1902 Robert Wiley Hancock succumbed to a heart attack, "stricken in his

15. "Reflections."

16. "Biographical Sketch of Reverend Robert Wiley Hancock, 1862–1902."

17. Mae, Eloise, Ruth, Sloan, and Richard Carroll. Interview with Mrs. Mae Hancock Garner, June 18, 1974, Greensboro, North Carolina.

pulpit." For the family, bereaved and distressed, this was an irreparable loss. Only the help of relatives kept them from becoming destitute. Gordon moved into the home of a great uncle. Some of the children went to their half-sister Edith, then Mrs. Ezra Gilchrist, while Georgia and the others were cared for by her father. Intermittently ill, Georgia died in 1906. "She was unlearned," Hancock declared of her in 1934, "but she taught me in the ways of the Master."[18]

In spite of the oppressive milieu, Gordon exemplified vitality, curiosity, and a sense of purpose. Together with his brothers and sisters, he chopped wood for the fire and weeds from the field and went to a one-room, weather-beaten schoolhouse. The teachers told him that faith in God, knowledge, and self-reliance were prerequisites for life, lessons he never forgot. Among the Reverend Mr. Hancock's books on history and theology, he commented, "I learned to read unusually well." Under the instruction of S. A. Neeley of Ninety-Six he delved into the classics and developed the flair for metaphoric expression which would permeate his oratory and journalistic writing. Almost every Sunday morning, moreover, he heard his father preach bold sermons on Christ, thrift, and racial advance.[19] These values, as well as his father's role in religious and educational affairs, made indelible impressions on him. From them he derived courage, pride, idealism, and a tenacious faith. This rich spiritual heritage, deepened by tragedy and poverty, found outlet in his efforts to solve race problems.

After scoring a high mark on the test for prospective teachers in 1902, Gordon earned a first-class certificate and began teaching. For two years in China Grove and Edgefield, twelve and five miles from home respectively, he encountered the grim realities of dilapidated buildings, a two-month term, too few books, inadequate instruction, indolence, underpaid personnel, and general invisibility. To counteract these invidious conditions, he urged blacks to petition the county and consolidate their limited financial resources. At China Grove he rallied the people behind a statement to the county board, raised money, and had the term extended to five months, no ordinary

18. Hancock to Mrs. Francis J. Torrance, July 27, 1934, Hancock Papers.
19. "Reflections."

feat in a decade when black attendance averaged sixty days per year.[20]

Nowhere did Hancock confront racial discrimination more consistently than in Negro schools, and he felt that much more could be done to correct abuses. Throughout the Southern states appropriations for black pupils and teachers were uniformly low. In 1900, South Carolina's expenditures amounted to $1.30 per black pupil and $5.55 for each white one, even though well over half the children in public schools were black. The $202,171 spent on Negro education that year represented a meager 22 per cent of the total fund. The black teacher's annual salary was $80.68, approximately 46 per cent of what his white counterpart received. Not a single four-year high school for Negroes existed, and the South Carolina Department of Education labeled the more than nineteen hundred Negro schools as third-class institutions, the lowest possible rating. There were not twenty-five upper-level students in the combined enrollments of Columbia's Benedict College and Orangeburg's Claflin University, the only places where blacks came close to having bona fide college courses. Unhappily, 52.8 per cent of South Carolina's 782,321 blacks ten years old and over were illiterate, and the educated Negro remained a rare breed.[21] Surrounded everywhere by such willful neglect, Hancock was inevitably moved "to seek training to help Negro people." [22]

In 1904 he matriculated at Benedict College, founded during Reconstruction by the American Baptist Home Mission Society and the philanthropy of Bathsheba Benedict of Providence, Rhode Island, and incorporated under South Carolina law in 1894. The Home Mission Society, six white and three black trustees, a white president, and a largely white staff governed its operations. By 1895 it had eleven faculty members, all churchgoers in good standing, a 20-acre campus, 4 attractive buildings, and a library which housed 2,300 books and 1,000 pamphlets. Twenty years later there were 12 blacks among 30 teachers, and its registration of 507 included 254 elemen-

20. "Reflections."

21. See Louis R. Harlan, *Separate and Unequal: Public School Campaigns and Racism in the Southern Seaboard States 1901–1915* (New York: Atheneum, 1968), pp. 170–209, 248–269; Newby, *Black Carolinians*, pp. 85–86, 88–89, 106–107.

22. "Reflections."

tary, 205 secondary, 45 college, and 3 divinity students. The curriculum combined the fundamentals of reading, writing, and arithmetic with the classics, history, science, and handicrafts. Each student worked an hour each day for the school in order to learn "that an education puts no man or woman above work," participated in daily devotional exercises, and cultivated "habits of virtue, morality and godliness, and the highest type of Christian manhood and womanhood."[23] Failure to live up to these requirements resulted in certain expulsion.

Twenty years old and quite serious, Hancock readily adjusted to the new setting, deporting himself much like a black puritan in the devout academic climate. Working to pay his keep, he studied three years in the academy and went on to complete his A.B. in 1911 and B.D. in 1912 *summa cum laude*, excelling in philosophy, history, rhetoric, and religion. "The struggle to get an education was the best part of my education," he stated reminiscently in 1959. "I had the good fortune to earn every dollar of it."[24]

The capital city, located seventy-five miles east of Ninety-Six, made its impact on Hancock too. The state's second most populous urban area, Columbia had 11,250 white and 9,858 black inhabitants in 1900,[25] and a harsh color line. When the city council adopted an ordinance requiring Jim Crow seating on passenger cars in 1903, Negroes retaliated with a boycott. But the enthusiasm for it soon dissipated and street cars and trains remained segregated. Black life in Columbia alternately depressed and inspired Hancock. The Negro masses lived in overcrowded and unsanitary slums where petty thieves, confidence men, prostitutes, bootleggers, and other charlatans preyed upon the innocent. To find Negroes living in squalor and apathy on such a large scale disturbed Hancock, as did the fact that neither whites nor respectable blacks cared. A farm boy himself, he naturally assumed that opportunities for land ownership, cohesive families, and good health

23. Benedict College, *Catalogue and Announcements 1895–96*, pp. 8–10, 15–17; Newby, *Black Carolinians*, pp. 112–114.

24. Quoted in Bardolph, *The Negro Vanguard*, p. 172. Mrs. Mae Hancock Garner doubted that he did everything himself, however, remembering that "Ezra Gilchrist, Edith's husband, right many times borrowed on his crop to send 'GB' book money." Interview, June 18, 1974.

25. *Twelfth Census of the United States: 1900*, I, 354, 680.

among rural Negroes, by contrast, made them better off. Even though these somewhat romantic agrarian notions posed a conflict with his own attachment to the city, he would someday popularize them under the caption of "Back to the Farm." On the bright side, Hancock saw that black Columbians were enterprising. In 1905, they operated 23 of the 29 barber shops, 50 of 200 grocery stores, and 13 of 21 shoemaking firms. There were 22 Negro eating houses, 2 newspapers, and myriad other businesses, artisans and professionals, including a coterie of teachers, ministers, physicians, lawyers, and funeral directors.[26] This small though significant middle class embodied the race's highest potential, in Hancock's view; its chief mission, he felt, was to help Negroes in the streets. He never departed from this position.

As a race-conscious college student, Hancock observed Negro leaders and occasionally read their works. He found the Reverend Richard Carroll of Columbia an altogether remarkable man. A former slave from Barnwell County and graduate of Benedict College and Shaw University in Raleigh, North Carolina, Carroll was then the most peripatetic advocate of self-help in the state. An indefatigable organizer of race conferences, Carroll admired Booker T. Washington and twice had him to speak in Columbia. Addressing a conclave in 1907, Washington encouraged blacks to become diligent workers and, above all, save their money. Greatly impressed, young Hancock never forgot the speech on efficiency and thrift or the Tuskegeean's commanding presence. Besides Washington's autobiography, moreover, Hancock read *The Aftermath of Slavery*, by William A. Sinclair. Born a slave in 1858 at Georgetown, Sinclair had attended South Carolina College and received degrees from Andover Theological Seminary and Meharry Medical College. The financial secretary of Howard University from 1888 to 1903, he participated in Du Bois' Niagara Movement, helped to launch the NAACP in 1909, and became a leading anti-Bookerite. Sinclair's history broke with standard white interpretations, as he condemned slavery and the hypocrisy of

26. Newby, *Black Carolinians*, pp. 134, 138, 159; *Columbia City Directory 1904–1905*, pp. 411–511; W. E. B. Du Bois, ed., *The Negro in Business*, Atlanta University Publications No. 4 (Atlanta: Atlanta University Press, 1899), pp. 27, 34–35; Asa H. Gordon, *Sketches of Negro Life and History in South Carolina* (Orangeburg, S.C.: Privately printed, 1929), pp. 144–145.

Reconstruction and strongly denounced Negro disfranchisement. "Never among any civilized people has there existed a condition wherein oppression was so heartless and widespread," he wrote of Southern racism in 1905. "[Never were] withering wrongs so multiplied; and human life so cheap."[27] This perspective increased Hancock's awareness of oppression in ways which Carroll's and Washington's did not.

Ordained for the ministry in 1911, Hancock became pastor of Bethlehem Baptist Church in Newberry, not far from Columbia.[28] The same year he married Florence Marie Dickson, a well-to-do young woman whom he met at Benedict. Not much can be said of the church, except it had a membership of "over 1,200 souls" and that gospel preaching was its central attraction. Hancock stayed only a year, but he keynoted the annual meeting of the State Baptist Convention and won considerable recognition for his forceful delivery. Born July 31, 1893, Florence Marie Dickson grew up in Society Hill township, Darlington County. Joseph Samuel Dickson, Sr., her mulatto father, ran a mercantile business, owned large tracts of farm land, and employed more than fifty black and white tenants. Frequently regarded as a "white man trying to be colored," he gave his schoolteacher wife, seven daughters, and six sons a comfortable life. The Dicksons were the sole Negro family living in Society Hill proper, customarily a haven for well-to-do whites. The children were privately tutored by Mrs. Lizzie Saunders, a refined Negro lady who had graduated from a Northern college. Florence Marie attended Browning Home, an exclusive elementary school for colored girls in Cam-

27. Interview with Hancock, October 21, 1968; Newby, *Black Carolinians*, pp. 99–101, 163, 169–184; Columbia *State*, January 25, 1907, March 16, 1909; William A. Sinclair, *The Aftermath of Slavery: A Study of the Condition and Environment of the American Negro* (Boston: Small, Maynard and Co., 1905), pp. 106–107.

28. Interview with Hancock, November 15, 1968; "Reflections." By going into the ministry, Hancock followed a well established practice. Of the 1,312 Negro college graduates about whom Du Bois gathered information in 1900, 53 per cent were teachers and 17 per cent were preachers. He did not give the percentage for those who combined the two professions. See W. E. B. Du Bois, ed., *The College-Bred Negro*, Atlanta University Publications No. 5 (Atlanta: Atlanta University Press, 1900), pp. 16–17. Also, see Ralph J. Bunche, "A Brief and Tentative Analysis of Negro Leadership" (September 1940), p. 16, in the Carnegie-Myrdal Study of the Negro in America, Duke University Library, Durham, North Carolina.

den, before entering the academy of the State College for Negroes in Orangeburg. She transferred to Benedict in 1908, received a diploma in 1910, and taught home economics. Sheltered from hardship, well educated, she was undoubtedly ambitious, but she also evidenced sympathy for the downtrodden and a passion for thrift, qualities which endeared her to Gordon Hancock for fifty-nine years.[29]

In 1912 the Oconee Baptist Association's board of trustees named Hancock principal at Seneca Institute, a private coeducational boarding school in Seneca, South Carolina, one of several such institutions founded to provide high school instruction for Negroes.[30] The Institute had six faculty members, mostly Benedict graduates, offered pre-college classical courses, fielded athletic teams, paraded a brass band, and faced perennial budgetary problems. Thomas Jesse Jones, a white Federal Office of Education investigator who visited Seneca in 1914, said it was "a school of elementary and secondary grade doing fairly good work . . . , maintained almost entirely on the income from board and tuition . . . [and] owned by a Baptist Association too small to support it." There were 127 students.[31] Hancock, anxious to upgrade it, quickly made the institution solvent through extensive fund raising. By 1916 he had solicited enough money to construct Dunbar Hall, a three-story classroom and dining facility which cost $20,000. During the remainder of his tenure, he accelerated the curriculum to include advanced electives in science, mathematics, civilization, elocution, and social ethics. Regular Sunday vesper services were supplemented with required evening study

29. Interview with Mrs. Hancock, August 16, 1973. "Funeral services for J. S. Dickson, Sr., 80, successful merchant and farmer for the past fifty-five years and father of thirteen children, some of whom are leading figures in this and other states, were held at Union Baptist Church [in Society Hill] last week, the Rev. S. B. Thompson, pastor, officiating." Unidentified newspaper clipping, May 10, 1941, Hancock Papers.

30. Others included Schofield Normal, Aiken; Voorhees Industrial, Denmark; Penn Normal, St. Helena Island; Avery Institute, Charleston; Brainerd Institute, Chester; Brewer Normal, Greenwood, and Mather Academy, Camden. U.S., Bureau of Education, *Negro Education: A Study of the Private and Higher Schools for Colored People in the United States*, Bulletin 1916, No. 39, II (Washington, D. C.: Government Printing Office, 1917), pp. 471–526; Newby, *Black Carolinians*, pp. 103–106.

31. U.S., Bureau of Education, *Negro Education: A Study of the Private and Higher Schools for Colored People in the United States*, II, p. 499. Interestingly, Jones recommended "that more emphasis be placed on industrial work for both boys and girls."

hours, a merit system, and periodic exhortation. In 1918 there were three hundred pupils, including one hundred boarders, with the teachers receiving an annual salary of $1,620.[32]

At Seneca, Hancock stressed black pride, self-help, and Christian character, themes in his later sermons and hallmarks in the age of accommodation. Ideologically, however, he eluded simple categorization. Overshadowed by the Washington-Du Bois schism of the period, he pragmatically avoided taking a hard line on either. Negroes, he agreed, should learn vocational skills, acquire property, and cultivate white good will, but not at the expense of losing their manhood. Still, he believed that the burden of Negro uplift rested heavily on the shoulders of highly educated leaders, a Talented Tenth. This synthesis came from his exposure to the climate of contemporary Negro thought. He never met Washington but treasured *Up From Slavery* and heard the Tuskegeean speak. Although he did not meet Du Bois until 1928, he knew about the famous critique "Of Mr. Booker T. Washington and Others," the Niagara Movement, and the NAACP. Hancock also read Du Bois' Atlanta University Publications No. 14, a scientific investigation of Negro social betterment, which stimulated his initial interest in studying sociology.[33]

Seneca served as a proving ground where Hancock formed guiding assumptions and culminated the search for a career. Besides taking care of daily operations, he made the Institute a model of racial advancement. In visiting the local white schools and in asking white merchants to contribute to Seneca Institute, often without success, he made his first wavering steps toward interracial cooperation. He concluded that blacks, while remaining open to sympathetic white support, must ultimately sustain their own institutions. He also proposed that "color prejudice" was the fundamental reason for "the Negro's proscribed and disadvantaged status," a point on which most articulate blacks agreed. As a statistician for the National Baptist Convention

32. *Reference List of Southern Colored Schools*, Trustees of the John F. Slater Fund Occasional Papers No. 20, 1918, p. 8.
33. Interview with Hancock, October 21, 1968. Blacks in Columbia, for example, organized South Carolina's first chapter of the NAACP in 1916. W. E. B. Du Bois, ed., *Efforts for Social Betterment among Negro Americans*, Atlanta University Publications No. 14 (Atlanta: Atlanta University Press, 1910), was the book which he read.

from 1914 to 1917 he was the first person to discover that Booker T. Washington had once been a licensed Baptist preacher. Furthermore, he developed keen insight into the economic potential of the Negro church, which he urged blacks to use.[34]

In 1914, on a tour financed by the National Baptist Convention, Hancock traveled to England, Ireland, Scotland, Wales, France, Italy, and Switzerland. There, far from the provincialism of South Carolina, he saw a different world. He saw Europe torn by nationalist strife, fear-ridden, and nearing the brink of war. Simultaneously inspired and disturbed, Hancock returned to Seneca more determined than ever, he said, "to further the emancipation of my stricken race." Yet as World War I engulfed Europe and American intervention appeared inevitable, he decided to leave Seneca Institute and South Carolina for what turned out to be a challenging interim of study and ideological formulation.

Gradually, worsening race relations, feelings of isolation, pressure from Marie, and his own desire for greater security and recognition impelled Hancock to seek higher ground. Sometime in the winter of 1917, soon after he preached in a country church near Greenville urging blacks to band together and help themselves, rumor spread that he was out to turn "niggers against white folks." When he learned that Ku Klux Klansmen were planning to discipline him, he declined all invitations to speak in the Greenville area. Though dauntless in faith, he refused to be impractical about life and limb. As wartime tensions caused more mob violence in the state, and with visions of Phoenix on his mind, Hancock continued the now unspectacular routine of running Seneca Institute. Despite the execution of thirteen black soldiers accused of starting the Houston riot of September 1917 and resistance to black demands throughout the nation, currents of hope were moving within the black world. Restless, separated from the mainstream of black activity, Hancock wanted to flow with those currents, to play a larger role. Marie D. Hancock, who never adjusted well to Seneca, provided the clincher when she persuaded her husband to relocate, hopefully in a place where he could exercise the full range of his talents. So, in consultation with Marie and two white professors at Bene-

34. "Reflections"; interview with Hancock, October 21, 1968.

dict, both Colgate men, Hancock applied for admission at Colgate University in Hamilton, New York, pursuing the day when he would do an even greater work for his people.[35]

Despite his two degrees from Benedict, Hancock entered Colgate in 1918 as a junior. He had to satisfy senior requirements in the college before going into the seminary. Thirty-four and disciplined, he performed exceptionally well, earning another A.B. in 1919 and a B.D. in 1920. Undergraduate humanities and social science added little to his substantive knowledge, except the confidence that he could compete with white students. As a seminarian he held a Smith Scholarship, the most coveted academic award, became class vice-president, and delivered the valedictory at graduation exercises. Liberal, humanistic, and practical divinity studies enlarged his perspective on the role of organized religion in human situations, and he wrote his B.D. thesis on "Christian Education and the Negro Problem." Christianity, in his view, was the custodian of society, ministering to man's spiritual and temporal needs, especially the need to be free. Theologically, this interpretation touched base with the "social gospel" of the black church which he had witnessed in his father's ministry, confirmed by becoming a minister himself, and preached at Bethlehem Baptist at Newberry. The two traditions would become syncretized in Hancock's later efforts to involve the Southern clergy in race relations.[36]

For Hancock the real meaning of Colgate lay in its effects on his racial attitudes. White men encouraged him to apply, a white family rented him an apartment, and Mrs. Hancock, using her sewing skills, earned subsistence income from the wives of the white intelligentsia. In fact, Hamilton was lily white. The Census of 1910 reported no Negroes among its 3,825 residents. Only 4 Negroes were there in 1919, the Hancocks and the Parkers, a couple also affiliated with the university. Never before had Hancock lived in such close proximity to whites. Sensitive but not timid, he moved in a twilight zone between uncertain tolerance and forced isolation, openly avoided by

35. Newby discusses World War I racial conditions in *Black Carolinians*, pp. 185–193; interview with Mrs. Hancock, September 23, 1972.

36. "Reflections"; Miles Mark Fisher, ed., *Virginia Union and Some of Her Achievements* (Richmond: Virginia Union University, 1924), p. 11.

white Southerners and kept at a respectable distance by white Northerners. "I deplored the fact that no Negroes were to be found at Colgate," he said to a fellow alumnus in 1944. "I was not surprised, however, for I knew about President Cutten's attitude toward Negroes." The professors were polite, if condescending, and a few became Hancock's genuine friends, Marie Hancock recalled. "Several of Gordon's teachers had us in their homes on certain occasions, but I don't think the Parkers were ever invited out." Experience in South Carolina, not to mention Northern race riots in 1919, taught Hancock to beware of white people. Nevertheless, it is probable that the kindness and unprejudiced behavior exemplified by some whites did soften his suspicions. "Some of my high opinion of white men and my indisposition to curse out the whole lot because a few are lynchers is based largely on the fact of the fine men I met at Colgate," he testified. "I have outlived hatreds. I am free to respect and love all men." [37] By braving Colgate's covert racism and finding evidence of white sincerity, Hancock had turned an important corner on the road "to the promulgation of brotherhood." One more step awaited him before he continued the journey.

On the strength of excellent scholarship and enthusiastic recommendations, Hancock enrolled at Harvard University in 1920. A graduate fellow in sociology under the direction of Professor James Ford, he completed the M.A. degree in August, 1921. His thesis, "The Interrelationship of the Immigrant and Negro Problem," examined Irish-Negro antagonisms in Boston. Essentially, as he explained, both groups were city migrants. The Negroes—Southern born, ignorant and poor—arrived flood tide during World War I in search of economic opportunity. The Irish—Catholic, white and working class—came largely a generation earlier, secured jobs, and now resented the Negro newcomers. What made them hostile was not the issue of social equality, he said, as much as employer use of Negroes to break strikes and depress wages. This competitive situation sparked Irish-Negro violence. Although the groups were "a sub-

37. *Thirteenth Census of the United States: 1910*, I, 199; interview with Mrs. Hancock, September 23, 1972; Hancock to Judge Orrin Judd, March 13, 1944, Hancock Papers.

merged element," he concluded that economic competition, postwar recession, and the "ominous color question" would combine to drive the "Negro masses into unemployment . . . and permanent subordination."[38] Harvard's environmentalism, which postulated that individual or group behavior is predicated more upon social forces than heredity, gave Hancock the conceptual parameters of his own eclectic approach to sociology. Black social conditions could be effectively analyzed, he reasoned, by correlating their economic, cultural, and political underpinnings.[39]

As noted, Hancock's interest in sociology began at Seneca when he read Du Bois' book on Negro social betterment. More immediately, in the wake of postwar riots as traumatizing for him as Phoenix had been in 1898, he began pondering the socio-economic causes of race conflict. These related concerns help to explain, to some extent, his choice of a thesis topic and perhaps why he chose Harvard. A leader in the emerging field of sociology, Harvard was surpassed in the 1920's only by the University of Chicago and Columbia University. Once Pitirim Sorokin, Carle C. Zimmerman, and later Talcott Parsons were imported to its department, however, Harvard gained international recognition in social theory. Chicago remained pre-eminent in urban studies and social psychology, while Columbia held distinction in research methodology and social work.[40] Practically all the eminent black sociologists of Hancock's times were trained in the three schools. Du Bois and Allison Davis went to Harvard; Charles S. Johnson, E. Franklin Frazier, Horace Cayton, St. Clair Drake, Bertram Doyle, and Oliver Cox studied at Chicago; George E. Haynes and Ira DeA. Reid attended Columbia. Typically, they researched Negro migration, urban violence, racial adjustment, Negro institutional development, and ethnic relations.[41]

38. Fisher, ed., *Virginia Union and Some of Her Achievements*, p. 11; interview with Hancock, February 5, 1969. Harvard University misplaced the only available copy of Hancock's M.A. thesis.

39. Interview with Hancock, March 7, 1969.

40. *Ibid*; Robert E. L. Faris, *Chicago Sociology 1920–1932* (San Francisco: Chandler Publishing Co., 1967), pp. 123–133.

41. John H. Bracey, Jr., August Meier, and Elliott Rudwick, eds., *The Black Sociologists: The First Half Century* (Belmont, Calif.: Wadsworth Publishing Co., 1971), pp. 1–12; Bardolph, *The Negro Vanguard*, pp. 317–318. For one excellent example of

In an era of intense black intellectuality, radiating from the Harlem Renaissance, a militant Negro press, and rising Negro colleges, Harvard catapulted Hancock into the discipline of sociology. He fit well William Pickens' description of the New Negro as being "a sober, sensible creature, conscious of his environment, knowing that all is not right . . . but, at any rate, he is resolved to fight." [42] On this foundation Hancock would become one of the most articulate and outspoken analysts of race relations and black social problems in the South. After 1921, in spite of other commitments, he continued at Harvard, taking required courses for his doctorate in the summers, 1922–1925, [43] but he never completed it.

Soon after earning his M.A., Hancock declined an offer to teach in a Northern college and accepted a professorship at Virginia Union University in Richmond, Virginia, where in September, 1921, he took up his duties. The white president, William J. Clark, was very anxious to recruit Hancock, but three other factors made Union a good place to teach. Through a reputable program in liberal arts and theology, it enjoyed prestige in the black academic world; [44] terms of the appointment stipulated that a department of economics and sociology would be organized; and Richmond, a booming urban center of the upper South, provided a laboratory for racial research. "I came here deliberately after turning down a thirty-five hundred dollar job on the theory that educated Negroes born in the South should not run away and leave the submerged Negro to fight it out as best he can," Hancock said of his decision. "When I came to Virginia Union I was getting only twelve hundred dollars as a salary." [45]

these black sociologists' works, see Allison Davis, *Deep South: A Social Anthropological Study of Caste and Class* (Chicago: University of Chicago Press, 1941). Also, see James E. Blackwell and Morris Janowitz, eds., *Black Sociologists: Historical and Contemporary Perspectives* (Chicago: University of Chicago Press, 1974), pp. 121–228.

42. William Pickens, *The New Negro: His Political, Civil, and Mental Status, and Related Essays* (New York: Neale Publishing Co., 1916; reprinted New York: AMS Press, 1969), p. 239.

43. Interview with Hancock, March 7, 1969.

44. W. E. B. Du Bois, ed., *The College-Bred Negro American*, Atlanta University Publications No. 15 (Atlanta: Atlanta University Press, 1910), p. 12, lists Virginia Union sixth among eleven "First Grade Colored Colleges."

45. Hancock to President John M. Ellison of Virginia Union, October 16, 1948, Hancock Papers.

In choosing Virginia Union Hancock had indeed returned to the South, to the neglected arena of Negro education and struggle. Never again would he live in his native state. Being one of the 147,000 blacks who left South Carolina between 1900 and 1920, he also cast his lot with the long line of her black expatriates who enjoyed outstanding careers elsewhere. Among the best known were Archibald H. Grimké, consul to Santo Domingo; his brother, Francis J. Grimké, minister; Mary McLeod Bethune, educator; William Pickens, NAACP official; Benjamin E. Mays, president of Morehouse College; Benjamin G. Brawley, scholar; Kelly Miller, dean at Howard University; Ernest E. Just, biologist; T. McCants Stewart, lawyer; G. C. Gomillion, Tuskegee Institute administrator; and Robert N. C. Nix, a Pennsylvania congressman. All except Just owed their prominence to leadership in racial causes. For Hancock, now thirty-seven, much time had passed. Most men would have been involved in their professions long before, provided they were not born black and poor, and he had definitely known poverty and adversity. Although he had long since begun his career as a minister and as a teacher, in one sense, he was beginning. Schooled in Christian ethics, he wanted to "serve the race . . . and redeem the South." [46] Over the ensuing forty years he strove to implement these high ideals.

46. Newby, *Black Carolinians*, pp. 193–197; interview with Hancock, March 7, 1969.

II. Union, Moore Street, and Richmond Negroes

In an open letter to President Warren G. Harding, November 29, 1921, Kelly Miller of Howard University gave a rebuttal to an address by the chief executive in Birmingham, Alabama, which had justified Jim Crow on grounds of indelible differences between blacks and whites. "The immediate effect of your declaration has been to bring the eternal Negro question once more to the forefront of current discussion," the wily educator wrote. "The Negro finds himself in a segregated social world. He is making the best he can of this situation. He is not clamoring for so-called social equality, and would be wholly unable to assert his claim even if he were clamorous. But surely it cannot be expected that the race will . . . affirm its belief in and acceptance of 'fundamental, inescapable and eternal differences.' " [1] The Negro could live with color discrimination, but would never assent to inherent inferiority. Most black intellectuals who attempted to stem the tide of anti-Negro thought after World War I, with few exceptions, veered toward Miller's pragmatism. During the 1920's Hancock espoused this position and he faced the dilemma which it entailed.

Upon arrival in the former seat of the Confederacy, Hancock and his wife Marie[2] went directly to the president's house on the Virginia Union campus. A somewhat irate white woman answered the bell and told the anxious couple to go to the back door, but they refused. An embarrassed Dr. Clark rushed to the front porch, apologized for the conduct of his sister-in-law, and invited the Hancocks in. He also asked them please to conceal what happened.[3] Interestingly, both the incident and the request underscored the delicate nature of interracial feeling at Union, where whites and blacks had worked in harmony and mutual respect for years.

1. Kelly Miller, *Is Race Difference Fundamental, Eternal and Inescapable? An Open Letter to President Warren G. Harding, November 29, 1921*, pp. 2, 16. Pamphlet Collection, Duke University Library, Durham, North Carolina.
2. She used Marie instead of her first name, Florence.
3. Interview with Mrs. Hancock, September 23, 1972, Richmond, Virginia.

Like all educational institutions for freedmen, the school emerged from humble beginnings. Richmond Theological Seminary opened in 1865, with its first permanent accommodations at Lumpkin's Jail, a facility once used for imprisoning and punishing disobedient and refractory slaves. Wayland Seminary and the National Theological Institute were established in Washington, D. C., the same year, and in 1869 they were combined. The American Baptist Home Mission Society, the parent body, merged these Washington, D. C., and Richmond enterprises in 1899 under the name of Virginia Union University.[4] Nine gray granite buildings, artistically spaced on thirty acres along North Lombardy Street and Brook Turnpike, and the adjacent campus of Hartshorn Memorial College,[5] virtually made Union a Richmond tourist attraction. It represented "that broader, nobler conception of education which, while not neglecting the preparation of its pupils for the homely duties of life, seeks to train as well for professional careers," General T. J. Morgan said during dedication ceremonies, "and also offers to the gifted few an opportunity for the development to its highest form and degree whatever of talent God has entrusted to them."[6]

Within the limits of their resources, the founders endeavored to carry out that mission of higher learning for which W. E. B. Du Bois became chief advocate. Of the Old Dominion's four other Negro Colleges—Hampton, St. Paul's, Virginia State, and Virginia Seminary—none matched Union academically.[7] "Christian living and service" and "right habits of conduct," understandably, received much emphasis on

4. Charles H. Corey, *A History of the Richmond Theological Seminary, with Reminiscences of Thirty Years' Work among the Colored People of the South* (Richmond: J. W. Randolph Co., 1895), pp. 36–50; "A Century of Service to Education and Religion: Virginia Union University 1865–1965," *Virginia Union Bulletin*, LXV (June 1965), 5–20; hereinafter referred to as *V.U.B.*, Centennial Issue.

5. A school for Negro women which received aid and supervision from the American Baptist Home Mission Society, Hartshorn coordinated its curriculum with Union's in 1922. Formal merger occurred in 1932.

6. "Virginia Union University: What it Signifies, An Address Delivered by T. J. Morgan, LL.D., at the Dedication of the New Granite Buildings on May 18, 1900," *Virginia Union Bulletin*, LXX (October 1969), 6–16.

7. Emma Wesley Brown, "A Study of the Influence of the Philosophies of Accommodation and Protest on Five Colleges Established in Virginia for Negroes, 1865–1940" (Ed.D. Dissertation, Columbia University, 1967), pp. 113–114.

her "hallowed grounds." But admissions and scholastic regulations favored those who could make the grade. "An examination in reading, spelling, or composition may be given to any student at any time," one rule stated, "and if the results are unsatisfactory he will be required to enter classes in these subjects." The university consisted of three divisions, including an academy of preparatory instruction and manual crafts, a liberal arts college, and a theological department. The general curriculum covered English grammar, composition, and literature; the classics, with Latin, Greek, Hebrew, French and German; European and American history; natural sciences; mathematics; and Bible. Industrial training in the Academy never got much attention. There were 14 faculty members and 156 students in 1900. Most pupils did "an hour's work a day" to defray part of their expenses. By 1910, when Du Bois rated it sixth among the top 11 black colleges, the school had a faculty of 15 and a student body of 240.[8] In 1921 she boasted an endowment of $100,000, 19 teachers, and a total enrollment of 459.[9]

The young men and women who attended Virginia Union usually deported themselves well. They were not overtly militant or rebellious, but self-respecting and proud, eager exemplars of middle-class virtues. "You may own everything else and be nothing worth while unless first of all you own yourself," the Reverend H. B. Gross of the Home Mission Society remarked at one assembly. "That is the aim and end of the true education—to make every man owner and master of himself."[10] Statements along these lines, if anything, heightened the students' consciousness of color and alerted them to existing controversies about race.

8. Virginia Union University, *Annual Catalogue 1899–1900*, pp. 5–18, 56; *Annual Catalogue 1910–1911*, pp. 5–6, 60; W. E. B. Du Bois, ed., *The College-Bred Negro American*, Atlanta University Publications No. 15 (Atlanta: Atlanta University Press, 1910), p. 12.

9. Virginia Union University, *Annual Catalogue 1920–1921*, pp. 5–6, 10, 62. The school continued to grow. When Hancock retired in 1952, its endowment was $1,015,596, and it had 56 teachers and 805 students. In 1972 it reported revenues of $2,890,107 and 85 faculty members and 1,405 students. See Mary Irwin, ed. *American Universities and Colleges* (Washington, D. C.: American Council on Education, 1952), p. 977; and W. Todd Furniss, ed., *American Universities and Colleges* (Washington, D. C.: American Council on Education, 1972), pp. 1661–1662.

10. H. B. Gross, "The Essential Factors of Race Education," *University Journal*, I (January 1901), 6.

One such controversy involved the Baptist State Convention and the Baptist General Association, both black, and the resulting schism between Virginia Seminary of Lynchburg and Union. The seminary, founded by the State Convention in 1888, would have experienced an early demise if the Home Mission Society had not rescued it financially. While management remained in Negro hands, the institution gradually lost its autonomy to the society, and Gregory W. Hayes, the bold charismatic president who earned his M.A. at Oberlin, resented it. When the society announced plans to build a university in Richmond, in a consolidation program which proposed to make the seminary only an affiliate academy, Hayes absolutely refused to acquiesce. The 1899 meeting of the Baptist State Convention at Lexington occasioned such a bitter contest between delegates backing Hayes and a group of divines led by Z. D. Lewis and J. E. Jones of Richmond that students called it "the Battle of Lexington." Amidst cries of Negro independence, Hayes prevailed and the Convention broke all ties with the Home Mission Society. The Lewis-Jones faction withdrew in protest and organized the Baptist General Association, pledging cooperation with the society and support for Virginia Union. In the aftermath the rival church bodies and schools vilified each other, but the Seminarians were no more committed to Negro elevation than Unionites. Sidestepping the conflict, the Class of 1901 looked at the long road ahead: "If our race is to rise . . . it must have leaders, men of sterling character, thorough education, and lofty purpose. . . . 'Give us men.' " [11]

Another issue which provoked discussion on campus was the question of industrial versus liberal education. Booker T. Washington, who studied a year at Wayland Seminary of Washington, D. C., following his graduation from Hampton, visited Union in 1901, looked through the buildings, and delivered an address to the students. "We are expected to render services to our race commensurate with our opportunities," he said, avoiding any reference to vocational training. He challenged them to go where they were needed, "to the parts where there is the greatest poverty, greatest ignorance, and hence where we

11. Frank P. Lewis, "A History of the Baptist General Association of Virginia, Colored" (B. D. Thesis, Virginia Union University, 1937), pp. 44–94; "Our Place and Work in the 20th Century," *University Journal*, I (January 1901), 8.

can do most good." [12] Afterwards, a student editorial suggested that it might be a mistake to regard Mr. Washington as an enemy of colleges like Union, but added: "The progress of this race depends largely on . . . broadminded, well trained leaders, and . . . such leaders can be expected to come only from schools for the higher education of the race." When the students formed a Du Bois Literary Society and presented a portrait of Du Bois to the University in 1903, and later enthusiastically attended the scholar's lecture, they showed unequivocally whose side they were on.[13]

Consistent with their support for Du Bois, Unionites contributed significantly to the Talented Tenth. Of the University's 618 graduates from 1900 to 1932, 25 received doctorates and many others achieved professional distinction. The ablest, literally comprising a who's who among the Afro-American intelligentsia, included presidents Samuel H. Archer of Morehouse, Ferdinand D. Bluford of North Carolina A. & T., John M. Ellison and Thomas H. Henderson of Virginia Union, John Bacoats of Leland, and Robert P. Daniel of Shaw. Adam Clayton Powell, Sr., and J. Raymond Henderson became nationally acclaimed Baptist ministers; Eugene Kinckle Jones and T. Arnold Hill directed the National Urban League, while Miles W. Connor, Howard H. Long, William, Vattel, and Walter Daniel, Charles H. Thompson, Henry A. Bullock, Henry J. McGuinn, and Marie E. Carpenter distinguished themselves as college educators. Sociologist Charles S. Johnson, economist Abram L. Harris, historian James Hugo Johnston, physicist Victor C. Smith, biologist Limus D. Wall, and journalist Robert L. Vann won outstanding recognition in their fields.[14]

For Hancock this small black university—its fabric interwoven with bourgeois standards of respectability and success—proved

12. "Booker T. Washington at Virginia Union University," *University Journal*, I (March 1901), 10; Louis R. Harlan, *Booker T. Washington: The Making of a Black Leader 1856–1901* (New York: Oxford University Press, 1972), pp. 96–98.

13. "Booker T. Washington and Higher Education," *University Journal*, I (December 1901), 2–3; Brown, "A Study of the Influence of the Philosophies of Accommodation and Protest on Five Colleges Established in Virginia for Negroes, 1865–1940," p. 113; "Du Bois Literary Society," *University Journal*, III (May 1903), 11.

14. Charles S. Johnson, *The Negro College Graduate* (Chapel Hill: University of North Carolina Press, 1938), pp. 29, 95–97; *V.U.B.*, Centennial Issue, 47–51.

amenable to a vigorous focus on race. Under his chairmanship, the Department of History and Sociology grew rapidly, converting in 1927 to Economics and Sociology, but still including history. Essentially, it was an interdisciplinary experiment in social science. In 1922 there were 2 electives each in history, economics, and sociology; 1 in political science. By 1930 economics entailed 9 offerings; sociology, 9; history, 12; political science, 1; and anthropology, 1.

Contending that "the problem of race relations is crucial if American democracy is to survive," Hancock organized one of the first courses on the subject at any Southern school. Members of the class not only assessed tensions between blacks and other minorities, they also studied black and white leaders, the social effects of race mixture, and agencies working for interracial cooperation in the South. While Negro life occupied an important place in the curricula of many black colleges at the time, largely because of the pioneering works of Du Bois and George E. Haynes of Fisk, little systematic analysis of black-white interaction existed. Hancock, in attempting to balance the scale, stressed the intergroup processes of competition, conflict, compromise, cooperation, accommodation, acculturation, amalgamation, and assimilation, as well as black institutional development. Charles S. Johnson, then associate director of the Chicago Commission on Race Relations, worked along similar lines. Unless Negro youth grasped the subtleties of race, Hancock did not see how they could successfully meet the Darwinian challenge presented by the white world. He told his students, often in dramatic lectures, that "races vie in a fierce struggle for existence." Race prejudice forced the Negro into a caste status, denied him manhood, and threatened his economic survival.[15]

More melioristic than scientific, Hancock meshed teaching and writing with racial advocacy, a common practice among black academicians. He maintained that the Negro college could not wink at

15. *V.U.B.*, Centennial Issue, 64–65; John H. Bracey, Jr., August Meier, and Elliott Rudwick, eds., *The Black Sociologists: The First Half Century* (Belmont, Calif.: Wadsworth Publishing Co., 1971), pp. 14–55; Chicago Commission on Race Relations, *The Negro in Chicago: A Study of Race Relations and a Race Riot* (Chicago: University of Chicago Press, 1922), pp. 436–519; copies of syllabi for Race Relations, Economics 204, and Sociology 1, n.d., Gordon Blaine Hancock Papers, Richmond, Virginia.

lynching and mob violence, or the black exodus taking place beyond its walls, but should align itself with liberal movements like those promoted by the Commission on Interracial Cooperation. Founded in Atlanta during the riot crisis of 1919, the commission promoted black-white dialogue through a Southwide network of state and local committees. Ethically committed to cooperation, Hancock criticized those Negro educators who said white people were no longer needed in Negro schools. Besides white philanthropy, he explained, Negro education demanded the services of the best prepared teachers regardless of color. Whites might be rejected "because they are incapable or unsympathetic or condescending, but not because they are white."[16]

At the same time, he defended the Negro against the charge of inferiority. According to popular racist theories, the Negro sprang from a dark continent where he lived in barbarism and primitive passion. European slave traders and colonizers converted him to Christianity and introduced him to civilization. This interpretation found no sanction in history or archaeology, said Hancock, whose own study of Africa yielded different conclusions. He revealed that the eastern, central, and western tribes of Uganda, Mashonaland, and Yorubaland developed strong moral codes, complex forms of artistic expression, and viable political systems before the arrival of the white man. Unfortunately, slave raiding severely depleted the population and weakened native institutions, and hence retarded cultural progress. On another occasion, Hancock attacked the notion that low-income groups, including blacks, were innately criminal. Using a variety of statistics gathered from business reports, periodicals, police and penal records, he demonstrated that advertising, which then generated $250,000,000 per year, drove poor people to steal and commit other crimes in order to satisfy their wants. Unless submerged groups had a better chance to earn money to buy the products widely advertised, he contended, they would become restless and form a dangerous segment in society. In this analysis, which attempted to explain how the system caused behavior deviating from prescribed patterns

16. *Union-Hartshorn Bulletin*, XXIII (January 1923), 5, 14; *ibid.*, XXIV (June–November 1923), 13, 18–19.

of conduct, Hancock anticipated sociologist Robert K. Merton's strain theory of deviance. The social structure, Merton would argue later, exerts definite pressures upon certain persons and groups to engage in nonconforming rather than conforming conduct.[17]

Eclectic in social outlook, confident of the Negro's possibilities, the educator remained vigilant. Discussing the deteriorating economic status of Southern blacks in *Opportunity*, official organ of the National Urban League, he pointed out that the unskilled Negro laborer was hard pressed even for the roughest kinds of work, both by reason of the white man's changing attitude toward work and by the gradual mechanization of the South. Not only were higher level employment opportunities closed, but the Negro's technical qualification and equipment were still inadequate for a complex industrial order. Three other problems aggravated this situation. First, the steady growth of the Negro professional class, dependent upon the patronage of black workers, increased the danger that the latter might be exploited by the former. Second, Negroes lived beyond their means, frequently spending too much for luxuries. Third, pretentious building programs were alienating the masses from the black church, usually because of their inability to bear the financial burdens which membership entailed. For the foreseeable future, Hancock urged collective restraint and race solidarity. Speaking to a Hampton Institute commencement audience, he eloquently recommended Booker T. Washington's "misunderstood and at times maligned" doctrine of thrift, property, efficiency, and character; for the Negro, survival had become the question of the hour.[18] A Negro educator who concentrated his thinking almost entirely on race problems, constantly seeking solutions, was unorthodox even in black college circles. Hancock, overstepping the restraint which many of his colleagues preferred, enjoyed being an agent provocateur. Fraternal, religious, and civic groups were moved by his oratory, and the local press acclaimed him as a black spokesman. John

17. Gordon B. Hancock, "Three Elements of African Culture," *Journal of Negro History*, VIII (July 1923), 284–300; and Hancock, "The Commercial Advertisement and Social Pathology," *Social Forces*, IV (June 1926), 812–819. Also, see Robert K. Merton, *Social Theory and Social Structure* (New York: The Free Press, 1949), pp. 131–160.

18. Hancock, "When the Manna Faileth," *Opportunity*, VI (May 1928), 133–135, 147; and Hancock, "Thinking in Ultimate Terms," *Southern Workman*, LVIII (July 1929), 291–297.

Mitchell, Jr., militant editor of the Richmond *Planet*, considered him Virginia Union's ablest teacher. But older black professors like Joshua B. Simpson and John W. Barco would have disagreed. For more than two decades prior to Hancock's arrival the two were dominant at Union. "Josh" Simpson, besides Greek and literature, had taught sociology, while Barco combined history, Hebrew, and Latin. Erudite pedagogues, they felt that the younger men on the faculty, including Hancock, were more concerned with individual reputation than effective teaching. To them, classroom performance, not outside involvement, was the best route to Negro elevation. Hancock respected Simpson and Barco, but not this somewhat provincial and isolationist position. Educated Negroes, he believed, should not be aloof or wait for their students to change the world.[19]

Despite the subtle competition for status among Unionites and his introverted nature, Hancock enjoyed cordial relations with his colleagues. West Indian born Clarence M. Maloney, A.B., M.A., Syracuse, LL.B., Dalhousie, was his closest associate. A professor of economics, French, and history, and debating team advisor, Maloney, a bachelor, spent many idle moments in the Hancocks' Kingsley Hall apartment, mostly eating and discussing football. Hancock and Maloney were not above helping the players through tough courses, and they occasionally abandoned their classes to attend road games. In a more serious vein, the two men were joint mentors of young Abram L. Harris, known to them as "Abe," who later earned the Ph.D. in economics from Columbia and held professorships at Howard and the University of Chicago. Also, each man contributed uniquely to stimulating intellectual inquiry among Union students. Hancock used oratory, conventional wisdom, and methodical ideas. Maloney relied upon argument, debate, and personal éclat.

Out of the Hancock-Maloney camaraderie emerged a strong bond of loyalty. Although he considered Hancock too wrapped up in religion, theology, and the mystique of Virginia Union, Maloney vigorously defended Hancock when men like Charles T. Russell, Union's bursar,

19. Richmond *Planet*, April 25, 1925; Richmond *News Leader*, March 17, 1926; Richmond *Times-Dispatch*, June 8, 1929; *V.U.B.*, Centennial Issue, 3–4, 62–64; pamphlet, *By Their Fruits* (Richmond: Virginia Union University, 1939).

criticized him. Russell, the Negro power broker within the administration, resented Hancock's ambitiousness and popularity. On the other hand, Hancock interceded but could not save the quick-witted, outspoken Maloney. At the 1924 annual meeting of the Association for the Study of Negro Life and History in Richmond, Maloney rebuked Dr. James E. Gregg, the white president of Hampton Institute, for telling blacks to keep quiet on race questions. Many influential white people were present. Not long afterward college officials received word from the State Department of Education that unless Maloney were removed from Union's faculty all summer school funds would be terminated. He left in 1925 at the end of the spring semester.[20]

Miles W. Connor, A.B., Virginia Union, M.A., Howard, and Miles Mark Fisher, A.B., Morehouse, M.A., Chicago, were also congenial toward Hancock. Connor headed the education department. Fisher was professor of church history, a Baptist minister, and writer. Fisher and Hancock did much to undermine Biblical fundamentalism at Union. Each subscribed to the theory of evolution and, to them, the virgin birth had only a symbolic meaning. The Baptist General Association rose in holy wrath against this alleged heresy and, although unsuccessful, demanded their resignations. Once Hancock found himself in the middle of a Fisher-Maloney argument on the slave songs and spirituals. Fisher, author of *The Master's Slave, Elijah John Fisher* (1922) and *Life of Lott Carey* (1922), said they manifested African culture and, above all, a desire for freedom. Maloney accepted Fisher's point on freedom, but considered the music a sociological response to enslavement, more American Negro than African in meaning. Hancock did not take either side. "Josh" Simpson backed Maloney. During a Richmond showing of the movie *The Birth of a Nation* in 1923, student leaders Wendell P. Dabney and James W. Ivy invited Fisher and Maloney to critique it. Fisher did not show up. English professor Clarissa Kyles Dillard, one of a few black women on the faculty at the time, said Fisher and Hancock typically avoided people who challenged them. On the contrary, William L. Ransome,

20. Interview with Clarence M. Maloney, September 13, 1974, Lynchburg, Virginia; Richmond *Planet*, September 27, 1924. Following his departure from Virginia Union, Maloney was appointed assistant attorney general for the State of New York at Buffalo.

then instructor in Bible, recalled that they were bold, modern, and controversial.[21]

Hancock's encounter with Rayford W. Logan, also a colleague, accorded more with Ransome's view. The son of Washington, D. C., domestics, Logan graduated from Williams College, was a second lieutenant in World War I, and, following his discharge, stayed on in France until 1924. While serving as secretary-interpreter at the American Embassy, he attended the Pan-African Congress in Paris and absorbed the protest philosophy of Du Bois and Walter F. White of the NAACP. He joined the Union faculty in 1925, offering courses in United States, European, and Negro history, as well as French and Spanish. Logan openly criticized Union's emphasis on faith and character, and ridiculed black Richmonders for accepting the statement that they were "the best Negroes in the world." He initiated efforts to place Negro names on the voting list and Negro personnel in Negro schools, and he zealously denounced colonialism, imperialism, and racism. Several people accused him of being too radical and a Communist.[22]

Hancock inadvertently told Logan that Negroes needed more than protest. Using the platform of Coburn Chapel, where students assembled for weekly devotions, Logan attacked Hancock for this cautious attitude. Invoking the spirit of Frederick Douglass, he said those who would be free must strike the first blow. Hancock conceded that agitation had a place in the Negro's fight for citizenship, but unless it was studied and constructive it might become a stumbling-block rather than a stepping-stone. Speaking on other occasions, Logan derided segregation, especially in the schools, and scorned Negroes who acquiesced in it. Hancock rejected the notion of inferiority which forced

21. Miles Mark Fisher, ed., *Virginia Union and Some of Her Achievements* (Richmond: Virginia Union University, 1924), pp. 7–18; *Union-Hartshorn Bulletin*, XXIV (June–November 1923), 14; interview with Maloney, September 13, 1974; interviews with Clarissa Kyles Dillard, June 27, 1974, and William L. Ransome, June 26, 1974, Richmond, Virginia. Fisher assumed the pastorate of White Rock Baptist Church, Durham, North Carolina, in 1932. He earned the Ph.D. in religion from the University of Chicago and published *Negro Slave Songs in the United States* (Ithaca, N. Y.: Cornell University Press, 1953).

22. V.U.B., Centennial Issue, 62, 64–65; interview with Rayford W. Logan, July 11, 1974, Washington, D. C.

separation presupposed, but felt the Negro would have to tolerate overt discrimination. For separate schools, whether in Virginia or Washington, D. C., were symptoms of one insidious disease—race prejudice. Of course, neither man could propose an airtight plan to abolish it. Going further, despite the difficulty, Logan demanded an end to white control of black colleges. Enough qualified blacks could be found, he said, to fill every available presidency and professorship. President Clark was naturally disturbed by these contentions. Reportedly, he also knew about Logan's low estimate of his ability. Hancock insisted that ending white control would mean the loss of white philanthropy, which would practically doom black higher education. Driving out whites, he further asserted, would certainly boomerang on the Negro. He made no specific defense of President Clark, who, in June 1930, politely asked Logan to find a job somewhere else. Different in outlook, Hancock and Logan, even after Logan left Union, remained foes.[23]

Just as he spoke his mind on Negro problems at Virginia Union, Gordon B. Hancock preached a message of racial uplift in his sermons at Moore Street Baptist Church. Located a few blocks from Union's campus in Jackson Ward, Richmond's largest black section, this impressive red brick edifice was built in 1908. Its lofty steeple overlooked establishments of the black bourgeoisie on Clay Street, crowded tenements lining Jackson Street, and white businesses along Broad Street. Founded in 1875 by a small group of dissenters from a neighboring congregation, the church changed ministers five times before Randall O. Johnson of Hampton stabilized it in 1895.[24] Johnson served until 1925, when he retired as pastor emeritus on a modest pension provided at Hancock's suggestion. There were over six hundred members when Hancock succeeded Johnson, and they prided themselves on being a

23. Interviews with Hancock, February 5, 1969, and Logan, July 11, 1974; *Union Hartshorn Bulletin*, XXX (November 1929), 7–8; interview with Henry J. McGuinn, June 12, 26, 1974, Richmond, Virginia. McGuinn, A.B., Virginia Union, M.A., Ph.D., Columbia, served on the faculty with Logan and Hancock, and remembered the details of their debate. In 1938, having earned M.A. and Ph.D. degrees from Harvard, Logan became professor at Howard University and a distinguished historian of the American Negro.

24. "Moore Street Missionary Baptist Church, Richmond, Virginia: Some Historical Notes Compiled by Deacon W. P. Burrell, Oldest Living Member of the Congregation, 1933," Hancock Papers.

cross section of the black community. On Sunday morning at Moore Street teachers and students from Union rubbed shoulders with hundreds of uneducated workers, while the church's day care center, industrial school, and adult education program offered strong testimony to the idea of betterment in this world. Hancock accepted the pastorate because he believed in an earth-centered church, and he expected Moore Street to play an even greater role in providing social services and promoting social justice.[25]

Hancock enjoyed autonomy and identity as undisputed father of his flock, combining intellect and emotion, old-time religion and social gospel, lower-class sympathies with middle-class training and station. A man of the people, he easily equaled the prestige normally accorded only the pastors of First African and Ebenezer, Richmond's silk-stocking Negro Baptist churches. If the congregation grumbled when he rearranged and shortened the services, they beamed over the many new members and visitors whom he attracted.[26] A trumpet prelude, antiphonal hymn, religious poetry, and benevolent offering highlighted the revised order of worship. Praying and preaching were standard features, but Hancock made each more interesting with his unusually resonant voice. Appealing to the interest of the informed and the confidence of the lowly, he tackled topics like "The Gospel According to Physicians, Dentists, and Nurses" or "The Gospel According to the Hardworking Men and Women."[27] Although dynamic, these were no red-hot down-home sermons. Like his father, Hancock inspired enthusiastic religion but did not countenance pandemonium. He inculcated a deep respect for Negro spirituals, glorified the folkways of the country church, and emphasized the traditions of mutual aid and self-help in Afro-American Christianity.[28]

25. Interview with George B. Winston, a member of Moore Street since 1914, June 26, 1974, Richmond, Virginia.

26. Benjamin E. Mays and Joseph W. Nicholson, *The Negro's Church* (New York: Institute of Social and Religious Research, 1933; reissued New York: Russell and Russell, 1969), p. 194, reported that Moore Street had twelve hundred members in 1931.

27. Interview with George B. Winston, June 26, 1974; Richmond *Planet*, February 18, March 11, 1928.

28. Interview with Hancock, February 5, 1969. Hancock wrote the words and music to "Contrition," a devotional hymn which he introduced into Moore Street's services, and two spirituals—"Our Long Home" and "Our Journey Home." When he retired in 1963 there were more than 2,500 members and an annual budget of $85,000. A $150,000

Under his leadership Moore Street sponsored relief, recreation, a day nursery, evening courses, and an employment bureau. As a rule the church was the institutional locus of the black community, with multiple functions in Negro life. Hancock made his own parish both a spiritual haven and a settlement house, for conditions in Jackson Ward necessitated an action-oriented ministry. He visited the sick and the indigent, and he used his influence downtown to arrange parole for members of his congregation in trouble.[29] He likened the church to one link in the chain that must lift the race from the depths where slavery left it to the sunlit heights of freedom. To him, the Negro's everyday life provided numberless opportunities to help, encourage, inspire, arouse enthusiasm, contend, and conquer. Spurred on by this ethic of service, blacks could achieve full citizenship, organize for mutual protection, and work out their own salvation.[30]

Consistent with his training in liberal theology at Colgate, Hancock was of this world rather than other-worldly in his thinking. In moving cadence, he forewarned Moore Street that he would cry loud against injustices, prejudices, oppressions, crimes, and murder, sins in high places, compromising churches, money-inspired preachers, time-serving teachers, devastating wars and rumors of wars, nations rising against nations, decadent families and divorce, hunger and distress, luxury for the few and suffering for the many. Citing the Old Testament example of Caleb and Joshua, who urged Israel to go up at once and possess the land, he admonished blacks to overcome fear and democratize society. To do this, they must dare to hope and take advantage of the breaks in the game of life. God set the world before man like a vast table, Hancock explained, and no one had the right to deny another his place as an equal at the table. Whether by implication, illustration, symbol or substance, the whole idea of uplift permeated his religious rhetoric.[31]

---

expansion project, which added a Social Center to the main sanctuary, was also paid off. See Hancock, "Back to Benedict—An Abbreviated Account of My Stewardship," n.d., Hancock Papers.

29. Interview with George B. Winston, June 26, 1974.

30. Richmond *Shepherds' Voice*, December 1925; January 1926.

31. Copies of undated sermons: "What's Right with the World," "Looking on the Sunny Side," "Getting the Breaks," and "When God Sets the Table," Hancock Papers.

Characteristically polite, Hancock nevertheless became involved in some undignified squabbles. For evolution, the virgin birth, bodily resurrection, and proper baptism, not to mention personal jealousies and rivalries, kept the local brethren at odds.[32] W. H. Stokes of Ebenezer, William L. Ransome of First Baptist, and Hancock were by far the leading polemicists. For example, when the *Planet* reported that Dr. James S. Hatcher, pastor of Bethel A.M.E. Church, had preached from the subject "The Sun Does Move" to more than seven hundred people on the fourth Sunday night in March, 1925, it ignited an interesting debate. Fifty years before, the intrepid John Jasper of Richmond, the nineteenth century's foremost Negro pulpiteer, achieved worldwide fame with his sermon "The Sun Do Move."[33] Yet, many blacks wondered why Hatcher was reviving this outmoded thinking. Within two weeks, E. Rice McKinney, a Northern Negro minister, and Hancock delivered the first blows. Out of the fulness of his ignorance, McKinney said, John Jasper believed in a moving sun and a four-cornered earth. He doubted if Hatcher shared these beliefs, but since times were tight and the collections were falling off, a new "selling" talk was needed to make receipts balance the tremendous overhead of the church—including the pastor's board and keep. Hancock contended that clerical gowns and degrees and Jasper sermons were incompatible. If Hatcher did not sincerely believe what he was preaching, he desecrated Jasper's memory. If he held to a theory which had been invalidated for nearly five hundred years, he forfeited his claims to a respectful hearing from intelligent people. Hancock also proposed a code of ministerial ethics as one way of ending such obvious show-boating.[34]

In replying to McKinney, Hatcher stated that Jasper was inarticulate but not ignorant. He denied the need for financial gimmicks, since Bethel raised over $8,000 per year. He charged science and scholarship with trying to undermine the Almighty and affirmed his faith in Biblical miracles, even that God spoke through Balaam's ass. He added sarcas-

32. Interviews with Hancock, February 5, 1969, and William L. Ransome, June 26, 1974.
33. Richmond *Planet*, March 25, 1925; Federal Writers' Program, *The Negro in Virginia* (Hampton: The Hampton Institute, 1940), pp. 250–251.
34. Richmond *Planet*, April 11, 1925.

tically that "dumber asses than Balaam's have spoken and written." [35] Similarly, Hatcher chafed at Hancock's unwarranted attack on his motives and reputation, claiming that the learned professor wanted to destroy him. He expressed shame that Hancock, who disputed the Holy Word, should call himself a Christian minister. Besides, he asked, why howl down a man who simply endeavored to do good works? [36] Hancock, in turn, severely ridiculed Hatcher as an erstwhile eminent divine, modern in dress and ancient in mind, shrinking like a gas bag before the immortal Jasper. He considered Hatcher more popular than pertinent, and wished to save him for the cause of intelligence. Hancock said that he was howling out against Hatcher because a possible minister had become an impossible fame-hunter, exploited the memory of John Jasper, run short on fundamentals, and embarrassed the Negro community. Anyone converted on Hatcher's doctrine deserved salvation, he noted, for he would need great faith—greater than was ever found in Israel. Finally, he castigated Hatcher as a chronic affliction and an inconvenience, warning him to behave himself before Richmond in sheer self-defense demanded it. [37] One Sunday afternoon not long afterward, amidst all the publicity, Hatcher drew a mostly black crowd of three thousand to the City Auditorium, where he reiterated his position, cited Biblical proofs and scientific theories, and thanked his critics for making the occasion possible. [38] Hancock made no further statements.

A less vitriolic but far more insightful religious debate involved V. F. Calverton, Jewish author and editor of the *Modern Quarterly*, Kelly Miller, and Hancock. Writing as early as 1919, black Socialist publishers A. Philip Randolph and Chandler Owen of *The Messenger* announced the failure of the Negro church. They said it had failed to educate the people to the modern problems of capital, labor, unionism, and politics, and seldom, if ever, used its power against disfranchisement and lynching. [39] Their strong denunciation initiated a continuing dialogue in *The Messenger*, mostly with black churchmen. In 1927

35. *Ibid.*
36. *Ibid.*, April 18, 1925.
37. *Ibid.*, April 25, 1925.
38. *Ibid.*, May 2, 1925.
39. "The Failure of the Negro Church," *The Messenger*, II (October 1919), 6.

Randolph and Owen selected and invited three popular thinkers to discuss whether religion and the church handicapped or helped Negro progress.

Calverton wrote that an extraordinary religiosity, rooted in slavery and sustained by oppression, enveloped the Negro's entire institutional life. The Negro preacher remained chief protagonist in the community, the ministry still ranked high as a profession, while the Negro colleges and press were strongly influenced by their church-related constituencies. Yet, because it instilled other-worldliness instead of this worldliness in blacks, presented myth instead of science, and canonized Jesus instead of Marx, orthodox Christianity was a backward force. Calverton doubted if Christian values of forbearance and forgiveness, submissiveness and meekness would equip Negroes to survive in America's modern capitalist society, where class-struggle, race prejudice, and economic exploitation were rampant. As part of the urban proletariat, therefore, they needed to divest themselves of any and all beliefs which impeded the process of social change and economic revolution.[40]

Miller scoffed at the Bolshevik line in Calverton's reasoning. Viewing the broad sweep of history, he conceded that the church as a human institution had made many mistakes, evinced reactionary and progressive tendencies, and yielded slowly to scientific knowledge. But it also raised the peasants and serfs of the ancient world to the pinnacle of triumph over Rome and enabled blacks to endure the cruelties, torture, and terror of slavery. Through its philanthropy the Negro received both his education and highest aspirations. Miller rejected the thesis that religion weakened the Negro's will. For the legacies of Denmark Vesey, Nat Turner, Frederick Douglass, and countless others proved the contrary. The Negro's spiritual emotionalism might at times be excessive, he said, but it provided necessary psychological release and did not blind him to social and economic realities. Indeed, if Christianity handicapped the Negro, Miller concluded, then every Negro church and school, YMCA and YWCA, and the fraternal associations,

40. V. F. Calverton, "Orthodox Religion, Does It Handicap Negro Progress?" *ibid.*, IX (July 1927), 221, 236.

insurance companies, and businesses fostered by its spirit should be abolished. Unquestionably, the race would never recover.[41]

Hancock offered a critical synthesis of Calverton and Miller, because he felt the question could not be answered absolutely yes or no. If progress meant adjustments whereby the Negro participated more fully in the mainstream of society, he opined, religion might be helpful. Disagreeing with Calverton, he said the mere fact that Christianity had been conservative did not warrant its destruction. Acknowledging the antireligionist's argument that the hopes of oppressed groups rested upon the radical elements in society, Hancock nonetheless considered it unsafe and unwise for the Negro to ally himself with any of the current "isms." Except slogans, radicals had little or nothing to offer, being themselves at the mercy of an overwhelmingly conservative social order. Alluding to Miller's point, he said Negroes had gained much, and were still gaining from Christian philanthropy. Although this too was conservative and a poor substitute for equality, its cessation would definitely set the race back. Insofar then as Christianity cautioned the Negro against casting away the old for the new, set forth the indispensableness of religion in his upward struggles, and recognized the necessity of a stabilizing force in the social process, it did not handicap Negro progress. He reminded Calverton that atheism and irreligion were negative, while religion was positive, and the progress of a race could not be intelligently predicated upon a negation. Yet this did not mean that blacks must look for their pie in the sky. Rather, Hancock urged the Negro church to awaken from its lethargy. For the Bible did not rule out science, the economic interpretation of history, or an attack upon racial exploitation. In place of so much shouting and theological quibbling, the Negro needed a social gospel—and a church committed to social justice.[42]

The dialogue with Calverton and Miller, though instructive, failed to concentrate forcefully on the nagging issue of Christianity and white racism. Segregation within the universal fellowship, where all believ-

41. Kelly Miller, "Orthodox Christianity, Does It Handicap Negro Progress?" *ibid.*, IX (August 1927), 254–255.

42. Hancock, "Orthodox Christianity, Does It Handicap Negro Progress?" *ibid.*, IX (September 1927), 278–279.

ers were suppose to be brothers and sisters, troubled the Moore Street pastor. Writing in 1928, he called upon Christians everywhere, especially white Southerners, to destroy race prejudice. He observed that in spite of the extravagant claims of its devotees, Christianity, after nearly twenty centuries, looked upon a world where morality was subordinated to money, where the many were exploited for the advantage of the few, where nationalism produced on the horizon war clouds more ominous than ever, where idealism was decadent and the tide of materialism at its height. In the contest for world supremacy the Western nations were offering their Eastern counterparts Christ and trade and the sword, forms of conquest not different from those of Alexander or Caesar. Since all were closely related to colonialism and the fortunes of the white man, the champion of Christianity, millions of the darker peoples seriously distrusted a religion which sanctioned such evils. In America, moreover, nothing set the church apart as a leader in attacking caste or the ever present hostility between black and white. Unless Christians practiced what they professed, he stated, the masses could become alienated and driven to Communism. No double standard existed in the teachings of Jesus; there should be none in the church. Christianity must crush prejudice, Hancock warned, or it would itself be crushed.[43]

In making this declaration, though, he did not say whether the abolition of race prejudice logically meant disbanding the independent Negro church. If that citadel of black culture and social concern had to be preserved, as he believed, how could the kingdom of God—neither white nor black—come on earth? Furthermore, were feelings of racial antipathy stronger than overt segregationist practices, or vice versa? Whatever the case, a Christian offensive against racist attitudes was likely to produce only slow, minimal changes in the economic and political superstructure. Pulled between the ultimate principle of brotherhood and the practical fact of separation, Hancock, like most black ministers,[44] encouraged Negroes to work within the biracial framework. In Richmond, of course, Negroes knew a lot about

43. Hancock, "The Challenge to Christianity Today," *Home Mission College Review*, I (March 1928), 25—29.

44. See the discussion of the Negro minister's message in Mays and Nicholson, *The Negro's Church*, pp. 58–93.

biracialism. For the capital city contained two societies, one black, one white—separate and unequal.

Richmond had 171,667 residents in 1920, 117,574 whites, 54,041 blacks, and 52 other nonwhites. Before the end of the decade, the total number of residents increased by 11,262.[45] According to an early promotional publication, white Richmonders were a homogeneous people, largely native born, patriotic, law abiding, and industrious. The colored inhabitants, it said, were descendants of "the old Virginia 'darkies.' " "A superior class of negroes," they were a valuable factor in the domestic and industrial life of the community.[46] Later, in addition to advertising the absence of labor disturbances, the city claimed that its Negroes were quick to learn, easily managed by those who understood them, tractable of temper, home loving, and ambitious.[47] This obvious condescension typified black-white relations, demonstrating how completely the old patterns persisted in the new economic order. Object of myth, possessing the glamour of colonial traditions and of its role in the Civil War, Richmond also symbolized the New South of business and industry. It had the South's largest insurance company, paper bag manufacturer, automobile jobbers' supply house, engraving plant, lithographing establishment, chewing gum factory, and mail order service. Simultaneously, it boasted the world's largest wood works, baking powder, flour, blotting paper, bottled extract, locomotive, fertilizer, and tobacco industries.[48] Producing five hundred million cigars and forty billion cigarettes annually, it far surpassed Durham in the volume and variety of its tobacco products and capital assets. Second only to Atlanta as the fastest growing urban center below the Potomac, its bank clearings in 1921 alone exceeded $3,000,000,000.[49]

New South magnates, true exemplars of white superiority in the eyes

45. U.S., Bureau of the Census, *Fourteenth Census of the United States: 1920. Population*, III (Washington, D. C.: Government Printing Office), 1074; *Fifteenth Census of the United States: 1930. Population*, I (Washington, D. C.: Government Printing Office, 1931), 29.

46. *Richmond, Virginia—Yesterday and Today* (Richmond: The City of Richmond and The Chamber of Commerce, 1913), p. 69.

47. *Richmond City Directory 1923*, pp. 11–12.

48. *Ibid.*, p. 10.

49. *Richmond City Directory 1921*, p. 7.

of the rank and file, ruled this corporate domain. But Democratic party bosses like Congressman Andrew J. Montague and cultured aristocrats such as John Stewart Bryan, newspaper publisher and later president of William and Mary College, and Douglas Southall Freeman, author and editor of the Richmond *News Leader*, shared the pinnacle of power.[50] All members of the elite were uniformly paternalistic on the Negro question, however, and shunned the company of liberals in the Interracial Commission, including L. R. Reynolds and Lucy Randolph Mason.[51] Although it sponsored discussions, mostly at black schools and churches, the Commission could not halt deteriorating race relations in the postwar period. General black assertiveness, summed up in Lucian B. Watkins' "My God is Black,"[52] hardened white resistance. In December 1920 the Ku Klux Klan staged a full-dress downtown parade.[53] Within two years, a small group led by the noted Richmond pianist John Powell organized the powerful Anglo-Saxon Clubs to lobby for stricter segregation laws. The Virginia legislature responded to their formidable campaigns with a 1924 statute forbidding interracial marriage and one in 1926 requiring separate seating of the races at public functions.[54] Disillusioned by these developments, as well as frequent instances of mob violence, blacks retreated, accommodating themselves to segregation while working to undermine and overcome it. Frustrated in their poverty, ably represented by leaders who could seldom deliver through tangible gains, they were forced to compromise in order to survive.

Richmond Negroes, however, never forfeited their self-respect. Overshadowed by the city's opulence, victims of its racist hysteria,

50. Virginius Dabney, *Virginia: The New Dominion* (New York: Doubleday and Co., 1971), pp. 463, 472–473, 504–506.

51. A member of a socially prominent Richmond family, L. R. Reynolds served as director of the Virginia Commission on Interracial Cooperation. Lucy Randolph Mason, an activist in the Richmond League of Women Voters, was general secretary for the YWCA.

52. Richmond *Planet*, February 21, 1920.

53. *Ibid.*, December 11, 1920.

54. Charles E. Wynes, "The Evolution of Jim Crow Laws in Twentieth Century Virginia," *Phylon*, XXVIII (Winter 1967), 419–420; June Purcell Guild, *Black Laws of Virginia: A Summary of the Legislative Acts of Virginia Concerning Negroes from Earliest Times to the Present* (Richmond: Whittet and Shepperson, 1936), pp. 35, 148–149.

they simply endured. World War I, in which many of them served, had indeed sharpened racial frustration. "We want full rights unfettered and unproscribed," declared the Reverend W. B. Reed at Shiloh Baptist Church's Emancipation Day observance in 1922. "If this is social equality, we want it."[55] On the other hand, Marcus M. Garvey, charismatic head of the Universal Negro Improvement Association, speaking to Richmond's largest Negro gathering ever, denounced mere agitation. "If . . . you Negroes are tired of being abused, misrepresented, Jim Crowed, lynched, burned at the stake and persecuted," he fumed, "then get up and do something for yourselves."[56] Although they applauded him enthusiastically, black Richmonders were not ready for Garveyism. John Mitchell, Jr., who introduced the Jamaican, liked the idea of race unity but disagreed with his Back-to-Africa philosophy. Hancock thought that few in the audience accepted Garvey's extreme black chauvinism or booked passage on the Black Star Line, or planned to liberate Africa forcibly. What most wanted, he averred, was freedom in Richmond.[57]

After all, a proud black subculture existed behind the wall of segregation whose traditions and values, no less than those of white Richmond, were rooted in the past. Aware of their place in Negro history, black Richmonders knew the importance of Jamestown, where the first Africans were enslaved, and Appomattox, scene of the South's surrender and the real birthplace of Negro freedom. They immortalized the memory of Gabriel Prosser, Nat Turner, John Jasper, and Booker T. Washington as heroes, while William Washington Browne, John Mitchell, Jr., and Maggie L. Walker were their most esteemed local leaders.[58]

In 1882, Browne, an ex-slave, founded the Grand United Order of True Reformers, the most significant Negro benefit society up to the formation of North Carolina Mutual Life Insurance Company eighteen years later. Expanding his work in 1888, Browne organized the first Negro-owned bank in the country. The Order also published a weekly,

55. Quoted in Richmond *Planet*, February 11, 1922.
56. Quoted in Richmond *Planet*, July 8, 1922.
57. *Ibid.*; interview with Hancock, February 5, 1969.
58. Federal Writers' Program, *The Negro in Virginia*, pp. 292–305; interview with William L. Ransome, June 26, 1974.

the *True Reformer*, whose circulation averaged five thousand copies. From these origins emerged an extended family of Negro churches, mutual-aid societies, banks, insurance enterprises, cemetery and realty associations, newspapers, funeral homes, barber shops, and retail stores.[59] Mitchell, son of slave parents, in 1884 established the Richmond *Planet*, the first black paper to circulate nationally. Known for his "race rights" policy and prominent in politics, he opened the Mechanics Savings Bank in 1902. When Virginia Negroes launched the "lily black" Republican Party in 1921, a valiant effort to bolt the "lily white" regulars, Mitchell was their unsuccessful candidate for governor. His major support came from Richmond, where only 2,800 Negroes were qualified voters.[60] Browne and Mitchell worked for blacks' economic uplift and first-class citizenship, but were contrasts in leadership. They varied in response to the common reality of caste. Using Robert K. Merton's modes of adaptation to strain, Browne was an innovator who accepted the goals of material prosperity, seeking these through black self-help and racial solidarity rather than individualism. Mitchell was a rebel whose simultaneous acceptance and rejection of prescribed goals and means evidenced itself in militant protests to end racial discrimination within the system.

Born July 15, 1867, Maggie Walker, in 1899, became executive secretary of the Independent Order of St. Luke. By 1910 she had increased the membership from 700 to 20,000, set up the St. Luke Penny Savings Bank, a department store, and the *St. Luke Herald*, which sold 10,000 copies per week. A race benefactor and the grand

59. W. P. Burrell and D. E. Johnson, Sr., *Twenty-Five Years History of the Grand Fountain of the United Order of True Reformers 1881–1905* (Richmond: United Order of True Reformers, 1909), pp. 11–15, 35–44, 95–107; Abram L. Harris, *The Negro as Capitalist: A Study of Banking and Business among American Negroes* (Philadelphia: American Academy of Political and Social Science, 1936), pp. 62–74; Walter B. Weare, *Black Business in the New South: A Social History of the North Carolina Mutual Life Insurance Company* (Urbana: University of Illinois Press, 1973), pp. 12–16.

60. Federal Writers' Program, *The Negro in Virginia*, pp. 245, 284–285; Harris, *The Negro as Capitalist*, pp. 74–84; Ann Field Alexander, "Black Protest in the New South: John Mitchell, Jr. (1863–1929) and the Richmond *Planet*" (Ph.D. Dissertation, Duke University, 1972), pp. 127–184; Andrew Buni, The Negro in Virginia Politics 1902–1965 (Charlottesville, University Press of Virginia, 1967), pp. 84–89. For Merton's modes of adaptation, which include conformity, innovation, ritualism, retreatism, and rebellion, see his *Social Theory and Social Structure*, pp. 140–157.

darling of the Negro community, she sponsored a school for delinquent colored girls and scholarships for needy students at Virginia Union.[61]

Among other worthies was Giles B. Jackson, lawyer, Republican maverick, Negro business publicist, and Mitchell's number-one rival. Born in 1852, he served as Grand Attorney for the Order of True Reformers and drafted its original bank charter. Granted $100,000 by the United States Congress, he masterminded the nationally acclaimed Negro exhibit at the Jamestown Ter-Centennial in 1907, which displayed Negro achievement in practically every phase of art, industry, and education. In 1908 Jackson and D. Webster Davis, black poet and preacher, produced *The Industrial History of the Negro Race*.[62] According to the gossip columns, Jackson and Mitchell were natural competitors. Mitchell held office in the Knights of Pythias, a fraternal order whose relations with the True Reformers were always stormy. Each defended his lodge. Also the *Planet* editor had once vigorously criticized the accommodationist tactics of his Republican brother.[63] Hancock, who did not know either Jackson or Mitchell well, stood beyond the pale of Richmond's Negro upper-crust. Much the outsider needing approbation, he cultivated a good image with both the bourgeoisie and blacks in the street. Through his work at Union and Moore Street, including articles for the *Planet* and *St. Luke Herald*, he made himself known. He openly praised Mitchell's crusading journalism and Maggie Walker's inspiration to the race, on one occasion giving her an appreciation service at Moore Street.[64] To some, this smacked of opportunism.

In his community activities Hancock stressed the Negro's low economic status, and contemporary sources testified to the acuteness of the problem. Although many people considered Richmond the most progressive Negro business center in the nation next to Durham, the facts warranted a different appraisal. Very few Negroes, for example, were in the professions. In 1921 blacks comprised 31 per cent of the

61. Wendell P. Dabney, *Maggie L. Walker and the Independent Order of Saint Luke: The Woman and Her Work* (Cincinnati: Dabney Publishing Co., 1927), pp. 15–54; Federal Writers' Program, *The Negro in Virginia*, pp. 292–293.

62. Buni, *The Negro in Virginia Politics*, pp. 39–40; Federal Writers' Program, *The Negro in Virginia*, pp. 281–282, 297–298.

63. Buni, *The Negro in Virginia Politics*, pp. 65–66.

64. Richmond *Planet*, December 27, 1930.

population but accounted for 1 of the city's 23 architects, 12 of 273 attorneys, 13 of 412 notaries, 7 of 99 dentists, 1 of 20 opticians, 15 of 233 registered nurses, and 24 of 268 physicians. In Durham, a much smaller city with 7,654 blacks out of a total population of 21,715 for 1921, blacks contributed 2 of 27 attorneys, 3 of 46 notaries, 2 of 14 dentists, and 8 of 40 physicians. While blacks in Durham were doing better proportionately, progress in neither city was roseate.

In the city of Richmond a small number of blacks worked in skilled trades. There were 3 auto mechanics, 5 butchers, 3 bakers, 4 contractor-builders, 1 locksmith, 13 blacksmiths, 1 paperhanger, 3 photographers, 3 plasterers, 6 printers, 9 tailors, 1 house painter, 3 upholsterers, and 4 cabinet makers. The 4 banks, 3 newspapers, 14 funeral homes, 5 theaters, 65 churches, 9 insurance companies and mutual benefit societies which funneled the flow of Negro capital were dwarfed by a plethora of individual enterprises—135 barber and beauty shops, 20 clubs and pool halls, 72 dry cleaners and laundries, 33 coal and wood dealers, 55 dressmakers, 57 eating houses, 17 fish markets, 51 shoe repairmen, 43 courier services, and 139 retail grocers.[65] Unquestionably, these were the traditional black businesses which emerged largely in response to institutionalized discrimination and exclusionary economic practices.

Ultimately dependent upon white capital, lacking a foothold in manufacturing or industry, excluded from craft unions, blacks were also plagued with an 18.3 per cent illiteracy rate for those twenty-one years old and over.[66] Consequently, most ended up in the heaviest, lowest paying jobs of the mills and tobacco factories. A good many others were maids, janitors, yardmen, bellboys, bootblacks, cooks, waiters, and messengers. Three-fourths of all blacks occupied rental housing, and lived at or below the line of minimum subsistence.[67] Postwar inflation and rising unemployment reduced even more to poverty.

Negro leaders did not have the resources to solve these problems,

65. *Richmond City Directory 1921*, pp. 141–210. *Durham, North Carolina City Directory 1921*, pp. 45–90.

66. U.S., Bureau of the Census, *Abstract of the Fourteenth Census of the United States 1920* (Washington, D. C.: Government Printing Office, 1923), p. 439.

67. Federal Writers' Program, *The Negro in Virginia*, pp. 336–341; *Abstract of the Fourteenth Census of the United States 1920*, pp. 470, 503.

but they were determined. The Richmond and Virginia Union chapters of the NAACP, though ignored by white authorities, issued complaints against jury discrimination, voting restrictions, unequal school funds, and police brutality.[68] In 1923 Hancock, William N. Colson, Ora Brown Stokes, J. Milton Sampson, Wiley A. Hall, and a handful of white people founded the Richmond Urban League. Colson and Sampson were Virginia Union professors and pillars of the Richmond Negro Welfare League. Mrs. Stokes was president of the Negro Neighborhood Association. Hall, born in Alabama and a 1917 Union graduate, earned his M.A. from the University of Pittsburgh. Focusing on jobs, health, housing, and community services, the League complemented the NAACP's program of legal redress. Using the facilities of Leigh Street YMCA, Moore Street Baptist Church, and Virginia Union University, it functioned as a combination employment agency and information bureau on Negro life. In 1929, after six unspectacular years of operation, it hired Wiley Hall as executive secretary, and one office helper.[69]

The Urban League lacked the resources to reach the seat of the problems, unfortunately, and the Negro remained desperate. "Both brickbats and bouquets are seemingly as scarce as hen's teeth," commented the *Planet*. "We wonder when the storm will break."[70] Consonant with this mood was Hancock's own critique of Negro living conditions in Richmond, which, to his surprise, appeared uncut in the *News Leader*. He said that if white people faced up to the responsibility of improving opportunities for blacks the ghost of racial intermixture which haunted segregationists would be banished. Being a Negro in Richmond, he explained, was both irksome and embarrassing. It meant slurs in conversation and ridicule in the press, life in the most sordid

68. Buni, *The Negro in Virginia Politics*, p. 127; NAACP, *Eighth and Ninth Annual Reports 1917 and 1918* (New York: National Office of the NAACP, 1919), p. 85; Richmond *Planet*, July 31, 1921; Norfolk *Journal and Guide*, July 31, 1921.

69. J. Harvey Kearns, "Social and Economic Conditions in Richmond, Virginia as They Affect the Negro and An Evaluation of the Richmond Urban League," March–April, 1966, p. 8; "Statement Prepared by Wiley A. Hall, Executive Secretary, Richmond Urban League, to the Study Committee of the Richmond Area Community Council," April 14, 1954, pp. 1–2; clippings, Richmond *News Leader*, January 12, 1952, Richmond *Times-Dispatch*, February 24, 1955, Urban League Scrapbook. All of these are located in the Urban League's Files, Richmond, Virginia.

70. Richmond *Planet*, January 19, 1924.

part of the city where sanitation was at its lowest efficiency, riding on Jim Crow buses and waiting for trains at the Main Street station in a room marked "colored," disrespect for Negro women and bitter censure for their moral delinquencies, poor educational facilities and theories of mental inferiority. It meant "first paging" the Negro crimes and "last paging" Negro achievements, legislation "to keep him in his place" rather than laws to make him a first-class citizen. Finally, it meant being used as a means to an end and treated as a social menace. In closing, he expressed the hope that the races might cooperate in making Negro life more pleasant and profitable.[71]

Happily, when the Richmond Council of Social Agencies appointed a Negro Welfare Survey Committee in 1928, blacks and whites worked together. Seventy-five people—divided into task forces on economic status and dependency, health and housing, recreation, education, and behavior—observed, interviewed, and analyzed Richmond Negroes. Ora Brown Stokes, Union professors Henry B. Hucles, Robert P. Daniel, and Henry J. McGuinn, and rural educator Virginia Randolph were prominent among Negro participants. Lucy Randolph Mason, L. R. Reynolds, Jackson Davis, an official of the Rockefeller Fund, and June Purcell Guild, a social worker and director of the project, typified the whites. In November 1929, following many meetings, private conferences, changes, additions and omissions, the final report was published.[72]

A compendium of telling facts, it revealed, among other things, that Negroes lived 15 years less, were arrested 3 times more, and had a rate of illiteracy 14 times higher than whites. Negro illegitimacy was 198.5 per 1,000 as opposed to 30.7 for whites. In stillbirths, infant mortality, tuberculosis, venereal disease, homicide, blindness, and every other instance of social pathology, the black minority far outstripped the white majority. Few Negroes earned a decent family wage. Most stayed in over-crowded homes and had limited access to medical services. Wholesome recreational facilities were not available to Negro children, nor were kindergartens or day care centers. Richmond spent $50.79 per capita for instruction in white schools and $23.72 in

71. Richmond *News Leader*, March 17, 1926.
72. *The Negro in Richmond, Virginia* (Richmond: Richmond Council of Social Agencies, 1929), pp. i–ii, 1–4.

black ones, and white teachers received $550 to $800 more pay than black teachers. There were no Negro principals or special classes for the mentally and physically handicapped in Negro schools. The document concluded that an "inferior economic status . . . is the outstanding and most pressing social problem of Richmond Negroes, and is directly related to almost every other social problem of the group." Higher wages, greater regularity of employment, increased education and opportunities, it said, must be implemented immediately. Other key recommendations included fair Negro representation in decision-making, municipal funding for the Urban League, a receiving home for dependent Negro children, hospital practice for Negro physicians and nurses, construction of clean, low-rent housing, equalizing teacher salaries, and hiring Negro probation officers in the courts.[73]

If it told Negroes what they already knew, the survey presented information heretofore evaded by whites. For Hancock, who almost singlehandedly wrote the section on economic status and dependency problems, the entire project was a *cause célèbre*, tangible proof that black and white Southerners could bury the hatchet in a common cause. Moreover, it represented a step toward social change along lines which revealed a fundamental ambivalence in his thinking about strategy for achieving that change. Like Charles S. Johnson and W. E. B. Du Bois in the 1920's, Hancock believed that unbiased research and intelligent dissemination of the facts would spark greater interracial understanding and cooperation. In turn, coalitions of black and white leaders would push for progressive laws, compensatory programs, and a climate of public opinion conducive to fair implementation. Clearly, this strategy combined the legalistic philosophy of the NAACP with the economic adjustment approach of the National Urban League.

Segregation, of course, created problems which strained the efficacy of Hancock's strategy. Separation by law limited contacts to all but select groups of race reformers, so the entire legal corpus had to be changed before new laws, programs, and attitudes could emerge. Yet *The Negro in Richmond, Virginia* made no reference to ending segregation. Being pragmatic, or at least accommodationist, Hancock and his

---

73. *Ibid.*, pp. 5–8, 16–46, 89–96, 108–130.

coworkers hoped and allowed for the possibility of change despite the absence of such a reference. Hancock expected white Richmond to act with dispatch, presumably within the biracial framework. If not, Negroes would continue to be hopelessly trapped, and he wondered how long they would endure.[74]

Hancock was not insistently committed to biracialism. He thought that integration would supplant segregation in the future. For a while, however, he concealed his doubts about the effectiveness of his own strategy and adopted a positive attitude. He began a weekly column for the Associated Negro Press in 1929 which appeared in 114 Negro newspapers throughout the country, including the *St. Luke Herald* and Norfolk *Journal and Guide*. Generally, his early releases emphasized interracial understanding and Southern redemption. A better South, he prophesied, was gradually being born. Hancock encouraged blacks to hope.[75] "I used to be afraid about the Negro problem but now I am calm about it," he declared at the 1929 meeting of the Virginia Interracial Commission in Lawrenceville. "I realize that the white man must save us or he must himself be lost. You can't build the world upon the exclusive plan."[76]

Popular, in demand as a public speaker, having people like President Gregg of Hampton praise him as "a scholar, teacher and preacher who has won deserved recognition,"[77] Hancock probably did feel a certain calm—but a calm like the one before a storm. He had emerged, and he doubtless enjoyed the emotional rewards of leadership. He also developed friendly, purposeful ties with other black leaders, notably Plummer B. Young, publisher-editor of the *Journal and Guide*, Luther P. Jackson, professor of history at Virginia State College, William M. Cooper, dean of Hampton Institute, and J. M. Tinsley, state secretary of the NAACP. Yet, events were in the making which soon jolted his apparent optimism and ushered in pessimism and gloom.

74. Interview with Hancock, February 5, 1969.
75. See Richmond *St. Luke Herald*, February 2, August 24, 1929; Norfolk *Journal and Guide*, January 12, 1929.
76. Quoted in Richmond *Times-Dispatch*, February 28, 1929.
77. Quoted in Richmond *Times-Dispatch*, June 8, 1929.

III. The "Gloomy Dean"

In the closing chapter of his much heralded book, Robert Russa Moton, Virginia-born president of Tuskegee Institute and a towering figure among Southern blacks, described a hopeful outlook for the 1930's. He saw new forces at work, creating a positive interest in the Negro and a sympathetic attitude toward his problems. The word "nigger" was rarely heard in public, he noted, and even the asperities of segregation were mitigated by an accompanying smile of deprecation which deplored its necessity and ridiculed its absurdity. More than ever before, blacks and whites were recognizing their interdependence. Just as it was impossible for the white man to prosper without the labor and assistance of the black man, blacks needed the practical support and cooperation of whites in order to advance. Bound together by ties of a common suffering and sacrifice, he concluded, the two elements could be nothing less than allies in the future.[1] Economist Abram L. Harris, sociologist E. Franklin Frazier, and other younger Negro thinkers rejected Moton's optimism, as well as his over-reliance upon race adjustment. Negro dependence upon white good will and self-interest, they argued, guaranteed neither social recognition nor bread. It obscured rather than clarified the hard issues of economics and class which, in their judgment, were equal to, if not more important than, race in the lives of Negro Americans.[2]

The Great Depression widened the ideological rift between the old guard and the young radicals, and Hancock found himself increasingly in the middle. Closer to Moton's camp in age and temperament, he

1. Robert Russa Moton, *What The Negro Thinks* (Garden City, N. Y.: Doubleday, Doran, and Co., 1929), pp. 240–267.
2. Harris, Frazier, and the academic radicals criticized both the old Negro leaders and their white liberal friends. See Ralph J. Bunche, "The Programs, Ideologies, Tactics and Achievements of Negro Betterment and Interracial Organizations" (June 1940), pp. 147–148, in the Carnegie-Myrdal Study of the Negro in America, Duke University Library, Durham, North Carolina; Raymond Wolters, *Negroes and the Great Depression: The Problem of Economic Recovery* (Westport, Conn.: Greenwood Publishing Corp., 1970), pp. 219–229; and James O. Young, *Black Writers of the Thirties* (Baton Rouge: Louisiana State University Press, 1973), pp. ix–xii, 35–63.

hammered out the Washingtonian values of thrift, hard work, sacrifice, respectability, and individual enterprise. The neo-economic determinism of the radicals confirmed basic points in his own economic philosophy, but he spurned Socialism and Communism and emphasized race. If his continuing personal dilemma over segregation—exacerbated by deteriorating race relations and the increasing misery of the black masses—made him unduly pessimistic, he was still convinced that self-help and interracial cooperation offered a way out.

The thirties ushered in the worst economic crisis in American history. Agricultural prices fell by more than 60 per cent, industrial production declined 50 per cent, and a high of 12,000,000 Americans were unemployed. Negroes were the most disadvantaged major group in the country. The first fired and the last hired, they faced disproportionate joblessness, neglect, hunger, despair, and violent repression.[3] In devising strategies to combat these deplorable conditions, they turned not only to the question of rights but to the issue of survival. Bread and butter dominated Negro thought. Many black scholars and intellectuals studied Negro life and documented ways in which caste kept their race poor and ignorant.[4] To be sure, they continued their uneasy attachment to the American creed of freedom and equal opportunity. Some propagated the tenets of Marxism. Others invoked the maxims of Christianity. But all were interested in programs and institutions which assured permanent recovery and relief.

The national disaster sent shock waves of consciousness throughout the black world. At the Springfield, Massachusetts, meeting of the

3. Wolters, *Negroes and the Great Depression* pp. ix, 3–4, 83–86; John Hope Franklin, *From Slavery to Freedom: A History of Negro Americans* (4th rev. ed.; New York: Alfred A. Knopf, 1974), pp. 367–371; John Williams, "Struggles of the Thirties in the South," in Bernard Sternsher, ed., *The Negro in Depression and War: Prelude to Revolution, 1930–1945* (Chicago: Quadrangle Books, 1969), pp. 166–178.

4. For contemporary examples, see Charles S. Johnson, *The Negro in American Civilization: A Study of Negro Life and Race Relations in the Light of Social Research* (New York: Henry Holt and Co., 1930); Abram L. Harris's collaborative work with the white scholar, Sterling D. Spero, *The Black Worker: The Negro and the Labor Movement* (New York: Columbia University Press, 1931); and E. Franklin Frazier, *The Negro Family in Chicago* (Chicago: University of Chicago Press, 1932).

NAACP Annual Convention, A. Philip Randolph, Brotherhood of Sleeping Car Porters and Maids' president, urged the Association to give priority to the acute needs of labor and the Negro masses. Editor P. B. Young of the Norfolk *Journal and Guide* warned that a time of testing more severe than chattel slavery was upon the race. Negroes, he insisted, must learn to live within their means. One writer for the *Southern Workman*, official voice of Hampton Institute, decried the dearth of jobs and educational opportunities in Virginia. These privations, he feared, were having a deadening effect upon the whole outlook of Negro youth.[5] W. E. B. Du Bois, longtime advocate of civil rights, declared the Negro's economic condition to be the number-one problem of the hour. Urban League director T. Arnold Hill told the American Federation of Labor that unless it ended its narrowness and bigotry Negro workers would either scab or starve. W. C. Matney, a black economist, said the Negro suffered from conditions over which he had no control, victimized by the industrial and commercial order. Unable to pinpoint a remedy, he asked: "How can relief be obtained? What is the way out?"[6]

In the search for valid and usable answers to these questions, Hancock was not the cheerful minister whom Jackson Ward had known before. Now seldom preaching about the brighter side of life, he chose to describe the darkness. His terms, as expected, were graphic and picturesque. One sermon called "What To Do Next," delivered on November 9, 1930, drew comment from the *Planet*. The nation's storehouses were overflowing, Hancock lamented, but its children were crying for bread. Honest men could not live by honest toil, and the hungry millions were at the mercy of the charitable few. Nations talked peace and prepared for war, loved money more than mankind, and the races were divided and headed for ultimate doom. The best

5. NAACP, *Twenty-First Annual Report 1930* (New York: National Office of the NAACP, 1931), p. 33; Norfolk *Journal and Guide*, January 11, February 1, 1930; Thomas L. Dabney, "Local Leadership among Virginia Negroes," *Southern Workman*, LIX (January) 1930), 34.

6. See Du Bois' editorial in the *Crisis*, XXXVII (January 1930), 11; T. Arnold Hill, "Open Letter to Mr. William Green, President, American Federation of Labor," *Opportunity*, VIII (February 1930), 56–57; W. C. Matney, "Exploitation or Cooperation?" *Crisis*, XXXVII (January 1930), 12.

plans had failed, and the strong were bound. "And having done all," he advised the Moore Street congregation, "stand!"[7] In the context of this rich imagery, though, Hancock was responding to a variety of stimuli—Richmond's failure to implement welfare reform, mounting racial tensions, and economic depression. The connections were apparent. Just two weeks prior to his much talked about sermon, for example, he told the Annual Interracial Conference that over half of Richmond Negroes were on the brink of starvation. Without emergency relief, he said, there would be a serious moral collapse and ominous consequences for the city.[8]

Writing in *Southern Workman*, Hancock warned of "a definite Negro-displacement movement in the field of economic endeavor" which Negro leaders were either overlooking or ignoring. Like the ghost of Banquo, however, it was haunting the Negro's dream of survival in America. Migration to the cities and acute racial competition for employment, he thought, were chiefly responsible. Backing up his contention, he referred to a New Jersey summer resort where whites had replaced all the Negro help except one chef. Only one hotel in Boston employed Negroes, he demurred, and the Pullman headquarters were being stormed by young white men seeking places as porters. Virginia considered a bill in 1930 designed to destroy the Negro barber who catered to white trade. In Richmond, associations of window washers and furnace keepers excluded Negroes from jobs which they had held for generations. Throughout the South, moreover, whites were sweeping the streets, digging graves, waiting at table, driving taxicabs, cooking in restaurants, and chauffeuring. A few "positions" were opening up for educated Negroes here and there, he stated, but these did not offset the rapid loss of "jobs" at the lower level. Hancock criticized the apathy of the Negro church, and scorned the "speak up to and back at the white man" attitude of the Negro press. Neither provided the constructive leadership which the situation demanded. He contended that unless the problem of displacement received immediate attention, great tribulations would follow.[9]

7. Highlighted in Richmond *Planet*, November 15, 1930.
8. Editorial, "Virginia Conference on Race Relations," *Southern Workman*, LX (January 1931), 6; interview with Hancock, March 7, 1969.
9. Gordon B. Hancock, "Our Coming Captivity," *Southern Workman*, LIX (April 1930), 153–160.

Hancock dramatized the situation. "My class in Race Relations found that 85 per cent of the ads in metropolitan papers, East and South and West indicated direct demands for 'whites,' " he reported. "Unless this movement is counteracted, the whole plan of our progress in this country must be revised." [10] Speaking at Columbia University, he told a mostly white crowd that without adequate employment and wages Negroes would lose their fierce battle for survival in the cities. The speech prompted a comment from one of his listeners. "The immediate effect of your remarks upon the audience and especially upon our colored students was one of despair," Professor of Education Mabel Carney wrote to him. "Your warning and conviction that Negroes are being led into economic captivity is only too true." [11] Appearing in 1931 before a conclave of black leaders at Martha's Vineyard, Massachusetts, and the President's Committee on Unemployment in Washington, D. C., Hancock evoked similar responses. [12]

The Negro's plight involved race and economics. Frequently, though, Hancock slanted his own analysis toward race, as in his article on Negro labor. In his view, industrialization in the South, where over eight of America's eleven million blacks lived, vitally affected the status of Negro labor. In leaving agriculture for industry, the Negro had become a marginal worker—mostly unskilled and unorganized. By migrating from rural to urban areas, along with "the lowly whites," he chose to settle where life was most rigorous. For in the city he enjoyed little in the way of a labor market, except domestic service. Denied membership in unions and access to apprenticeship programs because of his race, he was forced to accept a perennially low wage. The changed attitude of the white South toward manual work threatened his monopoly of the so-called menial jobs. Negro business, lacking capital and volume, offered him virtually no succor. In fact, the future of race enterprises depended upon his income. Whether he should strive to enter fields barred by race prejudice or cling to the traditional ones constituted his profound dilemma. At any rate, he must face the

10. Clipping, Richmond *St. Luke Herald*, n.d., Gordon Blaine Hancock Papers, Richmond, Virginia; Norfolk *Journal and Guide*, March 22, 1930.

11. Program, "Lectures on Negro Education and Race Relations," Columbia University, New York, N. Y., February 4–April 15, 1931, p. 3; Mabel Carney to Hancock, March 30, 1931, Hancock Papers.

12. Hancock to Mrs. Francis J. Torrance, July 7, 1932, Hancock Papers.

ugly fact that white racism limited his upward mobility. Hancock there-fore advised that the overwhelming majority of Negroes hold fast to what jobs they had. The "Talented Tenth," on the other hand, should create and exploit new avenues and opportunities. Hancock recom-mended Negro cooperation with the labor movement, if possible. If not, Negroes should set up their own unions. He also insisted that national and state governments establish the necessary machinery to safeguard the Negro laborer's rights.[13]

Certain contemporary analyses supported Hancock's general as-sessment, but differed in emphasis. Black historians Lorenzo J. Greene and Carter G. Woodson examined the occupational experience of the Negro from 1890 to 1930, and were less than elated over their findings. In 1890, 87.3 per cent of black wage earners were agricultural or domestic workers; 6.8 per cent were employed in manufacturing or mechanical pursuits, 4.8 per cent in trade and transportation, and 1.1 per cent in the professions. Industrialization in the South and the black movement North, which reached flood tide during World War I, af-fected these categories only minimally. In 1930, 65 per cent of black workers were engaged in agriculture or domestic service, with 19.6 per cent in manufacturing or mechanical occupations. Negro ratios in trade and transportation and the professions, not surprisingly, remained under 5 and 2 per cent respectively. Insufficient skills, differential wage scales, exclusive craft unions, and white racism, the authors said, blocked the Negro's breakthrough to higher ground. The American labor movement had made no serious attempt to organize blacks, they charged, except where capitalists used them to intimidate white labor. Greene and Woodson saw a bleak future for the Negro wage earner, concluding that his fate rested upon industrial unionism, consumer consciousness, and the development of a working class ethos which demanded the protection of all laborers regardless of color.[14]

Economists Sterling D. Spero and Abram L. Harris looked at the Negro's relations with the American labor movement from the end of

13. Hancock, "The Changing Status of Negro Labor," *Southern Workman*, LX (August 1931), 351–360.

14. Lorenzo J. Greene and Carter G. Woodson, *The Negro Wage Earner* (Washing-ton, D. C.: Association for the Study of Negro Life and History, 1930), pp. 36–47, 337–353.

the Civil War to the Great Depression, focusing on the interplay between the slave heritage, craft–union structure and policy, Northern migrations, and the ideology of the Negro middle class. Of 120,000 Southern craftsmen in 1865 approximately 100,000 were black, but within a generation this figure declined both relatively and absolutely. The rise of trade unions placed blacks at a disadvantage in the labor market as competitors with white men, forced them to accept lower wages, and relegated them to the role of "an industrial reserve," a readily available supply of cheap manpower used during acute labor shortages and strikes. The massive numbers of rural, unskilled Southern Negroes who went North experienced new modes of living and employment, but were not absorbed by the labor movement. Some were members of segregated locals. Others, like A. Philip Randolph, organized independent black unions. Despite postwar racial hostility and continued oppression, the Negro masses did not embrace economic radicalism. Socialists and Communists, said Spero and Harris, overlooked the Negro's cultural background and his strong desire to integrate into American society. The Negro middle class, at the same time, was oblivious of labor alignments. Operating within the Booker T. Washington-NAACP tradition, most Negro leaders rejected a class analysis of the black community's problems, preferring instead the timeworn values of thrift, efficiency, character, and self-help. An "independent black economy," Spero and Harris stated, would further exploit the great majority of black workers. Industrial and political coalitions of the workers across racial lines offered the only real hope for the less favored.[15]

Sociologist Charles S. Johnson painted an unhappy portrait of black life, finding the Negro economically restricted, educationally deprived, politically disfranchised, and denied equal justice from the state. He proposed no panacea, but suggested that nothing short of immediate reform, enlightened public opinion, and increased interracial contact would end the nightmare of racial conflict, hatred, and fear. Turning to the impact of the depression, particularly on Negro employment in industry, Johnson said that mechanization and discrimination were combining to drive Negroes out. Using data from field studies and

15. Spero and Harris, *The Black Worker*, pp. 16–35, 53–86, 149–181, 385–469.

interviews of black and white employees, he found plants with under 25 per cent Negroes in the total working force reporting that they were responsible for 75 per cent of the turnover. Employers usually claimed that blacks were inefficient, unsatisfactory, not faithful, or took excessive time off. Johnson, however, discovered different reasons why blacks were being replaced—traditional plant policy not to employ Negroes; racial difficulties; disapproval of white workers; beliefs that Negroes were inferior, immoral, and lazy; fear of bringing Negroes into contact with white women employees; the Negro's lack of skills; previous unsatisfactory experiences with Negro laborers; the belief that certain jobs belonged exclusively to white people; additional expenses for segregated facilities; and objections of labor unions. These findings, he generalized, foreshadowed further unemployment.[16]

Greene and Woodson, Spero and Harris, and Johnson, like Hancock, were concerned with the black worker's worsening situation. Though race prejudice entered the picture, both Greene and Woodson and Spero and Harris made organized labor the chief culprit. They also postulated that a working-class ideology and program constituted the surest road for the Negro to travel, whereas Hancock, who remained dubious of the class analysis, fell back upon racial self-help and solidarity. He could not envision a black-white workers' alliance, but he saw the necessity of cooperation with white liberals. Johnson's tone was low-key when compared with Hancock's, yet the two men viewed the problems essentially in racial terms. Whether attributed to race or class, though, Negro unemployment rates were startling. Dr. Joseph H. Willits of the University of Pennsylvania, in his definitive study, calculated that 13.8 per cent of the whites and 19.4 per cent of the Negroes in Philadelphia were jobless in 1930; 24.1 per cent white and 35 per cent Negro in 1931; 39.7 per cent white and 56 per cent Negro in 1932! The National Urban League predicted no let up in either the South or the North. Only united, scientific, courageous, honest and sacrificial action by the "best brains" of the Negro community, A. Philip Randolph felt, would save the race.[17]

16. Johnson, *The Negro in American Civilization*, pp. 68–116, 355, 373.

17. See Charles S. Johnson, ed., *The Economic Status of Negroes* (Nashville: Fisk University Press, 1933), pp. 18–20, which summarizes and analyzes the materials presented by Professor Willits and others at the Conference on the Economic Status of

Monroe N. Work, the able Negro bibliographer and statistician of Tuskegee Institute, refused to despair. He thought black leaders such as Hancock had exaggerated the white takeover of traditionally "Negro jobs." He also questioned whether any jobs were historically "white" or "Negro," since the races overlapped in virtually every occupational category. There may be changes in some aspects of occupations, he said, but these did not necessarily indicate an economic loss to the race. The number of Negro barber shops catering to white trade was decreasing, Work explained, but those serving the needs of their own group were rapidly increasing. Unions of Negro barbers in Kansas City, Missouri, New Orleans, Richmond, Chicago, and New York testified to their strength in the trade. Further, the black waiter occupied somewhat the same position as his white counterpart with respect to competition from waitresses. The point overlooked, he argued, was that while there were fewer black male waiters the high percentage of black waitresses more than counterbalanced the decrease. While Work failed to point out that black waitresses uniformly received lower salaries than black waiters, which depressed the overall wage-earning capacity of black people, he did note a nationwide tendency in urban centers for white merchants to employ blacks in sales and clerical positions. He further prophesied that new job opportunities would multiply with the accumulation of Negro political strength.[18]

Hancock was too preoccupied with the clouds to see the silver linings that Work saw. Habitually apocalyptic, but possessing a keen eye for practicalities, he endeavored to arouse Negroes to the seriousness of their lot. Verbose, yet forceful, his statements ran the gamut from straight talk and common sense to race chauvinism and economic separatism. Most of his strategy through the early years of the depression can be summed up in three of his own popular slogans: "Hold Your Job," "Back to the Farm," and the "Double Duty Dollar."[19]

the Negro, held in Washington, D. C., May 11–13, 1933, under the sponsorship of the Julius Rosenwald Fund; Hancock, "The Changing Status of Negro Labor," 359–360; A. Philip Randolph, "The Economic Crisis of the Negro," Opportunity, IX (May 1931), 149.

18. Monroe N. Work, ed., Negro Year Book: An Annual Encyclopedia of the Negro 1931–1932 (Tuskegee: Negro Year Book Publishing Co., 1931), pp. 145–146.

19. Raymond Gavins, "Gordon Blaine Hancock: A Black Profile from the New South," Journal of Negro History, LIX (July 1974), 217–221.

For most blacks, Hancock believed, the question was to eat or not to eat. Negro leadership might seek to escape this harsh reality by gloating over a handful of new jobs, but token employment did not approach the magnitude of the problem.[20] He said that blacks like those who lived along Sophie's Alley in Richmond, where the one-room apartments were converted horse stalls without heat, water, or ventilation, hardly benefited from such misplaced optimism. Too poor to afford kerosene at five cents a jar or candles at a penny apiece, they roamed East Main Street begging bread.[21] Rather than giving priority to positions and offices for "a few capable Negroes," the race needed general improvement among the masses. Nothing helped the vast majority of Negroes more than the chance to work, Hancock said, although it appeared unlikely that most would be gainfully employed in the foreseeable future. Since unemployment had become a permanent part of American capitalism, he reasoned, business and industry would never again provide enough jobs to go around. In addition, automation, the steady contraction of manual-labor opportunities, increased competition, and widespread displacement threatened to eliminate the Negro from the economic order.[22] Weighing the odds, which were not good, Hancock argued that those Negroes who still held jobs must do everything possible to keep them. This involved being more efficient and diligent than native whites and immigrants of all races. Frequently, though, it meant racial abuse, accepting lower wages, and nonentanglement with labor unions—each a consequence of the Negro's unfortunate circumstances.

Fearing that Southern blacks could become indifferent under oppression and strain, Hancock launched a one-man crusade. "Negro, hold your job," he called out repeatedly.[23] Although he did not wish to imply that blacks were indolent and would not work, as his critics

20. Hancock, "Our Coming Captivity," 158; Norfolk *Journal and Guide*, March 22, 1930.

21. "Battling for Bread," a lecture delivered by Gordon B. Hancock at First Baptist Church, Norfolk, Virginia, March 30, 1930, Hancock Papers. Also, see Norfolk *Journal and Guide*, March 29, 1930; and Federal Writers' Program, *The Negro in Virginia* (Hampton: The Hampton Institute, 1940), p. 337.

22. Hancock, "The Changing Status of Negro Labor," 359–360.

23. For examples, see Norfolk *Journal and Guide*, January 11, 18, 25, February 22, 1930.

charged, he was pointing up the obvious fact that black survival demanded jobs. Salvation for the beleaguered Negro, in his view, necessitated a gospel of work. "By jobs and jobs alone shall Negroes live!"[24] After all, said Hancock, it was the income from jobs which enabled blacks to pay church dues, make bank deposits, patronize Negro professionals, buy from Negro enterprises, and maintain their self-respect. Surely the race, while forging ahead for better opportunities, could profit from a campaign designed to emphasize its fundamental and most valuable economic possession. Should twelve million Negroes become job-conscious, Hancock wrote, their casualties in "the bitter battle for bread" would be reduced.[25] As the mouthpiece of the job-holding idea, Hancock utilized a down-to-earth, anecdotal style. If Negroes told "fewer hard luck stories and more hard work stories," he said, they might boost racial morale. "Many a longwinded talker is a short-winded worker." In one column Hancock said that he was in a grocery store where a white man told the butcher that he wanted a chicken but not a black one. Noting the lesson from this interesting manifestation of the color line, he punned: "The black chickens had better get their heads together."[26]

In emphasizing job-consciousness, Hancock exhorted Negro workers to emulate middle-class standards and simultaneously criticized the Negro middle class. The Negro porter or maid who worked hard, saved money, and lived above reproach, he said, did as much to elevate the race as the professor or lawyer. Ordinary toilers were the Negro's offensive line in the football game of economic struggle. Their daily sacrifices made possible the race's hard earned touchdowns in business, the professions, and the education of Negro youth.[27] Regrettably, Hancock lamented, the Negro intelligentsia ignored the concerns of the lowly brethren. What these "give-me-taffy" Negroes failed to consider, however, was that unless the common work-a-day folks had jobs with which to patronize them, they were going to be less "upper-crust." If the so-called "big Negroes" were tired of his job propaganda,

24. *Ibid.*, April 12, 1930.
25. "Battling for Bread."
26. Norfolk *Journal and Guide*, January 18, 25, April 26, 1930. For a revealing commentary, see "The Job," *Southern Workman*, LXI (Jan. 1932), 4.
27. Norfolk *Journal and Guide*, January 25, February 22, 1930.

he said, then let them stop riding the backs of their people.[28] From the NAACP, which spent its time and money opposing the Supreme Court confirmation of Judge John J. Parker, to bourgeois black women in Washington, D. C., who spent $30,000 on furs for the Howard-Lincoln football game, Hancock scorned the neglect and pretentiousness of the black bourgeoisie. He claimed that Negro ministers who drove big cars and wore expensive suits were siphoning away the earnings of an impecunious people, while the Negro press, which over-publicized black-and-tan social events and black-white marriages, was undermining race unity.[29] Many people reacted bitterly to Hancock's alleged meddling. Editor Robert L. Vann of the Pittsburgh *Courier* and columnist William N. Jones of the Baltimore *Afro-American*, for example, strongly objected to his criticism of the Negro press on the grounds that Negro social activities constituted a major source of race pride for blacks in the streets.[30]

George S. Schuyler, a popular young black journalist and intellectual, dismissed Hancock's "constant yapping" about jobs as altogether unnecessary advice and an insult to the intelligence of the Negro worker. Nobody need tell the black toiler to hold his job, Schuyler stated, because he would if the white employer permitted him to do so. On the other hand, if the white employer decided to fire him, he had no power to prevent it. Thousands of excellent Negro workers were losing their jobs not because of inefficiency or indifference, Schuyler concluded, but because white employers wanted white employees. "If Hancock will devise some way of keeping white employers from throwing Negroes out of work, the dark brothers will hold their jobs all right."[31] Hancock, in replying, did not refute the fact of displacement

28. *Ibid.*, February 1, April 12, 1930.
29. *Ibid.*, April 19, May 3, 10, 1930.
30. Hancock responded to Vann and Jones in his column for May 10, 1930.
31. Pittsburgh *Courier*, May 31, 1930. "Gordon B. Hancock . . . seems to take all the Negroes for damn fools. Each week he harps on Negroes holding their jobs and prophesy dire catastrophies [*sic*] if they do not do so," Schuyler added. "When I go about the country and see the tens of thousands of Negro workers filing out of their hovels in the morning—making that time—to earn a mere pittance to keep the wolf from the door, it makes me sore to hear a cloistered professor bellowing to them week after week to hold their jobs."

or devise a scheme to stop it. Rather, he tackled the young writer on personal grounds. "Brer Schuyler," with his fourth-rate iconoclasm, cynicism, near-Menckenism and atheism, was deriding sound advice, Hancock explained. "His kind" would save Southern Negroes by leaving them the bag to hold while staying up North to indulge in derby hats, tuxedos and spats, and spout Socialist rhetoric. If Schuyler had something better to offer, he should give it. Otherwise, Hancock submitted, he was just one more "Black Nordic" out of step with "the poor struggling folks" in the South.[32] In a rebuttal, Schuyler got in a few digs himself. He said that Harvard wasted a lot of time trying to educate Professor Hancock, whose gloomy sociological deliverances contained little of scientific value. He denied aping H. L. Mencken in literary style and wit, confessed to being a Socialist and an atheist, and expressed shock that stylish dress made one an enemy of the Negro race. As for "speaking down" to Southern Negroes, Schuyler said he would never knowingly do it.[33] Ironically, the last word in this exchange came from P. B. Young instead of Hancock. Young considered the hold-your-job philosophy sound in spite of beliefs to the contrary, including Schuyler's. Hancock, he said, correctly understood "the habits, shortcomings and psychology of his Southern brethren."[34]

"Back to the Farm" touched some sensitive spots too. To its major advocates—Kelly Miller, President Benjamin F. Hubert of Georgia State Industrial College, P. B. Young, and Hancock—it was an expedient way of relieving Negro suffering. Hancock's involvement resulted primarily from his shifting position on what blacks ought to do. In January 1932, when he met with a group of economists to formulate a proposal to combat unemployment,[35] his views on Negro displace-

32. Norfolk *Journal and Guide*, June 28, 1930. "It is easy to criticize, in fact I know fifty fools who can out-criticize even our esteemed friend, but they have nothing constructive to offer," Hancock explained. "As an 'ear tickler' Brer Schuyler's line has financial possibilities, but as a constructive and practical philosopher he looks to us like a 'flat tire.'"

33. Pittsburgh *Courier*, July 12, 1930.

34. Norfolk *Journal and Guide*, July 19, 1930.

35. Held in New York City, the meeting brought together thirty-one economists, most of whom were professors, including Merryle S. Rukeyser of Columbia, Thomas N. Carver of Harvard, Paul H. Douglas of Chicago, William N. Loucks of Pennsylvania, and George R. Taylor of Amherst.

ment, captivity, and job-holding were well known.[36] The economists' plan, which he endorsed, recommended a $5,000,000,000 federal program of emergency public works. This measure, if dramatically introduced and effectively implemented, they stated, would end idleness, improve the environment, and stimulate business.[37] Copies of the plan were sent to President Herbert Hoover and the Congress, but were tabled until the coming of the New Deal. Hancock, meanwhile, thought Negroes were in for much harder trials. In Virginia, by the winter of 1932, the cities were disaster areas. Of the state's 650,165 blacks, fully 40 per cent lived in urban centers, while two-thirds of the entire black population were desperately poor. A continuous influx of black migrants from rural Tidewater and the Piedmont further overcrowded Negro slums and augmented the relief lines. Whenever blacks could find work, the pay scales were unconscionably low. Black tobacco workers in the Richmond factories averaged $6.40 per week, while white foremen in the same plants averaged $63.00 per week. Negro domestics in Lynchburg earned $4.00 for a work week of ninety hours. In Norfolk, Negro longshoremen received 25¢ an hour, with no extra pay for overtime.[38] Hancock, in face of these conditions, wondered if the Negro—like a used part—would be thrown upon the social junk heap of the nation. "Color prejudice will enventually force colored people out of the cities," he warned. "Our only hope is to go back to the Southern farms."[39]

Actually, as it appeared in his press releases, Hancock's farm idea seemed more a safety valve or escape hatch than a blanket solution to

36. His pronouncements were perhaps too well known to the Baltimore *Afro-American* which remarked in a column of October 27, 1931: "Like John Jasper, another Richmonder, who claimed the sun moves and the earth is flat, Mr. Hancock's views are outmoded and mossback; for him mist and gloom cover everything."

37. "Economists' Plan for Accelerating Public Works," New York, January 9, 1932, Hancock Papers.

38. Virginius Dabney, *Virginia: The New Dominion* (New York: Doubleday and Company, Inc., 1971), pp. 488–491; Federal Writers' Program, *The Negro in Virginia*, pp. 335–336; Ronald L. Heinemann, "Depression and New Deal in Virginia" (Ph.D. Dissertation, University of Virginia, 1968), pp. 2, 4, 6.

39. Norfolk *Journal and Guide*, January 16, 1932. The statement on the farm was made sometime during the summer of 1932 and appeared in an editorial of the Baltimore *Afro-American*, August 1, 1942.

black urban problems. There were advantages on the small farm and in country life which far outweighed the precariousness of the city, Hancock contended. Food and shelter of sorts were more often obtainable, with ample work in the fields. There were better opportunities for land and home ownership, cohesive families, good health, and almost no crime[40] —not a little reminiscent of his boyhood days in Ninety-Six and Greenwood County, South Carolina. For example, Negro security in rural Saluda, Virginia, as opposed to jeopardy in Harlem, New York, held strong possibilities for racial advancement.[41] The movement back to the farm, however, had to be orderly and planned. Individual Negroes with money, as well as businesses, churches, lodges, and fraternal orders, could buy the cheap farm lands being abandoned by whites in Virginia and other parts of the South. Resettled parties, ostensibly those who most wanted to relocate, would pledge themselves to cultivating the soil and the ideal of self-sufficiency. Blacks capable of adjusting in the city were advised to do so. Others, of course, were strongly urged to consider the country because the burden of feeding the impoverished millions would be greater than the municipalities could bear.[42]

Kelly Miller voiced a deeper distrust of the city, where white people monopolized every available avenue of opportunity and machines preempted Negro labor. Every time the white man abandoned a farm, Miller wanted to see a Negro take it up. Forty acres, a mule, and a cotton crop were infinitely more efficacious than being the object of charity or the surplus man. Only by outworking and underliving the arrogant majority could the Negro survive the depression.[43] Benjamin F. Hubert, echoing similar arguments, thought Negroes were sacrificing their superior agricultural heritage in quest of congested urban centers. Possession of fertile farms guaranteed the Negro a solid

40. Norfolk *Journal and Guide*, October 1, 1932.

41. Hancock, "Saluda, Virginia and Harlem, New York City," in *The Future of Negroes on the Farm: Articles and Editorials Reprinted from the Journal and Guide* (Norfolk: Association for the Advancement of Negro Country Life, n.d.), pp. 24–25.

42. Norfolk *Journal and Guide*, September 24, October 1, December 3, 1932.

43. Kelly Miller, "Back to the Farm," in *The Future of Negroes on the Farm*, pp. 17–18, and his "The Farm—The Negro's Best Chance," *Opportunity*, XIII (January 1935), 24.

economic foundation, he asserted, and preserved the values of discipline and self-help.[44] P. B. Young, who editorialized in favor of the farm, said the unemployed masses could not simply walk back and take up farming. He proposed the development of a rational plan, formulated and carried through by the government, under which Negroes might choose life on the soil as a means of making a living and rehabilitating the source of the nation's wealth.[45]

Critics were cynical, at times satirical, in attacking what they viewed as an anachronism. Rayford W. Logan, who interviewed many city-bound black farmers in his work at Atlanta University, said Hancock's back to the farm meant back to sharecropping, and no sensible Negro would go back.[46] George Streator, former managing editor of the NAACP's *Crisis* and a labor organizer, seized the opportunity to rebuke older race men. To him, Kelly Miller was an intellectual mossback, "a partisan of the hoe—for other men's children." Miller typified the "misleaders" who preached going back to the farms, he sneered, even though blacks were being killed in Alabama and Arkansas because they insisted upon $1 for a dawn-to-dark work day in the cotton fields.[47] W. E. B. Du Bois said he wanted to see the "Back to the Land" spokesmen sentenced to the Georgia Black Belt for about six months. This, he suggested, would certainly dull their romanticism.[48] Charles S. Johnson avoided ridiculing his Southern black compatriots, but his celebrated study of Negroes in Macon County, Alabama, the home of Tuskegee Institute, presented a shocking profile from the Cotton Belt. Tenancy, oppressive landlordism, apathy, fear, isolation, and a general cultural backwardness, he concluded, characterized this rural Negro community.[49]

44. Benjamin F. Hubert, "Country Life," in *The Future of Negroes on the Farm*, pp. 4–5.

45. P. B. Young, "The Farm Way Out," *ibid.*, pp. 27–28.

46. Interview with Rayford W. Logan, July 11, 1974, Washington, D. C. For Logan's assessment of the farm situation at the time, see his "Negro Status Under the New Deal," *Sphinx*, I (May 1937), 38–39.

47. George Streator, "In Search of Leadership," *Race*, I (Winter 1935–1936), 20.

48. W. E. B. Du Bois, "As the Crow Flies," *Crisis*, XL (September 1933), 197.

49. Charles S. Johnson, *Shadow of the Plantation* (Chicago: University of Chicago Press, 1934), pp. 208–212. For two other studies which examined rural Negro problems

On balance, nothing ever came of "Back to the Farm" in the way which Hancock and the others conceived it. Despite warnings, former black sharecroppers and tenant farmers continued their trek into the cities. Not many blacks had money to buy farms; even fewer wanted to. Judged from either side, blacks were torn between overcrowding, joblessness, and near starvation in urban ghettos, and tenancy, share-cropping, and utter hopelessness on the land. Each side gave a demeaning and emasculating view of the other; both perhaps overstated the facts. Subsequent Federal programs, however, backed the claims of farm advocates more than the critics cared to admit. Tenant purchase loans, rehabilitation loans, subsistence homesteads, and the establishment of rural communities under the Resettlement Administration and its successor, the Farm Security Administration, enabled thousands of blacks to stay on or return to the land.[50]

The "Double Duty Dollar"[51] complemented job-holding and back to the farm. Altogether, the three proposals formed a triangle of black economic priorities—job, land, and dollar consciousness. Specifically, Hancock based the latter on the assumption that Negroes could help themselves significantly by unifying their purchasing power. His rationale was simple. Because the Negro possessed little political clout, national, state, and local governments could ignore his complaints. Barred on the whole from membership in labor unions, he also lacked the right to bargain collectively. By spending where possible in Negro enterprises, the Negro could at least provide jobs for some members of his group and, at the same time, use his leverage as a consumer to coerce white merchants to hire Negroes. In short, the survival of black businessmen, professionals, and wage earners hinged upon the collective use of black dollars.

Abram L. Harris claimed that the doctrine of black support for black

without reaching harsh conclusions, see William H. Holtzclaw, "Present Status of the Negro Farmer in Mississippi," *Southern Workman*, LIX (August 1930), 339–344; and W. L. Leap, "The Standard of Living of Negro Farm Families in Albermarle County, Virginia," *Social Forces*, XI (October 1932), 258–262.

50. Wolters, *Negroes and the Great Depression*, pp. 66–73.

51. Hancock coined the phrase in 1925. See Gavins, "Gordon Blaine Hancock: A Black Profile from the New South," 216; interview with Logan, July 11, 1974.

business was a convenient way for entrepreneurs to advance themselves at the expense of the masses,[52] but Hancock framed his scheme in terms of improving the economic standing of the Negro community as a whole.[53] Speaking before the annual Tidewater Fair in Durham, for example, Hancock expressed concern that Southern Negroes were becoming mere objects of charity. Still, he noted, the National Recovery Administration's requirement of shorter hours and better wages was accelerating the displacement of Negro workers. Since demands for Negro labor were decreasing, he continued, it was time to stimulate that demand or create jobs within the black substructure. He proposed a program to create such jobs. When a Negro buys from a Negro grocer, Hancock said, "he not only gets a loaf of bread but helps to make a place of employment for some aspiring Negro. His dollar does double duty." If the Negro grocer, in turn, patronized professionals of his own race and so on, that dollar would ultimately benefit every segment of the community. "The question," he concluded, "is whether the Negro who possesses this dollar shall return it immediately to the white man or will he let other Negroes use it."[54]

The Negro's dollar for groceries, insurance, medical care, and other needs thus had to buy goods or services and boost the race. Frequently, Hancock criticized blacks who failed to heed the message. Middle-class blacks in Washington, D. C., he said once, were breaking their necks to get into Negro-insulting Jim Crow places of business, only to be pushed aside or downright refused, even though the city boasted many fine Negro establishments. This "turning white" and "thinking white," he said, undermined black hopes for a better day. Similarly, he rebuked educated Negroes for "whining and repining" about the "positions" which the white man refused to give them. He said that people who would not seize the opportunity to make jobs for themselves by

52. Abram L. Harris, *The Negro as Capitalist: A Study of Banking and Business among American Negroes* (Philadelphia: American Academy of Political and Social Science, 1936), pp. 177–179, 184; Young, *Black Writers of the Thirties*, pp. 43–45.

53. Especially see Norfolk *Journal and Guide*, January 24, 1931.

54. "The Double Duty Dollar," An Address by Gordon B. Hancock on Education Day, Tidewater Fair, Durham, North Carolina, October 20, 1933, pp. 1, 4, in Rare Virginia Pamphlets, University of Virginia Library, Charlottesville, Virginia.

building up their own commercial life deserved whatever they got.[55] Ira DeA. Reid, a young sociologist and staff member of the National Urban League, thought Hancock's statements were chauvinistic and economically unsound. Reid held that the separate Negro economy implied by the double-duty-dollar philosophy could not be successfully maintained within the larger system. Segregation restricted the flow of capital into the black community, he said, and doomed Negro business to a vicious circle of low capitalization, routine services, inferior facilities, inflated prices, small-scale employment, and exploitation of the poor.[56]

On the surface, Hancock acknowledged that "Mr. Reid may be right." However, he contended that even if his method was not foolproof, it still seemed better than nothing. As for Reid's point on segregation, Hancock echoed the pragmatism of the older race men: "Racially speaking . . . we oppose segregation, but economically speaking it forms the basis of our professional and business life. There is nothing at present to indicate . . . the slightest change in this bi-racial attitude." Hancock did not think that limited employment potential constituted valid grounds for condemning Negro business either, since any jobs would help. Racial solidarity and responsibility, he thought, would prevent exploitation of the Negro masses.[57]

Racial solidarity and responsibility, of course, had a variety of meanings. A. Philip Randolph, who believed the special problems of most Negroes were those of labor in general, urged blacks to organize as workers to fight crippling unemployment, long hours, and low wages.[58] Negro radicals like George Streator looked toward a coalition of the black and white working classes against capitalist employers, including

55. Norfolk *Journal and Guide*, January 18, December 13, 1930; Hancock, "Our Coming Captivity," 160.

56. Norfolk *Journal and Guide*, January 17, 1931. A more general overview of the problems is in Ira DeA. Reid, "Some Aspects of the Negro Community," *Opportunity*, X (January 1932), 19–20; and Harris, *The Negro as Capitalist*, pp. 182–183.

57. Norfolk *Journal and Guide*, January 17, 24, 1931, September 17, July 2, 16, 1932, January 10, 1933; Hancock, "The Double Duty Dollar in Principle and Practice," pp. 3–8, an unpublished and undated memorandum, Hancock Papers.

58. Randolph, "The Economic Crisis of the Negro," 146–148; Young, *Black Writers of the Thirties*, pp. 66–69.

black businessmen.[59] In Hancock's judgment, though, violent suppression of Negro attempts to organize, the bigotry of white workers, and the racist practices of labor unions precluded the effectiveness of those strategies in the South. Black consumer cooperation, he argued, was a far more practical alternative. Overall, the "Jobs for Negroes," "Don't Buy Where You Can't Work," "Buy Black," and other campaigns of the period, all efforts to promote racial uplift through economic solidarity, bore a close kinship to Hancock's doctrine.[60] Even the redoubtable Du Bois urged blacks to accept the reality of segregation and develop an "economic nation within a nation," a shift which underlay his break with the NAACP in 1934. Private profit would be eliminated under Du Bois' plan, with the proceeds going into expanding black consumers' cooperatives, industry, agriculture, and social institutions.[61] E. Franklin Frazier and Emmett Dorsey, two young Howard University professors, scoffed at the idea and called it the work of a confused Marxist visionary.[62] Hancock, amused by its striking resemblance to the double-duty-dollar program, remarked: "It is just about what Booker T. Washington would write if he were living." [63]

Like Du Bois, Hancock accepted the reality of segregation and continued throughout the depression to consider race the most significant issue in the South and nation. He agreed with Du Bois' dictum that the Negro's "greatest failure is inability to earn a decent living." [64]

59. For examples, see Streator, "In Search of Leadership," 19–20; Spero and Harris, *The Black Worker*, pp. 326–374; and Ralph J. Bunche, "Education in Black and White," *Journal of Negro Education*, V (July 1936), 353–355.

60. Harris, *The Negro as Capitalist*, pp. 180–181; John H. Bracey, Jr., "Black Nationalism since Garvey," in Nathan Huggins, Martin Kilson, and Daniel Fox, eds., *Key Issues in the Afro-American Experience* (New York: Harcourt Brace Jovanovich, 1971), II, pp. 262–266.

61. W. E. B. Du Bois, "Postscript," *Crisis*, XLI (June 1934), 182–183; and "A Negro Nation within the Nation," *Current History*, XLII (June 1935), 269. Also, see Wolters, *Negroes and the Great Depression*, pp. 230–265; and Young, *Black Writers of the Thirties*, pp. 23–27.

62. See E. Franklin Frazier, "The Du Bois Program in the Present Crisis," *Race*, I (Winter 1935–1936), 12–13; and Emmett Dorsey, "The Negro and Social Planning," *Journal of Negro Education*, V (July 1936), 108.

63. Norfolk *Journal and Guide*, October 26, 1935; Wolters, *Negroes and the Great Depression*, p. 251.

64. Quoted in Johnson, ed., *The Economic Status of Negroes*, p. 18.

As already illustrated by the hold-your-job, back-to-the-farm, and double-duty-dollar slogans, Hancock advocated a variety of racially oriented economic programs. During the course of the New Deal, while holding these themes intact, he proved himself to be a jealous guardian of black interests in face of white indifference, discrimination, and neglect. Although he seldom matched his Northern colleagues in stridency and suffered criticism for projecting a "Gloomy" view, Hancock was no less committed to Negro equality.

As he peeped beyond the black veil, Hancock recognized that the Negro had to do more than pull at his own bootstraps. Believing that minority groups should predicate their survival on strategy even as majorities based theirs on strength, he spoke in favor of the tried-and-true tactics of Negro voting, petitioning, fact finding, propaganda, protest, and participation in interracial dialogue—although he remained dubious concerning the effectiveness of these steps.[65] He vacillated. Politics could never be a panacea for the Negro's social and economic complaints, he thought, but it would help. Yet, he never ceased to depend upon government to safeguard Negro rights, appealing eloquently to the Fourteenth and Fifteenth Amendments of the Constitution and denouncing color barriers to economic advancement, political enfranchisement, educational opportunity, and simple justice.[66] Writing on the eve of the 1932 presidential election, for example, he said no right-thinking Negro expected much from either a Republican or Democratic success because the Negro's troubles were largely at the local level. Of course, if this meant having ten million Negroes turn to the South for "succor," he predicted, the road ahead was going to be rough. Notwithstanding, Hancock endorsed "Roosevelt and Relief," explaining that a Democratic administration headed by Mr. Roosevelt could hardly proscribe and deny Negroes the elemental decencies, opportunities, and rights of free citizens any more than did Mr. Hoover and the Republicans.[67]

Evidently Virginia blacks felt that way across the board. In 1932, following the advice of Hancock, P. B. Young, Luther P. Jackson, and

65. Norfolk *Journal and Guide*, November 26, 1932, April 29, 1933, January 26, 1935; Gavins, "Gordon Blaine Hancock: A Black Profile from the New South," 220.
66. Norfolk *Journal and Guide*, October 24, August 22, 1931.
67. *Ibid.*, November 12, 19, 26, 1932.

Roscoe C. Jackson, most of the state's twenty-nine thousand registered black voters supported Roosevelt and, once the new federal programs got off the ground, remained grateful converts to the Democratic Party.[68] Using the pages of the *Journal and Guide* and *Planet*, Negro leaders, including Hancock, staged a vigil on the "Roosevelt Reconstruction." They viewed the experiment favorably, but not uncritically. They applauded the appointment of influential blacks to "cabinet level" positions in New Deal agencies. By 1934 the Civilian Conservation Corps employed over two thousand Virginia blacks, although they were strictly segregated from white workers. The Resettlement Administration hired many Negroes at its Homestead Project for housing redevelopment in Newport News, while hundreds of young blacks financed their education through National Youth Administration scholarships. Federal construction of the Norfolk Community Hospital for Negroes and renovation of that city's Booker T. Washington High School and Eleanor Roosevelt's visit to Hampton Institute and her sympathetic interest in Negro welfare also won praise.[69]

The Negro's share of the booty in Virginia, however, was not only separate but grossly unequal. On the Works Progress Administration sites in Richmond and Hampton whites earned $86.50 monthly; blacks received $29.50.[70] "The white employers are doing as they please to either give the Negro a differential wage or his release," Hancock said, hushing the chorus of praise. "The defenseless Negro is being forced to accept both evils!" The National Recovery Administration minimum wage codes had thus boomeranged on the Negro. In addition to criticizing the Agricultural Adjustment Administration's denial of direct cash benefits to black tenant farmers under its acreage reduction program, Hancock accused Congress of betrayal. The Social Security Act, which omitted persons "in the lower brackets of labor," excluded 2,500,000 black domestics and 1,500,000 tenant farmers from cover-

68. Andrew Buni, *The Negro in Virginia Politics 1902–1965* (Charlottesville: University Press of Virginia, 1967), pp. 111–112. Roscoe C. Jackson, son of Giles B. Jackson, was the leader of a Richmond Negro voters league.

69. Norfolk *Journal and Guide*, March 17, 1934, March 9, February 23, 1935, February 29, April 1, 1936; Richmond *Planet*, September 29, November 17, December 1, 1934; Federal Writers' Program, *The Negro in Virginia*, pp. 343–344; Buni, *The Negro in Virginia Politics*, pp. 113–114.

70. Richmond *Planet*, October 24, 1936.

age. Moreover, continuing competition for public works jobs, political race baiting, and a rise in lynchings made the South a potential racial battleground, Hancock said, causing the disillusioned Negro masses "to depend upon white Communists . . . for bread which our so-called democracy does not provide."[71]

To be sure, Hancock rejected communism. Its atheism, advocacy of violent revolution, inflexible definition of the class structure of society, and ambiguity on the color question offered the Negro little hope. Bitter over the Communists' disruptive tactics in the Scottsboro, Alabama, trial of nine Negro boys accused of raping two white women, Hancock perceived them as a threat to black leaders. "It is not a disgrace to be hungry; it is not a shame to march in protest of hunger," he observed. "It is a shame, however, for the hungry Negro masses to depend upon white Communists for organization and leadership."[72] Although James W. Ford, the black vice-presidential nominee on the Communist ticket in 1932, Norman Thomas, the white Socialist presidential candidate, and the young black radicals monopolized the proceedings at the National Conference on the Economic Crisis and the Negro,[73] Hancock hailed the historic meeting. In his opinion, this conspicuous conclave reasserted Negro leadership of the Negro's cause. Carefully scrutinizing every presentation, he especially agreed with T. Arnold Hill, executive secretary of the Urban League, that "the Negro remains the most forgotten man in a program planned to deal new cards to the millions of workers neglected and exploited in the shuffle between capital and labor."[74] Some of the conferees founded the Communist front National Negro Congress, but Hancock refused to join. Yet the unwillingness of President Roosevelt and Southern

71. Norfolk *Journal and Guide*, December 17, 1932, December 2, 23, 1933, January 20, 1934, January 12, February 2, 9, May 4, July 27, 1935.

72. *Ibid.*, August 20, December 17, 1932, January 25, 1936.

73. Sponsored by the Joint Committee on National Recovery, it met at Howard University, Washington, D. C., in May 1935. Representatives of more than twenty black organizations attended, including Hancock. The hard-hitting presentations of John P. Davis, executive secretary of the Joint Committee, T. Arnold Hill, Ralph J. Bunche, A. Philip Randolph, James W. Ford, Norman Thomas, Emmett Dorsey, W. E. B. Du Bois, and others were printed in the *Journal of Negro Education*, V (January 1936), 1–125.

74. Norfolk *Journal and Guide*, March 14, 1936; T. Arnold Hill, "The Plight of the Negro Industrial Worker," *Journal of Negro Education*, V (January 1936), 40.

liberals to back the Costigan-Wagner antilynching bill practically quenched his New Deal spirit. He reluctantly endorsed Roosevelt for re-election, fully realizing what Attorney Charles Houston of Howard University meant when he asked: "Is the Democratic Party determined to make it impossible for self-respecting Negroes to support it in 1936?"[75]

Whether motivated by personal or racial self-respect, Hancock practically ignored the New Deal after 1936. Significantly, in 1940, he supported the Republicans' Wendell Willkie for president. He shifted temporarily to Republicanism partly because he thought blacks needed direct action and believed that Willkie, if elected, would deliver it. As a matter of strategy, too, Hancock hoped that his support for the dynamic and idealistic Republican challenger might help to force Roosevelt and the Democrats to redress black grievances. Willkie's forceful pledges to end racial discrimination, provide jobs, and continue public relief to those who could not work elicited enthusiastic responses from thousands of black voters tired of weak alphabet agencies, wearied by years of strife, and vexed over the failure of the New Deal to end their suffering.

To Hancock, who never achieved recognition by Roosevelt's black cabinet, it seemed futile to defend further a program which would not end racism. Obviously, the Negro received emergency relief from the Roosevelt administration, he conceded, "but relief can never be a desirable substitute for economic opportunity." After the expenditure of millions, he stated, "Unemployment is still the No. 1 Negro Problem!" Like the Negro radicals, he blamed the "iniquitous system" for racial exploitation. Unlike them, however, he saw no clearcut solutions to the problem in labor solidarity or proletarian alliances. For Negroes, race prejudice remained the major stumbling-block, and Hancock wondered if there was any way out. "The subjugation of the black man is nearing completion and . . . white domination of the world is nearing reality." Those who were too weak to strike back, he warned, would "be sentenced to the ghettos of the world." More and

75. Norfolk *Journal and Guide*, August 8, 1936; Gavins, "Gordon Blaine Hancock: A Black Profile from the New South," 221. Houston is quoted in William E. Leuchtenburg, *Franklin D. Roosevelt and the New Deal 1932–1940* (New York: Harper and Row, Publishers, 1963), p. 186.

more, students at Virginia Union called him the "Gloomy Dean." [76]

Hancock, not surprisingly, defended his dismal point of view. "There is always the danger that the few Negroes who are fortunately situated may become too optimistic of the color situation," he said, "and the success of these may blind the race to the struggle ahead." This pessimism was matched only by his apparent anger and his racial chauvinism. "We cannot exist half segregated and half free," he declared. "Let us have segregated schools, churches, businesses and everything else, if we cannot have all our freedom. We can build our own structure." Clearly, since segregation in the final analysis would still retard Negro economic advancement, what he really wanted was complete freedom—integration into the mainstream of national life. In 1938 he told the student body of Randolph-Macon College in Ashland, Virginia: "Segregation means death to the Negro race. It is a form of elimination that must be terminated if the Negro is to survive." [77] Hancock never said precisely how segregation could be abolished, but he maintained that black-white tolerance, understanding, and cooperation were absolutely essential first steps toward doing so. All during the depression, even as he promoted black self-help, these were central ideas in his philosophy of race relations.

76. Norfolk *Journal and Guide*, April 15, 25, 1933. March 14, 1936, March 6, 1937, January 8, 1938, May 13, August 26, 1939. Interview with the Reverend Gilbert C. Campbell, December 13, 1974, Richmond, Virginia. A former student of Hancock's at Virginia Union, Campbell is the current minister of Moore Street Baptist Church. For details on Willkie's campaign and his appeal to blacks, see Leuchtenburg, *Franklin D. Roosevelt and the New Deal 1932–1940*, pp. 317–323.

77. Norfolk *Journal and Guide*, February 22, 1936, October 16, 1937, and the editorial tribute of August 8, 1970.

IV. Race Relations

In 1932 Arthur P. Davis, a young Virginia Union professor and literary critic, complained: "Negroes talk too much about the race problem. It has really become an obsession with us." However, he confessed the difficulty of ignoring something which affected "our every thought, working or sleeping." Davis said he understood why blacks like singers Roland Hayes and Paul Robeson wanted to leave America, and suggested that only the Negro's stability or charity or cowardice, so far, had staved off violent revolt. But he berated the Negro who boasted pride in his blackness as "either a consummate fool or colossal liar." For Davis saw nothing in being handicapped by prejudice "to be so proud of." Commenting further that "'race' is too much with us" and noting the recent popularity of the moratorium idea, he proposed stopping all discussions and writings on the race question for ten years. This, he believed, would give black children a chance to grow up without having their minds too warped. On second thought, he doubted the practicality of his proposition because if it were effective "every so-called 'Big Negro' in the country would starve to death." Humorously, he added that "this would probably be a good thing." [1]

Gordon B. Hancock did not heed Davis's somewhat mocking call, or even comment on it. During the 1930's, in addition to popularizing his economic views and self-help schemes, Hancock wrote and spoke extensively on race relations. Generally, he accepted E. Franklin Frazier's statement that "the development of the Negro's status in the United States . . . has been bound up, in the final analysis, with the role which the Negro has played in the economic system," but he considered the racial character of the matter more important than did Frazier.[2] Although several black sociologists, including Frazier, theorized about a "struggle of white and black workers against the white landlords and capitalists," Hancock prescribed a different

1. Norfolk *Journal and Guide*, April 30, 1932.
2. See E. Franklin Frazier, "The Status of the Negro in the American Social Order," *Journal of Negro Education*, V (July 1935), 307; and Gordon B. Hancock, "Our Coming Captivity." *Southern Workman*, LIX (April 1930), 159.

remedy for the problem. He worked assiduously for interracial cooperation at every class level, particularly among educated blacks and whites. The broadest possible "union of intelligence," he assumed, would help to relax tensions, create good will, generate understanding, and change attitudes.[3] Believing in an integrated social system, he wished to eradicate white prejudice as well as to create viable black institutions. Continued segregation and exploitation of blacks strained this dual approach to biracialism, however, and Hancock, increasingly frustrated, shifted to a new militance in his views. Neither radical nor conservative in the context of contemporary black thought, he remained a tough, insistent moderate—a far cry from the "Uncle Tom" label usually affixed to Southern black leaders.[4]

Anthropologists defined race cautiously and broadly as a biological term based on blood relationship relating to transmissible physical characteristics and denoting a subdivision of the human species. Paradoxically, the scientific study of race had little to do with race relations, where, for all practical purposes, cultural and social phenomena were more important than genetic differentiation.[5] Hancock viewed race in its social context. "The color question is a social problem and, as such, is not essentially different from any other social problem," he wrote, "and by reason of this fact, it responds to the same processes of adjustment or maladjustment." He believed in racial equality, biologically, culturally, and socially. He subscribed to the credo that "neither color nor race determined the limits of a man's capacity or desert." The Negro's black skin, woolly hair, and other

3. Frazier, "The Status of the Negro in the American Social Order," 300; Norfolk *Journal and Guide*, April 29, 1933.
4. The "Uncle Tom" or accommodationist stereotype of the Southern Negro leader is discussed in Ralph J. Bunche, "A Brief and Tentative Analysis of Negro Leadership" (September 1940), pp. 10–11, 34–35, 81–82, 125–126, in the Carnegie-Myrdal Study of the Negro in America, Duke University Library, Durham, North Carolina; and Gunnar Myrdal, *An American Dilemma: The Negro Problem and Modern Democracy* (New York: Harper and Row, Publishers, 1944), pp. 768–780.
5. Willis D. Weatherford and Charles S. Johnson, *Race Relations: Adjustment of Whites and Negroes in the United States* (Boston: D. C. Heath Co., 1934), pp. 3–5; Peter I. Rose, *The Subject Is Race: Traditional Ideologies and the Teaching of Race Relations* (New York: Oxford University Press, 1968), p. 39; Myrdal, *An American Dilemma*, pp. 113–117.

physical peculiarities, therefore, did not make him inferior. These obvious traits were simply being used by the white majority to rationalize prejudice and discrimination. The myth of black inferiority and white superiority, he said, constituted the most emotional issue in black-white relations. In his opinion, both black and white scholars were under a moral mandate to destroy this diabolical belief.[6]

Conceptually speaking, Hancock found himself in the company of leading authorities. By 1930 Franz Boas of Columbia University had already challenged widely held assumptions about innate cultural, temperamental, and mental differences between the races. He demonstrated that cultural, and even some physical, differences were determined by environment, not heredity.[7] Hancock studied Boas, among others, at Harvard. Chicago's Robert E. Park, more than any one else, redirected race relations research away from the traditional emphasis on racial differences toward problems of caste, class, and status. To Park, racial antagonism resulted largely from an exaggerated social distance between whites and blacks, which would be bridged inevitably through the long, gradual process of assimilation.[8] Hancock did not say much about assimilation, but he drew generously upon Parkian theories, especially those on competition and conflict, in his teaching at Virginia Union. On the one hand, W. E. B. Du Bois, whose Atlanta University Publications were known throughout the world, dismissed race as a fallacy. He contended that the "logical end of racial segregation is Caste, Hate and War." Since the Negro could not change the situation by violent revolution, Du Bois thought, he must rely upon self-organization and an enlightened public opinion, the latter stemming from investigation and dissemination of correct knowledge.[9] Like

6. Hancock, "Race Relations in the United States: A Summary," in Rayford W. Logan, ed., *What the Negro Wants* (Chapel Hill: University of North Carolina Press, 1944), p. 218; Hancock to the author, May 26, 1968.

7. Thomas F. Gossett, *Race: The History of an Idea in America* (Dallas: Southern Methodist University Press, 1963), pp. 418–430; Rose, *The Subject Is Race*, pp. 39–40.

8. Park's ideas and his influence on Negro scholars are discussed in John H. Bracey, Jr., August Meier, and Elliott Rudwick, eds., *The Black Sociologists: The First Half Century* (Belmont, Calif.: Wadsworth Publishing Co., 1971), pp. 5–7. Also, see Robert E. L. Faris, *Chicago Sociology 1920–1932* (San Francisco: Chandler Publishing Co., 1967), pp. 26–55, 67–69, 106–111, 130–131; and Rose, *The Subject Is Race*, pp. 65–67, 71–72.

9. Bracey, Meier, and Rudwick, eds., *The Black Sociologists*, pp. 2–4; James O. Young, *Black Writers of the Thirties* (Baton Rouge: Louisiana State University Press,

Du Bois, Hancock exemplified a progressive faith. The facts, scientifically gathered and vigorously proclaimed, would "overwhelm" racial ignorance, hostility, and fear.

Hancock's efforts to proclaim the truth about race received a boost in 1931 when Mary Rachel Torrance, a wealthy white widow from Sewickley, Pennsylvania, visited Virginia Union. Reportedly she had journeyed South in search of a deserving cause. Her deceased husband, Francis John Torrance, had been a manufacturer, corporate executive, financier, and philanthropist. Evidently Hancock's class in race relations impressed her immensely, because she gave Virginia Union $10,000 to expand this work. With president Clark's approval, Hancock established the Francis J. Torrance School of Race Relations in Virginia Union University.[10] Its objectives were to examine race questions, raise black consciousness, develop leadership, promote good will, improve character and job efficiency. Operating essentially as a special program within the Department of Economics and Sociology, the school offered courses already listed in race relations, black history, anthropology, and social legislation, with psychology and industrial education added on. In 1931 alone, 308 students took advantage of these offerings. Four faculty members participated, two of them white. A musky little room on the third floor of Pickford Hall housed a "modest library" of five hundred volumes.[11]

Community outreach played a vital role. Students conducted better health, education, family life, and job-holding campaigns in local black churches. Teach-ins were staged at the colored YWCA and YMCA for domestics, home nurses, chauffeurs, porters, and laborers. For example, a six-week session on employer-employee relationships involved several black maids and their "white ladies," meeting in separate places. Hancock, who carried out the discussions with the groups, said that the experience provided a basis for racial understanding

1973), pp. 21–22; W. E. B. Du Bois, "My Evolving Program for Negro Freedom," in Logan, ed., *What the Negro Wants*, pp. 37–38, 45–50.

10. *The National Cyclopedia of American Biography*, XXII (New York: James T. White and Co., 1932), p. 146; *V.U.B.*, Centennial Issue, 66; Hancock, *Supplementary Facts Pertaining to the Centennial Issue of the Virginia Union Bulletin* (Richmond: Virginia Union University, 1966), p. 6.

11. Pamphlet, *The Francis J. Torrance School of Race Relations in Virginia Union University* (Richmond: Virginia Union University, n.d.), pp. 10–11, 14.

"where the contacts are thousands." Each side, at least, presented its case. While the white women desired tolerant, congenial, and efficient servants, the black women talked about "higher wages, prompt pay, reasonable hours of work, time to eat, frankness about duties, notice before dismissal, lady with good disposition." The school also sponsored interracial dialogues, which brought prominent whites to Union's campus, including Richmond social worker June Purcell Guild and Will W. Alexander, director of the Commission on Interracial Cooperation. Du Bois, Charles S. Johnson, NAACP executive-secretary Walter F. White, historian Luther P. Jackson, and editor P. B. Young typified the black visiting lecturers.[12] The activities, in sum, appealed to both the lowly and the learned, combining practical advice with academic preparation.

Hancock wanted his brainchild to grow, but in-house difficulties and loss of financial support caused its early demise. Shortly after her initial gift, Mrs. Torrance, claiming "failing health" as her reason, withdrew her pledge of future contributions. George Burton, her black chauffeur, told Hancock that she was really upset by the unsympathetic attitude of the president and certain professors at Union. "I would not show this letter to anyone connected with the school," Burton pled, "just keep it to yourself please."[13] Although the experiment lingered on until 1934, Hancock never forgave the "whispering clique" responsible for undercutting him. He did not name the parties who circulated the damaging statement that his "Aunt Jemima" program would get Virginia Union an "Uncle Tom" building. However, he reported: "Mrs. Torrance was so disgusted with what she learned about Negro intraracial jealousies that she refused to further sponsor a program which easily could have meant millions to Virginia Union."[14] According to campus rumor, Arthur P. Davis and education professor Robert P. Daniel were no admirers of Hancock. They considered the Torrance

12. Hancock to Mrs. Torrance, July 7, 1932; *The Francis J. Torrance School of Race Relations in Virginia Union University*, pp. 6, 8; Minutes, "Class in Interracial Relationships," n.d., Gordon Blaine Hancock Papers, Richmond, Virginia; Norfolk *Journal and Guide*, May 23, 1931.

13. Mrs. Torrance to Hancock, October 20, 1931, George Burton to Hancock, October 18, 1931, Hancock Papers.

14. Hancock, *Supplementary Facts Pertaining to the Centennial Issue of the Virginia Union Bulletin*, p. 6.

School a waste of time and money. Henry J. McGuinn, a young sociology instructor, liked the school but openly disapproved of its Booker T. Washington orientation. President Clark, on the other hand, feared that his authority might be undermined by Hancock's outside influence.[15] Unfortunately, any one or all of these men had enough influence to cripple the venture.

Plans for the Torrance School, though unfulfilled, revealed the range of Hancock's thinking. In one prospectus on development, he estimated that $125,000 would be required for a building to house a library, classes, and the practical arts; $200,000 for scholarships, community services, and an information bureau. He outlined ten new courses in subjects like consumer economics, civil rights, and the psychology of racism. Interestingly, he also wrote up a faculty-student exchange program for Virginia Union and the Richmond Division of William and Mary College—an idea whose time had not come.[16] These projections, if realized, would have made Virginia Union a clearinghouse in racial research and action on a scale unequaled by any institution in the South. Opponents suggested that Hancock's plans were visionary, grandiose, and showed "an idolatry of white people" that conflicted with double-duty dollars and self-help. Hancock, however, saw nothing contradictory in trying to close "the cultural gap that separates the races." To him, Negro self-help and interracial cooperation were variables in the same equation, not exclusive factors.[17] Despite his rationale, he continued to lose ground to the people who disagreed with him. A reorganization of the curriculum at Virginia Union in 1934–35, which established four divisions in place of departments, ended his reign in economics and sociology. President Clark named the following division directors: Arthur P. Davis, Languages and Literature; L. F. Jeffries, Natural Sciences; Robert P. Daniel, Education and Psychology; and Henry J. McGuinn, Social Sciences. Unlike Davis and

15. Interview with William L. Ransome, June 26, 1974, Richmond, Virginia.

16. These notions appeared in Hancock to William R. Conklin, April 16, 1932, Hancock Papers. A well-to-do associate of Mrs. Torrance, Conklin had considered the possibility of making a contribution. For course descriptions and the exchange program, see Hancock to Dr. H. H. Hibbs, Director of William and Mary College, Richmond Division, August 20, 1934, Hancock Papers.

17. Interviews with Arthur P. Davis and Rayford W. Logan, July 11, 1974, Washington, D. C., and Gordon B. Hancock, February 5, 1969, Richmond, Virginia.

Daniel, McGuinn did not yet hold the Ph.D. degree. Naturally, Hancock was hurt and disappointed about being overlooked for a younger, less experienced man.[18]

The Torrance School debacle and McGuinn's ascendancy in social sciences forced Hancock into temporary isolation. In 1934, when president Mordecai Johnson of Howard University selected E. Franklin Frazier to replace the aging Kelly Miller as chairman of the Department of Sociology, Miller declared war on his youthful successor. Hancock simply withdrew. For a long time afterwards, the fifty-year-old professor-divine, affecting a goatee and stylishly dressed, met his classes and hurried home. Occasionally he tarried with a curious student or attended a faculty meeting, but he preferred the solitude of the pastor's study in Moore Street or a quiet ride in his 1931 Packard. Social gatherings among Unionites, especially the parties at Slaughter's Hotel, did not interest him. Rather, he became active in editorial and planning activities for Omega Psi Phi Fraternity, where he established friendships with other fraternity brothers well beyond the confines of Virginia Union and Richmond. Indeed, Marie's company and companionship sustained Hancock through the troubles at Virginia Union, and P. B. Young, a trusted friend, encouraged him onward. Fortunately, during the time of his retreat from Union, Hancock renewed his sense of purpose. "In the cause of race relations I have found my life's work," he confessed to Mrs. Torrance, "and it is this work that I shall leave off when the time of my departure is at hand." [19]

Seemingly in search of approbation, Hancock projected himself into that "cause" with relentless enthusiasm. During the mid-thirties he addressed hundreds of educational, religious, and civic groups. Simul-

18. *V.U.B.*, Centennial Issue, 66–67; interview with Henry J. McGuinn, June 12, 1974, Richmond, Virginia.

19. Young, *Black Writers of the Thirties*, pp. 7–8; interviews with Clarissa Kyles Dillard, June 27, 1974, and John M. Ellison, June 12, 1974, Richmond, Virginia; interviews with Henry J. McGuinn, June 12, 1974, and Arthur P. Davis, July 11, 1974; Hancock to Mrs. Torrance, June 27, 1934, Hancock Papers. Omega Psi Phi was founded at Howard University in 1911, the first fraternity at a Negro College. For an overview of its activities and constituency, including Hancock's role, see Robert L. Gill, *The Omega Psi Fraternity and the Men Who Made Its History: A Concise History* (Washington, D. C.: Omega Psi Phi Fraternity, Inc., 1963), pp. 17–30.

taneously, he lectured to more than forty college and university audiences—white and black, North and South. Seven white institutions in Virginia were included: the University of Richmond and its affiliate, Westhampton College; Union Theological Seminary and the Presbyterian Training School, both in Richmond; Randolph-Macon College, Ashland; Randolph-Macon Woman's College, Lynchburg; and the State Teachers College, Farmville. "It must not be thought that only the whites listened to me. That somehow smacks of 'Uncle Tomism' or could be so construed by my traducers," Hancock stated, recalling his itinerary. "It is also true that I spoke at such Negro colleges as North Carolina A. & T., North Carolina College, Hampton, Shaw, Benedict, Allen, Virginia State, Maryland State, West Virginia State, Howard, and many others." [20] Even if he did not silence the critics with his impressive display of oratorical and journalistic skill, Hancock succeeded in establishing a reputation as a black spokesman that went far beyond Virginia Union.

To white people, Hancock donned the image of Negro savant and reformer par excellence. Neither timid nor overly aggressive in style, he was frank and insistent upon "next steps." His statements were a potpourri of plain talk and moral injunctions, which ran the gamut from condemning human decadence and oppression to commending ethnic tolerance and communication. "In all I held to the possibilities of interracial cooperation until integration could be effected," he explained, "and this seemed a long way off." [21]

Ever mindful of his goal, Hancock left few sensitive spots untouched. At Princeton University, for instance, he spoke out against black-white marriages because they incited white fears and, in the long run, held Negroes back. Intermarriage also comprised a threat to "racial integrity," a matter of importance to the white man and the Negro. Although blacks had been enslaved and brainwashed and were now segregated, he argued, they still possessed the consciousness which impelled them, like whites, to marry within their own group. The self-respecting Negro, he said, "wants a man's chance, not amalgama-

20. Hancock to the author, May 26, 1968; interview with Arthur P. Davis, July 11, 1974.
21. Hancock to the author, May 26, 1968.

tion." [22] Similarly, he advised against casual liaisons between Negroes and whites. George S. Schuyler, who wed the daughter of a white Texas banker, did not. In fact, Schuyler delighted in saying that "the most cordial and profitable race relations are sex relations." Periodically, his column in the Pittsburgh *Courier* either promoted racial commingling or featured amorous escapades between black men and white women.[23] Hancock excoriated Schuyler for playing up such "nauseating" sexual feats, and coolly reminded him that these indiscretions could only mean "death at the burning stake" to black men in the South. Moreover, in a letter to world heavyweight boxing champion Joe Louis, Hancock implored the pugilist to keep his head, talk sparingly, stick to the gloves, and, above all, avoid white women. Indeed, he reprimanded the Negro press for its "degrading" and "recreant" exulting of black-white social affairs. It affronted Negro pride.[24]

In contrast, Hancock approved of racial contacts and endeavors which implicated better treatment and opportunity for blacks, including conferences, forums, lectures, luncheons, joint research and publicity, but he recognized their limitations. He once criticized interracial luncheons because they were never held in Negro hotels or restaurants or serviced by Negro caterers, claiming that very few whites who attended these culinary extravaganzas would invite blacks to their homes or considered blacks social equals. Negroes, therefore, should not take the formality of "eating with the white man" so seriously.[25] Accordingly, Hancock looked at whites through clouded lenses. He openly acknowledged and encouraged white liberals, who usually incurred the wrath of their community in efforts to befriend Negroes. Yet the subtle paternalism of this "better class" frequently vexed him. If he saw poor whites as "the scum of the white race" or as the chief bigots and lynchers, he surmised that they were simply acting out the anti-Negro impulses of white employers, labor unionists, landowners,

22. Details of the Princeton speech were in Hancock to Mrs. Torrance, June 27, 1934, Hancock Papers.
23. Pittsburgh *Courier*, September 19, 1931, February 18, 1933, September 15, 1934, March 16, 23, April 20, 1935; Young, *Black Writers of the Thirties*, pp. 89–90.
24. Norfolk *Journal and Guide*, March 31, 1934, April 2, May 4, July 13, 1935.
25. Hancock, "The Double Duty Dollar in Principle and Practice," p. 2, an unpublished and undated memorandum, Hancock Papers; Norfolk *Journal and Guide*, March 23, June 23, 1934, March 9, 1935, October 17, 1936, January 16, 1937.

politicians, educators, journalists, and churchmen. Prejudice against the Negro cut across all institutional and class lines, he said. Respectable whites reaped its profits while poor whites incurred the blame.[26] Meanwhile, believing that Negro advancement hinged both upon self-help and eradicating prejudice, Hancock challenged articulate and influential whites to "divest themselves of the superiority complex" and demonstrate fairness to blacks. A progressive at heart, he assumed that if white leadership acted responsibly toward the Negro it would create greater tolerance and hasten economic, political, and social change.[27]

The spirited professor did not hesitate to train his guns on the white conscience in his attempts to refute racist attitudes. To more than two hundred young people at Grace Covenant Church in Richmond, he stated that the dearth of white men and women with sufficient moral courage to work for racial justice constituted the South's most tragic flaw. Echoing this theme before the city's white ministerial alliance, he maintained that if Christians shunned the quest for human rights the Negro's blood would be upon the church. Speaking to a Southern leadership conference, he told the delegates that paternalism was outmoded and that nothing short of fraternalism could ensure racial peace.[28] Evidently he conveyed his message well, because the editor of the Richmond *News Leader*, in a personal response, promised "to see to it that no underprivileged person can ever say to me that, within the limits of my ability, I did not do battle on his behalf." [29] The members of the Virginia Social Science Association, who voted unanimously in favor of birth control and were, in turn, bombarded by Hancock's arguments against it, reacted negatively. White advocates of birth control really supported its use to impede the Negro at a time when he most aspired to be a first-class citizen, said Hancock. To tamper with

26. Hancock to the author, September 4, 1969; Norfolk *Journal and Guide*, February 17, June 23, 1934, January 5, May 4, 1935, April 25, 1936, January 16, April 3, 1937.

27. Hancock, "The Double Duty Dollar in Principle and Practice," pp. 2–3, Hancock Papers. Norfolk *Journal and Guide*, October 13, 1934, January 7, March 11, May 13, 1939.

28. Hancock to Mrs. Torrance, June 27, 1934; speech texts, "The Economic Plight of the Negro," n.d., and "Two Master Plans of Rebuilding the Social Order," 1935, Hancock Papers.

29. Douglas S. Freeman to Hancock, January 4, 1935, Hancock Papers.

the biological balance of an underpopulated abundant world and nation, he suggested, would be the ultimate in selfishness and folly. Besides, he concluded, the near famine for the unemployed which accompanied the depression resulted from "faulty principles of wealth distribution" and could not be corrected by unilaterally limiting the birth rate. By the same token, he condemned lynching as a "Southern crime specialty," rooted in racial exploitation and competition. Like most black leaders, he campaigned for a Federal antilynching law.[30]

Hancock did not say a great deal about segregation in white circles, undoubtedly a tactic necessitated by Southern whites' disposition to rationalize it "as something necessary and sacred." But in spite of possible reprisals, he did state his resentment of this "crown of thorns." Addressing students of the State Teachers College in 1935 shortly after Donald Murray became the first Negro to gain admission to the University of Maryland Law School, he proudly announced that segregationists were on the defensive. Three years later at Randolph-Macon, still convinced that the demise of Jim Crow was imminent, he pointed out that only if segregation were abolished could Negroes survive.[31] To him its flagrant evils were the assumption of black inferiority, brutal suppression, and the denial of economic opportunity. Unfortunately, lacking power, Negroes could not overthrow legalized caste by force, but should work little by little for the day when it would be ended through the constitutional process and public opinion.[32] Insistently, Hancock waged a flank attack on racial injustice. Whites needed to know that blacks were not slaves or good darkies, but men and women who rejected the racial status quo. "Democracy is obviously a failure," he said at Randolph-Macon Woman's College, alluding to the Negro's sub-citizen status. "Discrimination before the law is a cancer that will eventually eat away the vitals of the nation." Among the despicable examples of America's colorphobia, none surpassed her refusal to protect black Ethiopia against Italy's fascist aggression.

30. Norfolk *Journal and Guide*, January 20, March 31, 1934, February 2, 9, 16, 1935.

31. Charles S. Johnson, *Into the Main Stream: A Survey of Best Practices in Race Relations in the South* (Chapel Hill: University of North Carolina Press, 1947), p. vi; interview with Hancock, February 5, 1969.

32. Norfolk *Journal and Guide*, July 21, September 15, 1934, October 16, 23, 1937; Raymond Gavins, "Gordon Blaine Hancock: Southern Black Leader in a Time of Crisis, 1920–1954" (Ph.D. Dissertation, University of Virginia, 1970), p. 128.

Hancock called it "the most glaring example of international hypocrisy of the century." To a white congregation, he suggested that Negroes out of sheer desperation just might choose Communism with some rights over democracy where they had none. His obvious attempt to dramatize the situation created a stir in the church, and led to his interrogation by the police.[33]

To black people, Hancock played the role of counselor and critic plenipotentiary. Vigilant, occasionally picayune, he spoke to them without the restraint exercised before whites or the fear of violent retaliation.[34] Judging from his rhetoric, he was a "race man" who deprecated racism, a social scientist who preached common sense, and a leader who disclaimed any desire to lead. If he talked most often about the callousness of the Negro middle class, he also articulated the concerns of the Negro masses, whom the writer Richard Wright described metaphorically as "that vast, tragic school that swims below in the depths, against the current, silently and heavily, struggling against the waves of . . . a common fate."[35]

Segregation and prejudice were ubiquitous facts of life for Southern Negroes, and Hancock responded to the exigencies of both, thus demonstrating his deep philosophical ambivalence regarding accommodation to segregation and advocating parallel structures among blacks and his commitment to racial integration. "We know that segregation is a bad thing, but . . . the consequences of not accepting it may be worse," he told a Benedict College audience. "Herein lies the pity!" Of course, he explained, mere accommodation to Jim Crow meant little, if blacks looked and worked toward its ultimate termination. After all, the NAACP, Urban League, Negro advisors in New Deal agencies, and Northern Negro radicals, notwithstanding their bitter protests, followed the same pragmatic strategy. He said Southern

33. Norfolk *Journal and Guide* February 3, September 8, 1934, April 27, July 20, September 21, 1935, July 17, 1937; Federal Writers' Program, *The Negro in Virginia* (Hampton: The Hampton Institute, 1940), p. 261; interview with Mrs. Hancock, September 23, 1972, Richmond, Virginia.

34. This dual standard was not unnatural for the Southern Negro leader. See Bunche, "A Brief and Tentative Analysis of Negro Leadership," pp. 34–35, and Myrdal, *An American Dilemma*, pp. 772–773.

35. Richard Wright, *12 Million Black Voices: A Folk History of the American Negro* (New York: The Viking Press, 1941), p. 5.

Negroes should not be blamed or look down upon themselves for doing what Northern Negroes do with grace.[36]

Extending his argument, he applauded Du Bois' rapprochement with segregation as a fact and a condition to which blacks must adjust for their own well being, calling it "the most momentous development in Negro affairs within the last fifteen years." Also, he supported Du Bois' contention that Negroes, instead of trying to crash the doors of white society, should solidify the black economic, educational, and cultural substructure.[37] For a start, Hancock demanded that only persons "of African descent" preside over state institutions for Negroes in Virginia, which irritated Governor George C. Peery not a little. Sidestepping his praise of Du Bois' realism, Hancock criticized Paul Robeson's naïveté on prejudice. When the famous Negro actor and singer moved to England in order to get away from color caste, Hancock accused him of deserting the millions who must stay behind and fight to the bitter end. No Southern black who migrated North had ever escaped white prejudice, and he doubted if Robeson could by leaving the country. Having himself experienced discrimination aboard transatlantic steamers, isolation during summer study at Oxford, and a plethora of snubs throughout his European and Asian travels, Hancock submitted that white men everywhere resented the Negro's presence.[38]

The Negro's fortress against white antagonism or indifference really inhered in self-help and solidarity, Hancock thought, recapitulating the themes which earned him the mocking title of "Gloomy Dean." As the decade wore on, he promoted Negro job and consumer consciousness, high thinking and plain living, with back to the farm receiving considerably less emphasis. Most often, he peddled his double-duty-dollar philosophy. Whether citing the failure of Negro-operated Lawntown

36. Norfolk *Journal and Guide*, July 21, 1934, May 1, 1937; Myrdal, *An American Dilemma*, p. 770.

37. Norfolk *Journal and Guide*, April 7, 1934, October 26, 1935; Young, *Black Writers of the Thirties*, pp. 24–27; W. E. B. Du Bois, *The Autobiography of W. E. B. Du Bois: A Soliloquy on Viewing My Life from the Last Decade of Its First Century*, ed. by Herbert Aptheker (New York: International Publishers, 1968), pp. 295–299.

38. Norfolk *Journal and Guide*, September 15, 1934, September 11, October 16, 23, 1937, August 27, 1938; Paul Robeson, *Here I Stand* (Boston: Beacon Press, 1971), pp. 48–62.

Shoe Store in Richmond as an outright disgrace, or chiding Howard University student strikers for making not one whimper about the hundreds of Negroes being fired from Federal departments, or deploring the tendency of educated Negroes to view their poorer brethren with contempt, he drove home the selfsame point: "Our own lack of accord and unity is far more threatening than the discriminations and injustices we protest!"[39]

Frequently, and in scathing terms, he denounced Negro class pretentiousness and the practice of overblaming the white man for black apathy, wastefulness, and neglect. Facetiously, Hancock wondered if the Negro's habit of patronizing white rather than black enterprises and his distrust of Negro competence could be cured by "pascho-therapy," which in Greek meant treatment by suffering. The Jews underwent it, he noted, and developed a group cohesiveness and commercial life unparalleled in the western world. Purposefully ignoring differences between the two minorities, he asked Negroes to emulate Jews. Furthermore, in the interest of black unity, Hancock called for a reordering of the race's priorities. When the hapless Negro learned to value lowly jobs as well as positions, dollars as well as votes, modern vocational education as well as liberal arts, the passion of youth and the wisdom of age, protest plus program, black culture in Harlem and black business in Durham, responsible leadership and responsive followership, concluded Hancock, he could command white cooperation and respect.[40]

Unlike E. Franklin Frazier, Ralph J. Bunche, and Abram L. Harris, who were sophisticated and detached scholars, Hancock remained a popularizer of Negro thought whose perspectives had a common touch. Very much in the style of historian Carter G. Woodson, he sought to instruct whites about blacks and, even more important, to inculcate a dynamic pride in blacks themselves.[41] While accepting the scientific fact of racial equality, he believed that there were significant

39. Norfolk *Journal and Guide*, March 17, April 14, 28, 1934; interview with Hancock, February 5, 1969.
40. Norfolk *Journal and Guide*, February 24, March 3, 17, April 7, 14, 28, October 20, 1934, March 2, 16, 23, 1935, October 17, 1936, January 16, 1937.
41. On Frazier, Bunche, Harris and Woodson, see Young, *Black Writers of the Thirties*, pp. 41–58, 111–119.

psychological and cultural differences between whites and blacks which complicated their relationships. Because many articulate Negroes preferred to ignore Negro peculiarities, Hancock asserted during a panel discussion at Shaw University, they generally lagged behind other groups in self-esteem. To acknowledge the race's physical prowess, he observed, was not to admit its mental inferiority or the white man's intellectual superiority.[42] Somewhat chauvinistically, he enjoyed telling black college students about the exploits of boxer Joe Louis, Olympic sprinter Jesse Owens, singer Marian Anderson, or Richmond's own dancer, Bill "Bojangles" Robinson. They "bolstered the pride of the Negro race throughout the world." Listed on Hancock's honor roll of constructive black leaders were W. E. B. Du Bois, Robert R. Moton, Plummer B. Young, William C. Matney, Luther P. Jackson, Maggie L. Walker, Nannie H. Burroughs, Charlotte Hawkins Brown, and Mary McLeod Bethune. Except Du Bois, they were all Southerners.[43] Correspondingly, he discussed the beauty "of the full blooded Negro," black folkways, religion, and social behavior.[44]

In Hancock's rendition of Negro life, watermelon, fried chicken, jazz, and spirituals were as commonplace as fraternal orders, protest organizations, and Sunday morning shouting. Once, to the dismay of a Baptist congregation in Portsmouth, Hancock even praised black cult leaders like Elder Solomon Lightfoot Michaux, Bishop Daddy Grace, and Father Divine. Although he objected to their excessive ritual and personal aggrandizement, he said that they were helping Tidewater's Negro masses while the conventional churches inertly watched.[45]

42. Norfolk *Journal and Guide*, August 29, 1936, March 18, 1939. Columbia University psychologist Otto Klineberg corroborated Hancock's view in *Race Differences* (New York: Harper and Brothers 1935), pp. 341–349.

43. Norfolk *Journal and Guide*, May 5, 1934, July 13, October 26, November 9, 16, December 7, 1935, August 29, November 28, 1936, April 8, 22, 1939. Those persons not previously identified include William C. Matney, an economist and professor at Bluefield Teachers College in West Virginia; Nannie H. Burroughs, founder of the National Training School for Women and Girls, Washington, D. C.; Charlotte Hawkins Brown, president of Palmer Memorial Institute, Sedalia, North Carolina; and Mary McLeod Bethune, advisor to the National Youth Administration.

44. Interview with Arthur P. Davis, July 11, 1974.

45. Norfolk *Journal and Guide*, April 18, 1934, July 10, 1937. Also, see Federal Writers' Program, *The Negro in Virginia*, pp. 256–257.

Essentially, he depicted ordinary blacks pretty much the way Richard Wright did in *12 Million Black Voices*: simple inhabitants of the land or erstwhile urban toilers, surrounded by violence and fear, who found happiness within their segregated but "irreducibly human" world. Yet, while the noted novelist and Communist steered blacks toward a proletarian union with the white working class, Hancock felt that their survival ethos and distrust of whites, not to mention white prejudice, rendered such an alliance impossible. If labor unions rejected them, he said, blacks should scab or organize on their own.[46] If and when desegregation came, Hancock further noted, it would still be necessary for Negroes to preserve their unique identity. E. Franklin Frazier wanted blacks to adopt the values and mores of the whites, and to achieve salvation through assimilation, culturally and biologically. Hancock did not foresee the eventual disappearance of the Negro race. Attaching more significance than Frazier to the Negro's differences, including color, he actually espoused cultural pluralism. In his view, blacks could enjoy equal civil rights and economic opportunities with all other groups in America and, at the same time, retain their distinctive institutions.[47] Effecting a compromise between complete integration and total separation, this philosophy synthesized the racial exhortations of Washington and Du Bois.

As an active member of the Commission on Interracial Cooperation, Hancock participated in a continuing dialogue between leaders of the white majority and the black minority, acting on behalf of the two blocs. With the exception of these individuals, the "invisible glass plate" of which Du Bois spoke was in operation. Common whites and blacks saw one another through this glass, though usually as strange, dim stereotypes. They could not hear each other either, except faintly. If luckily they heard something clearly from the opposite side, they still

46. Wright, *12 Million Black Voices*, pp. 31, 46–47, 98–101; Norfolk *Journal and Guide*, May 8, 1937.

47. Hancock to the author, September 4, 1969; Young, *Black Writers of the Thirties*, p. 53; E. Franklin Frazier, *The Negro Family in the United States* (Chicago: University of Chicago Press, 1939), pp. 474–475, 486–488; Norfolk *Journal and Guide*, January 16, April 10, 1937. For another statement of the pluralist philosophy, consult James Weldon Johnson, *Negro Americans, What Now?* (New York: The Viking Press, 1934), pp. 12–18, 98–103.

would not understand or accept it.[48] Like foreign nations, they were compelled to interact through the medium of emissaries. Under this arrangement, Gunnar Myrdal has concluded, caste reduced the leadership contacts to a protracted process of accommodation, feigned good will, special pleading, and paternalistic reticence.[49] However, the Swedish social economist failed to explain that, given the violent nature of Southern race relations, interracialists took upon themselves a perilous task. The mere suggestion of fairness to Negroes precipitated white hostility.[50]

When Paul E. Baker, a white Southerner, evaluated the Interracial Commission in 1934, he described a loosely structured organization committed to the belief that "race conflict between Negro and white people can best be adjusted by cooperation." Organized in Atlanta during the riot crisis of 1919, the Interracial Commission now had state commissions over the entire South and local committees in eight hundred counties. Volunteers did much of the work, but there were paid staff members and field coordinators. The one Negro on salary kept his office in a black section of Atlanta and went to the downtown headquarters only for conferences. Financial backing came mostly from Northern philanthropy; there were also contributions from the religious, educational, public-service, and business agencies of the South. A predominantly white executive board determined policies, which did not include an endorsement of Negro equality. Accepting segregation, the commission sponsored no mixed social functions. Using the strategy of gradualism, ever searching for ways to meliorate grievances and ease tensions, it endeavored to keep just a step ahead of the people. Its four-part program embraced activities for women, schools and colleges, churches, and the press, ranging from crusades against lynching to better-race-relations Sundays.[51]

48. W. E. B. Du Bois, *Dusk of Dawn: An Essay Toward an Autobiography of a Race Concept* (New York: Harcourt, Brace and Co., 1940), pp. 130–131.

49. Myrdal, *An American Dilemma*, pp. 724–727.

50. Wilma Dykeman and James Stokely, *Seeds of Southern Change: The Life of Will Alexander* (Chicago: University of Chicago Press, 1962), p. 117.

51. Paul E. Baker, *Negro-White Adjustment: A Study of the Interracial Movement* (New York: Association Press, 1934), pp. 17–20, 211–225. Also, see Edward F. Burrows, "The Commission on Interracial Cooperation, 1919–1944: A Case History of the Interracial Movement in the South" (Ph.D. Dissertation, University of Wisconsin, 1954), pp.

Almost as if they were overlooking its low-key methods, blacks based whatever loyalties they felt toward the commission upon their respect for the executive director, Will Winton Alexander. A native of Missouri and a graduate of Vanderbilt University, Alexander, a minister, believed that agricultural improvement and widening industrial opportunities would hasten the solution of the race problem. His forthright opposition to mob violence, municipal neglect, legal injustice, and land tenancy heartened Negroes. It was he, for example, who first invited black leaders to help launch the commission. They were presidents John Hope of Atlanta University, Robert R. Moton of Tuskegee Institute, and John M. Gandy of Virginia State College; Isaac Fisher, publisher of the *Fisk University News*; and Robert E. Jones, a Methodist Episcopal Bishop and editor of the *Southwestern Christian Advocate*. Alexander became a lifelong friend of Hope and Moton, and maintained working ties with sociologist Charles S. Johnson.[52] Jessie Daniel Ames, a Texas-born white woman and former suffragette, established some rapport with blacks through the ASWPL.[53] As general secretary, she increased publicity and kept a clip file on the Negro press. Editor Carter Wesley of the Houston *Informer*, president Benjamin E. Mays of Morehouse College, Charlotte Hawkins Brown, P. B. Young, and Hancock were among her black correspondents.[54]

The Virginia Commission, founded in 1920, attracted a heterogeneous band of educators, editors, ministers, and businessmen.[55] In 1931 it

45–109; and Charles S. Johnson, *A Preface to Racial Understanding* (New York: Friendship Press, 1936), pp. 168–169.

52. John LaFarge, *Interracial Justice: A Study of the Catholic Doctrine of Race Relations* (New York: America Press, 1937), pp. 168–169; Dykeman and Stokely, *Seeds of Southern Change*, pp. 68–76, 185–187; Burrows, "The Commission on Interracial Cooperation, 1919–1944," p. 114; Charles S. Johnson, Edwin R. Embree, and Will W. Alexander, *The Collapse of Cotton Tenancy* (Chapel Hill: University of North Carolina Press, 1935), pp. 64–69.

53. This was the Association of Southern Women for the Prevention of Lynching, organized in 1930. For Mrs. Ames's role in it, see Jacqueline D. Hall, "Revolt against Chivalry: Jessie Daniel Ames and the Women's Campaign against Lynching" (Ph.D. Dissertation, Columbia University, 1974).

54. Dykeman and Stokely, *Seeds of Southern Change*, pp. 115–117; Johnson, *A Preface to Racial Understanding*, p. 181; Burrows, "The Commission on Interracial Cooperation, 1919–1944," pp. 266–287.

55. Prominent were Robert E. Blackwell, president, Randolph-Macon College; John L. Newcomb, president, University of Virginia; Douglas S. Freeman, editor, Richmond

reached an agreement with the North Carolina unit whereby L. R. Reynolds, the Virginia director, became coordinator for both chapters. Reynolds, a native Virginian, held this post until 1942 and proved himself to be a skillful conciliator.[56] Lucy Randolph Mason, daughter of an Alexandria, Virginia, clergyman and secretary for the Richmond YWCA, served in no official capacity, but she championed the rights of women, factory workers, and blacks.[57] By 1935 the state body had a thousand members, scattered throughout eighty counties, and a budget of $6,000. There were eight white and two black officers, with thirty-two white and nine black district representatives. Besides the annual meeting, its agenda for 1935 included a good will tour of white colleges by a Negro quartet, an institute on religion and race at the University of Virginia, speeches by Negroes to white church conferences, and race relations course suggestions to white schools.[58] Seen in terms of the "quiet, dignified, and factual" tactics used, in the context of white obliviousness, these activities were laudatory. At the time Virginia had only three white institutions that offered instruction on the Negro: William and Mary, Sweetbriar, and the State Teachers College at Farmville.[59] Segregation, voting restrictions, and job discrimination

---

News Leader; Jackson Davis of the General Education Board, Richmond Office; John M. Gandy, president, Virginia State College; and William M. Cooper, dean, Hampton Institute.

56. "History of the North Carolina Commission on Interracial Cooperation," n.d., North Carolina Commission on Interracial Cooperation Papers, Box 1, University of North Carolina Library, Chapel Hill, North Carolina. Reynolds's overlapping correspondence contained items which illuminate the history of the Virginia Commission, whose independent records have not been found. The State Committees portion of the Commission on Interracial Cooperation Papers, Atlanta University Library, Atlanta, Georgia, has very little on Virginia.

57. Margaret Lee Neustadt, "Miss Lucy of the CIO: Lucy Randolph Mason, 1882–1959" (M.A. Thesis, University of North Carolina, 1969), pp. 1–17; Lucy Randolph Mason, *Standards for Workers in Southern Industry* (New York: National Consumers' League, 1931), pp. 3–4, 7–9; and her *To Win These Rights: A Personal Story of the CIO in the South* (New York: Harper and Brothers, 1952), pp. 1–18.

58. The black officers were John M. Gandy, vice-president, and Lorenzo C. White of Hampton Institute, recording secretary. "Progress Report—Commission on Interracial Cooperation for Virginia and North Carolina 1935," Pamphlet Collection, Duke University Library.

59. North Carolina had seven, including the University of North Carolina and Duke; Georgia, four; and Texas, eleven. "Race Relations Survey of Southern Colleges," n.d., North Carolina Commission on Interracial Cooperation Papers, Box 2.

remained constant. Moving against the tide, albeit slowly, the commission eked out some accomplishments. The most significant of these were establishing a Negro kindergarten, swimming pool, and high school in Richmond, a community center in Chatham, and library in Alexandria; placing a few Negro principals in Negro schools; adding two Negroes to the staff of the State Department of Education; and securing a state appropriation for an indigent Negro children's home.[60]

Yet there were inner tensions. Frequently impatient, blacks wanted to move faster than their white friends. The lynching of a Louisburg, North Carolina, black man prompted the usually mild mannered C. C. Spaulding, president of North Carolina Mutual, adamantly to recommend seeking swift punishment for the lynchers. While assuring him that the commission could only investigate the killing, L. R. Reynolds reluctantly conceded that Spaulding had a "strong basis for feeling that 'nothing will ever be done about it.'" Equally frustrating were the problems of Amanda E. Peele, a Hampton Institute faculty member, who could not register to vote in her home town of Carysburg, North Carolina, because she refused on three occasions to recite and write from memory sections of the state constitution. In a letter to the chairman of the Elections Board, she explained that the literacy test was illegal under North Carolina law and accused the registrars of using it to keep Negroes out of both the Democratic primary and the general election. When the Negroes of Weldon, North Carolina, openly challenged the Elections Board and the commission to end this humiliation, threatening to bring in the NAACP, Miss Peele "got through all right."[61]

Virginia Negroes actually brought in the NAACP, the dreaded colossus from up North. In August of 1935, Alice C. Jackson, a Rich-

60. Norfolk *Journal and Guide*, December 20, 1930; Josephus Simpson, "Are Colored People in Virginia a Helpless Minority?" *Opportunity*, XII (December 1934), 373–375; Charles E. Wynes, "The Evolution of Jim Crow Laws in Twentieth Century Virginia," *Phylon*, XXVIII (Winter 1967), 416, 421; "A Partial List of Some of the More Significant Work Done in Virginia since 1931 when the Joint Arrangement with North Carolina Started," n.d., North Carolina Commission on Interracial Cooperation Papers, Box 2.

61. C. C. Spaulding to L. R. Reynolds, August 24, 1935; Reynolds to Spaulding, August 26, 1935; Amanda E. Peele to Buxton Midyette, October 28, 1936; Weldon Civic Forum to L. R. Reynolds, November 3, 1936; Deposition of Amanda E. Peele, Northampton County, North Carolina, June 1936, North Carolina Commission on Interracial Cooperation Papers, Box 1.

monder and graduate of Virginia Union, applied to the University of Virginia Graduate School. This action, spearheaded by the Association as a test case of whether blacks could attend tax-supported institutions, jolted white liberals. Douglas S. Freeman, after noting that life would be intolerable for any Negro in a Southern white university and recommending the establishment of separate graduate facilities, asked why Virginia Negroes were deliberately pursuing a policy which alienated sympathetic whites. Writing confidentially to the University of Virginia's President John L. Newcomb, L. R. Reynolds informed him that Virginia Negroes, some of whom were in the commission, engineered the case, although they conveniently "put it on New York." He advised Newcomb to "stall off" the matter until January, when the commission would ask the General Assembly to provide out-of-state scholarships for Negro graduate and professional training. However, Miss Jackson's case never went to trial. The university soon rejected her application on a technicality: Virginia Union was not accredited by the Association of American Universities. Her exclusion, coupled with mounting Negro resentment, strained race relations. In 1936, during a two-day conference of the Richmond Public Schools, Negro teachers published a statement of protest and refused en masse to attend segregated sessions at Armstrong High School. Negroes and whites were "traveling in opposite directions," commented P. B. Young. "Such a course subjects liberalism to undue strain." [62]

Like Young, Hancock deplored the increasing polarization between black and white leaders, but he understood that without some line of communication the races would beat in vain against the "glass plate." This duality caused him to equivocate on whether Negroes should "go it alone" or cooperate with white liberals, who sometimes hindered as much as they helped. The fact that Southern Negroes were asserting themselves and whites seemed to be listening, the "Gloomy Dean" warned, did not mean that the white man would "relax his hold on power" or "afford economic opportunities for the generation of Negroes now in our colleges and universities." For blacks, racial solidarity and the double-duty dollar were yet in order. Concomitantly, he argued

62. Clippings, Richmond *News Leader*, August 28, 1935, November 6, 1936; L. R. Reynolds to John L. Newcomb, August 29, 1935, North Carolina Commission on Interracial Cooperation Papers, Box 1; Norfolk *Journal and Guide*, November 14, 1936.

that the diabolical forces of nationalism and racialism in America and the world necessitated the countervailing influence of internationalism and interracialism. Even if black-white cooperation in principle bowed to segregation in practice, those blacks and whites "mercilessly maligned" as "Uncle Toms" and "Nigger Lovers" were the moral hope of the modern South. Still, justifiably frustrated over the lack of real progress in race relations, Hancock criticized the time-worn habit of holding so many conferences. "We know what is the matter with the Negro and we know what is behind his problems; so why make further surveys?" he wrote. "Let us do something about it!"[63]

That injunction might well have been for the Interracial Commission, which failed to contain black defection. Hancock retained his membership, although he oscillated between affirmative support and a brooding wait-and-see attitude. Others came out against the commission. Richard H. Bowling, a Norfolk minister and member, denounced the statewide theme for 1939, "Going Forward Together." It meant "finding out what public sentiment is and going along with it," Bowling said. "There is no program, no effort that looks toward easing the economic disabilities of the race in Virginia." This obvious cynicism and discontent, Union professor John M. Ellison told the annual meeting, was rooted in "the biracial social system."[64] Undoubtedly, Virginius Dabney, Douglas S. Freeman, and Jackson Davis, who were seated in the audience, got the message. Down in North Carolina blacks were also highly critical of the commission. L. E. Austin, editor of the *Carolina Times*, scorned its silence on equal salaries for Negro teachers and the absence of Negro professional schools. "Unless some organization is courageous enough to protest," Austin pled, "the lot of the Negro in the state . . . will be only a little above that of a slave."[65]

Avoiding further reference to the Interracial Commission as the decade neared an uncertain end, Hancock turned his attention for a while toward resuming his studies. Except to prove to his opponents at Virginia Union that they had underestimated him, Hancock's belated desire to earn his doctorate seemed odd. At fifty-five, dedicated to his

63. Interview with Hancock, February 5, 1969; Norfolk *Journal and Guide*, January 16, April 10, July 17, 1937, May 28, 1938.
64. *Ibid.*, March 25, August 12, 1939.
65. Durham *Carolina Times*, January 22, 1938.

church and racial activities, ever preoccupied with the next speech or press release, he was hardly the younger man who had earned straight A's and written a master's thesis in one year. Having satisfied doctoral requirements in 1925, fourteen years before, he needed to update his knowledge, take comprehensive examinations, and write a dissertation. Partly in preparation, he had studied at Oxford and Cambridge during the summers of 1937 and 1938. However, his old Harvard mentor, James Ford, cautioned him against returning. "As for the question of continuing your work for the Ph.D. degree, I cannot help feeling that you have already achieved a distinction beyond that which the degree would confer," Ford wrote to him. "I still think your greatest contribution can be made in preparing some publishable study in the field of race problems." [66]

Concealing personal disappointment,[67] Hancock assessed the racial implications of the developing European war. By 1938, the international quest for colonies, natural resources, and power had already led to Japan's invasion of Manchuria, Italy's rape of Ethiopia, and civil war in Spain. Hancock said that Britain, France, and the United States were making a mockery of human decency by their outright appeasement of the brigands, particularly Germany. When Adolph Hitler used the plight of the German minority in the Sudentenland as a pretext for demands on the government of Czechoslovakia, apparently with the approval of Britain and the United States, Hancock denounced this "gentlemen's agreement." For even if war was averted, the "hellish doctrine of Nordic superiority" went unchallenged. At the same time, Hancock feared that white Americans were cultivating a racial hatred of the Japanese which made war against them imminent. To him, Japan was the last great power among the darker peoples of the world, and he asked that blacks "concertedly denounce" white America's anti-Japanese propaganda.[68]

Hancock became either more disenchanted or explicitly militant. Early in 1939 he damned the exclusion of Negro contralto Marian Anderson from Washington's Constitution Hall, and refuted the charge that blacks were naturally criminal. "Negroes who are segregated and

66. James Ford to Hancock, November 2, 1939, Hancock Papers.
67. Interview with Hancock, February 5, 1969.
68. Norfolk *Journal and Guide*, October 2, 9, 30, 1937; July 16, December 17, 1938.

relegated and aggravated and exploited and subjugated and dominated and repudiated are expected to have more crime," he exploded. "To make it appear that Negroes without a chance can equal whites with a chance is bologna!"[69] To the Baptist World Alliance, he declared, "This world must be brotherized or it will be brutalized." If the church backed down from confronting white racism, he contended, it would "seal its own damnation."[70] Finally, when World War II broke out late in 1939, Hancock predicted American intervention. In all probability blacks were going to take up arms and make the sacrifices incumbent upon them, he noted, but they would use their participation abroad as a leverage for equality at home.[71]

69. Norfolk *Journal and Guide*, April 8, 15, 22, June 3, 1939.

70. "The Color Challenge," An Address delivered by Gordon B. Hancock before the Baptist World Alliance in Atlanta, Georgia, July 1939. "A man who lives in the lion's den and beards that lion as you did in Atlanta should be honored as a hero." Adam Clayton Powell, Sr., to Hancock, August 4, 1939, Hancock Papers. Also, see Hancock, "The Color Challenge," *The Oracle*, XIX (March 1940), 5–6, 19.

71. Norfolk *Journal and Guide*, July 8, October 7, 1939.

V. Fighting at Home

World War II catapulted the nation into a bloody struggle against the Axis in Europe and Asia and catalyzed Negro frustrations. Having remained on the sidelines of economic life during the depression, experiencing rebuffs from industry and the armed services, blacks exploited the discrepancy between the defense of democracy overseas and the failure to practice it at home. Cynical but hopeful, they resolved to battle on two fronts. Added to protests over relief administration, lynching, and educational inequality were increasingly militant movements to secure fair employment, eradicate voting restrictions, and end segregation.[1] 'While the morale of the Negro, as an American, was low in regard to the war effort," writes one historian, "the Negro, as a member of a minority group, had high morale in his heightened race consciousness and determination to fight for a better position in American society."[2]

Down South, like the rest of the country, the war put people on the move to factories, shipyards, defense industries, training camps, and foreign battlefields. The climate and open spaces of the region were the magnets which attracted massive military installations. Of the $10,200,000,000 allocated for war plants, the South got $4,200,000,000 or 41 per cent, with Florida, Georgia, Mississippi, the Carolinas, and

1. See Robert H. Brisbane, *The Black Vanguard: Origins of the Negro Social Revolution 1900–1960* (Valley Forge, Pa.: Judson Press, 1970), pp. 161–183; Richard M. Dalfiume, *Desegregation of the U. S. Armed Forces: Fighting on Two Fronts 1939–1959* (Columbia, Mo.: University of Missouri Press, 1969), pp. 105–131; Lee Finkle, "The Conservative Aims of Militant Rhetoric: Black Protest during World War II," *Journal of American History,* LX (December 1973), 692–713; Herbert Garfinkel, *When Negroes March: The March on Washington Movement in the Organizational Politics for FEPC* (Glencoe, Ill.: The Free Press, 1959), pp. 15–36; Gunnar Myrdal, *An American Dilemma: The Negro Problem and Modern Democracy* (New York: Harper and Row Publishers, 1944), pp. 997–1024; Charles E. Silberman, *Crisis in Black and White* (New York: Random House, 1964), pp. 60–65; and Harvard Sitkoff, "Racial Militancy and Interracial Violence in the Second World War," *Journal of American History,* LVIII (December 1971), 661–681.

2. Richard M. Dalfiume, "The 'Forgotten Years' of the Negro Revolution," in Bernard Sternsher, ed., *The Negro in Depression and War: Prelude to Revolution, 1930–1945* (Chicago: Quadrangle Books, 1969), p. 301.

Virginia receiving the lion's share. The wartime recovery intensified established trends in politics and race relations, for blacks wanted to taste the fruits of prosperity too. Demands for integration and first-class citizenship fanned the flames of racist reaction. The "threatened cataclysm" drove black leaders to retreat, but they drafted a "new charter" for the South which challenged white liberals to act.[3] Gordon B. Hancock, Luther P. Jackson, and P. B. Young of Virginia were the chief architects of this endeavor.

From the beginning, Northern black spokesmen were critical of the war. Writing from London, essayist George Padmore called it a grand ploy to protect the empires of England and France from Hitler and perpetuate colonialism. Already, he warned, Africans, Indians, West Indians, and other darker races were becoming cannon fodder in the name of democracy. His sentiments were anti-colonialist and anti-imperalist. Elmer Carter, editor of *Opportunity*, wondered how the civilized white race could so soon forget the suffering which followed Versailles and commit mass murder and destruction again. Some blacks expressed a more isolationist position. George Schuyler, pondering the meaning of the war for colored peoples, considered it "a toss-up between the 'democracies' and the dictatorships." To them, he said, German rule in Austria was no worse than British rule in Africa. P. L. Prattis, another journalist, viewed the holocaust frankly as "a white man's war." It would be a blessing, he announced, to have whites just "mow one another down" rather than killing Africans, East Indians, and Chinese.[4]

Through the veil of racial inequality the war looked bad. Adam Clayton Powell, Jr., then a young Harlem politician, doubted that people who were politically disfranchised, socially ostracized, educationally deprived, and economically exploited would defend the country. Denouncing discrimination in industry and the military, How-

3. George B. Tindall, *The Emergence of the New South 1913–1945* (Baton Rouge: Louisiana State University Press, 1967), pp. 694–704, 716–719; Gordon B. Hancock, "Writing a 'New Charter of Southern Relations,'" *New South*, XIX (January 1964), 18–21.

4. George Padmore, "The Second World War and the Darker Races," *Crisis*, XLVI (November 1939), 327–328; "By the Sword," *Opportunity*, XVII (October 1939), 290; Pittsburgh *Courier*, September 2, 9, 1939.

ard University educator Charles Thompson argued that only if the Federal government implemented a policy of "complete integration" could Negro morale be improved. Vincent J. Browne, a Harvard doctoral candidate, reminded his readers that the Nazi creed of a master race had its domestic counterpart in class and color oppression. Negroes, wrote Browne, needed "a type of unity which has never been known before" to combat these sinister forces. Frequently, blacks excoriated white hypocrisy. American Negroes had nothing to die for, except to preserve a system which ridicules, demeans, and degrades them, Schuyler said. "Our war is not against Hitler in Europe, but . . . the Hitlers in America." The NAACP scoffed at "the hysterical cries of the preachers of democracy for Europe." Negroes, the Association declared, wanted democracy in Alabama and Arkansas, Mississippi and Michigan, the District of Columbia, and the Senate of the United States.[5]

Remembering World War I, when they adopted the strategy of subduing their complaints in order to give America full support, blacks assailed the national conscience. In World War II they looked upon the earlier stand as a great mistake.[6] "Sad experience proves that if the Negro forgets his grievances while the war is on," wrote the aged Kelly Miller, "the American people will ignore them when the war is over." The Negro's real enemies, proclaimed editor Robert L. Vann, were "oppression and exploitation from without and . . . disorganization and lack of confidence within."[7] Spurred on by the home-front idea, as war against Japan seemed inevitable, blacks resorted to direct action and mass pressure. During the height of defense mobilization in 1940,

5. "As the Negro Faces War," an address by Adam Clayton Powell, Jr., in Cleveland, Ohio, December 23, 1939, published in the Pittsburgh *Courier*, December 30, 1939; Charles H. Thompson, "The American Negro and the National Defense," *Journal of Negro Education*, IX (October 1940), 547–552; Vincent J. Browne, "A Program for Negro Preparedness," *Opportunity*, XVIII (August 1940), 230–231; Pittsburgh Courier, December 2, 1939, December 21, 1940; "Lynching and Liberty," *Crisis*, XLVII (July 1940), 209.

6. Kenneth B. Clark, "Morale of the Negro on the Home Front: World Wars I and II," *Journal of Negro Education*, XII (Summer 1943), 420–421, and his "Morale Among Negroes," in Goodwin Watson, ed., *Civilian Morale* (Boston: Houghton Mifflin Co., 1942), pp. 244–247; Horace R. Cayton, "Negro Morale," *Opportunity*, XIX (December 1941), 371–375.

7. Pittsburgh *Courier*, September 9, 1939, March 30, 1940.

Northern Negro leaders attempted to gain some concessions from the White House. President Roosevelt refused either to integrate the Army or guarantee fair employment. Various Negro organizations held rallies and meetings in protest, but to no avail. In January 1941 the veteran labor organizer A. Philip Randolph proposed that ten thousand blacks march on Washington, D. C. for jobs and freedom. The March on Washington Movement, which sprang from Randolph's suggestion, excluded whites from membership, increased the projected number of marchers to fifty thousand, and set July 1, 1941, as the target date. Only Roosevelt's agreement to issue an executive order establishing a Committee on Fair Employment Practice, which he did on June 25, led to a cancellation of the plans. Although government fiat hardly achieved what Negroes ideally wanted, FEPC symbolized a moral victory.[8]

Following the Japanese attack on Pearl Harbor and the nation's formal entry into World War II, protest escalated. Blacks agitated less against the war per se and more for equal participation in it. "Prove to us . . . that you are not hypocrites when you say this is a war for freedom," demanded Walter White of the NAACP. "Prove it to us and we will show you that we can and will fight like fury for that freedom."[9] Jealously guarding the interests of Negro soldiers and civilians, while channeling the hostility of the masses into a positive attitude about their role in the crisis, the Negro press popularized the "Double V" slogan, "victory over our enemies at home and victory over our enemies on the battlefields abroad."[10] Still, there was a certain ambiguity. Blacks appended their racial aspirations to America's official ideology during the same time that they labeled the war hypocritical

8. "White House Blesses Jim Crow," *Crisis*, XLVII (November 1940), 350–351, 357; Sitkoff, "Racial Militancy and Interracial Violence in the Second World War," 665–666; Pittsburgh *Courier*, December 7, 14, 21, 1940, January 25, 1941; Garfinkel, *When Negroes March*, pp. 37–61.

9. Walter White, "The Negro and National Defense," in Harry W. Laidler, ed., *The Role of the Negro in Our Future Civilization* (New York: League for Industrial Democracy, 1942), p. 40.

10. Pittsburgh *Courier*, February 14, 1942; Finkle, "The Conservative Aims of Militant Rhetoric," 694; Ralph N. Davis, "The Negro Newspapers and the War," *Sociology and Social Research*, XXVII (May–June 1943), 373–380; Lester M. Jones, "The Editorial Policy of Negro Newspapers of 1917–18 as Compared with That of 1941–42," *Journal of Negro History*, XXIX (January 1944), 24–31.

and racist. Even Schuyler, who had earlier denounced the war, thought Negroes in the long run would benefit from it. Roi Ottley, a free-lance writer, felt that its major advantage for the Negro lay in awakening white Americans from indifference.[11] On the negative side, however, whites were not indifferent. Resistance, conflict, and violence were unabated throughout the war and at times took on serious proportions. Soon after Pearl Harbor, there were race riots in Alexandria and New Orleans, Louisiana; Vallejo, California; Phoenix, Arizona; Florence, South Carolina; and Fort Dix, New Jersey. These were a prelude to the summer of 1943, when rioting erupted in Detroit and several other large cities and Army camps. Shocked by the white backlash, Harvard Sitkoff writes, "Negro leaders then retreated, eschewing mass movements and direct action in favor of aid from white liberals for their congressional and court battles."[12]

Southern Negroes were part of that tidal wave of race militancy which ebbed in late 1943, although their contributions have either been neglected or minimized by most students of the period.[13] Despite living in a culture of suppression, and usually without the psychological safety enjoyed by blacks in the Northeast,[14] they made a determined assault on the status quo. They spoke out. In 1939, for instance, the Atlanta *Daily World* reported that Negroes were worse off economically than their slave forebears. Under the old system slaves were

11. "Now Is the Time Not to Be Silent," *Crisis*, LXIX (January 1942), 7; "The Fate of Democracy," *Opportunity*, XX (January 1942), 2; Adam Clayton Powell, Jr., "Is This a 'White Man's War'?" *Common Sense*, XI (April 1942), 111–113; George S. Schuyler, "A Long War Will Aid the Negro," *Crisis*, L (November 1943), 328–329, 344; Roi Ottley, "A White Folk's War?" *Common Ground*, II (Spring 1942), 28–31.

12. Sitkoff, "Racial Militancy and Interracial Violence in the Second World War," 661, 668–669, 673–676. For support of Sitkoff's thesis on the retreat of black leaders, see Garfinkel, *When Negroes March*, p. 144; Adam Clayton Powell, Jr., *Marching Blacks: An Interpretive History of the Rise of the Black Common Man* (New York: Dial Press, 1945), p. 172; and Finkle, "The Conservative Aims of Militant Rhetoric," 711.

13. Notable exceptions to this generalization include Tindall, *The Emergence of the New South 1913–1945*; Dalfiume, "The 'Forgotten Years' of the Negro Revolution"; Wilma Dykeman and James Stokely, *Seeds of Southern Change: The Life of Will Alexander* (Chicago: University of Chicago Press, 1962).

14. Allison Davis, *Deep South: A Social Anthropological Study of Caste and Class* (Chicago: University of Chicago Press, 1941), pp. 373, 399, 427–428; Myrdal, *An American Dilemma*, pp. 722–724, 768–771.

extended some security without liberty, the Negro daily noted, but under the new wage slavery blacks had neither liberty nor security. Taking an early pro-Allied, equal-chance-to-fight position on the war, the paper also condemned lynching, segregation, and the absence of Negroes from draft boards, and avidly supported the March on Washington Movement. Following Pearl Harbor, it wavered between outright loyalty and skepticism.[15] Occasionally analogies were used to assert resentment. After commenting on Hitler's successes, the Charleston, South Carolina *Lighthouse and Informer* said that in the event of foreign invasion America would surely burn like Rome and France because she spent all her time fiddling—with race prejudice.[16]

As everywhere, Southern Blacks articulated a dual allegiance. The Durham *Carolina Times*, which initially claimed that America should ignore British propaganda and "stay out of European affairs," reflected this attitude. While deprived Negroes could and must be patriotic Americans, it contended, duty to themselves and posterity necessitated that they "be Negroes first and always." Notwithstanding, in mid-December of 1941, the Durham weekly asked Negroes to table their complaints for the duration of the war. Yet, even while closing ranks, the *Carolina Times* boldly called white racists, not Negroes, as many Southerners had assumed, the real "fifth column." Negro leaders who bowed to Jim Crow, it said, were "traitors to our race." When the University of North Carolina announced the enrollment of one hundred South American exchange students for a special course, the paper rebuked the university for denying similar privileges to blacks in the state, who were no darker in appearance than their Latin cousins. White people were simply "crazy," wrote the editor, if they thought Negroes wanted anything less.[17]

Black intellectuals from the South, whose candid and scholarly interpretations of current conditions appeared mostly in Northern journals, analyzed the Negro's changed mood. Horace Mann Bond,

15. Atlanta *Daily World*, December 12, 1939, August 13, September 16, 26, October 13, 20, December 20, 1940, June 29, December 12, 1941.

16. Charleston *Lighthouse and Informer*, quoted in Atlanta *Daily World*, September 14, 1940.

17. Durham *Carolina Times*, September 23, 1939, September 28, October 12, December 14, 1940, June 21, 28, July 5, December 13, 20, 1941.

president of Fort Valley State College in Georgia and a leading educator, related it to prejudice. He said many people considered blacks neither American Negroes nor Negro Americans, but a stateless minority beyond the pale of citizenship. Yet, by birth, tradition, ideals, hopes and aspirations blacks were indeed Americans, and would contend for freedom at home or abroad. At the same time, Bond saw among white Southerners the bitterness of a defeat suffered in 1865 which, along with eroded hills, warped cabins, scraggly fields, poverty and illiteracy, posed a continuing threat to Negro rights.[18] Sociologist Charles S. Johnson of Fisk University reported that increased color contacts and competition in wartime industries were producing sharp black-white conflicts in the South, where nearly four-fifths of the Negro population lived. The socio-political and ideological consequences of the resulting racial explosion, he intimated, were testing the very fiber of democracy.[19] J. Saunders Redding, distinguished author, literary critic and professor at Hampton, shared little of the detachment of Bond and Johnson. To him, the Southern Negro awakening reflected a deep distrust of white good will and "Uncle Tom" leadership. Not only were the black masses more class conscious but black leaders were openly opposing segregation. Although white liberals credited these developments to the unhealthy influence of "Northern Negro extremists," who were supposedly leading Southern Negroes into a blood bath, the stupendous cry for change was coming from the black South.[20]

Echoes of that cry resounded throughout the region. Moderate Negroes were no longer over-cautious. In 1940, during a much talked about radio speech, James E. Shepard, president of North Carolina College and an astute interracialist, upbraided the white power structure for hedging on educational opportunities and Negro participation in defense employment and the armed forces. There were public remonstrances. The Negro ministers of Atlanta, in 1941, unanimously en-

18. Horace Mann Bond, "Should the Negro Care Who Wins the War?" *Annals*, CCXXIII (September 1942), 81–84.

19. Charles S. Johnson, "The Negro and the Present Crisis," *Journal of Negro Education*, X (July 1941), 585–595.

20. J. Saunders Redding, "A Negro Speaks for His People," *Atlantic Monthly*, CLXXI (March 1943), 58–63.

dorsed the pressure tactics of the March on Washington Movement, and recommended their use in Georgia. Suits testing the constitutionality of white primaries and poll taxes stimulated black voter registration and political activity. Often, dissent spilled over into aggressive action. In 1941, when the black manager of an Elizabeth City, North Carolina theater was fired and replaced by a white man, angry local blacks ransacked the downtown area.[21] Reports were rife of Negro college students flaunting color barriers at soda fountains, in railroad dining cars, and aboard crowded buses. "It was as if some universal message had come through to the great mass of Negroes," wrote the white sociologist Howard W. Odum, "urging them to dream new dreams and to protest against the old order."[22]

Negro defiance sparked wild rumors of black soldiers taking over white women, an impending insurrection of Negroes with ice picks, and evil Communist plots. Whites retaliated unconscionably, but blacks fought back. Charles S. Johnson documented over a hundred cases of racial violence in the South for 1943 alone, each covered in the national press. Urban congestion, job competition, and the breakdown of traditional racial etiquette were the major causes.[23] Author Sterling Brown of Howard University traced the turmoil to alienation. On a trip to the South during the war, he found among Negroes "the sense of not belonging." In talking with black sharecroppers, union organizers, preachers, schoolteachers, newspapermen and bankers, he also discovered their bitter desperation and daring. "I found a large degree of militancy in Negroes who were Southern born and bred, some of whom have never been out of the South," Brown stated. "The protest I heard

21. Durham *Carolina Times*, September 14, 1940, November 29, 1941; Atlanta *Daily World*, July 25, 1941; Charles E. Wynes, "The Evolution of Jim Crow Laws in Twentieth Century Virginia," *Phylon*, XXVII (Winter 1967), 416; Ralph J. Bunche, "The Negro in the Political Life of the United States," *Journal of Negro Education*, X (July 1941), 573–579; Myrdal, *An American Dilemma*, pp. 486–490.

22. Tindall, *The Emergence of the New South 1913–1945*, p. 716; Dalfiume, "The 'Forgotten Years' of the Negro Revolution," p. 304; Howard W. Odum, *Race and Rumors of Race: Challenge to American Crisis* (Chapel Hill; University of North Carolina Press, 1943), p. 171.

23. Odum, *Race and Rumors of Race*, pp. 96–112, 142–155; Charles S. Johnson, *To Stem this Tide: A Survey of Racial Tension Areas in the United States* (Boston: The Pilgrim Press, 1943), especially pp. 22–39, 72–88, 118, 120–130.

ranged from the quietly spoken aside, through twisted humor and sarcasm to stridency."[24]

Clearly, Northern and Southern blacks mirrored a common frustration. Unfortunately, they were never able to convert such mass feeling into a unified national strategy. Despite the efforts of organizations like the NAACP, the Urban League, the March on Washington Movement,[25] and the Negro press, the Southern black vanguard faced a uniquely dangerous situation. In the South, where World War II shook and loosened many caste traditions from their deep moorings, the race problem was more personal and emotional. Every word, gesture, and act carried racial implications and, if offensive, could precipitate violence. If protest and defiant action were possible, compromise and cooperation remained necessary expedients.[26] The Southern black leaders who attempted to synthesize these four elements in a program of racial change were frequently pulled between the radicalism of their Northern counterparts and the conservatism of Southern liberals, but they asserted the right to speak for the black South. Three dynamic black Virginians—Hancock, Jackson, and Young—played a crucial role in this episode of the war years.

Luther Porter Jackson, in the estimation of columnist-critic Arthur P. Davis, was "the most valuable Negro leader in Virginia. . . . that rare combination of a scholar and a man of the people."[27] Born July 11, 1892, in Lexington, Kentucky, Jackson was the son of a dairyman and school teacher. His parents could afford only humble surroundings for

24. Sterling Brown, "Count Us In," in Rayford W. Logan, ed., *What the Negro Wants* (Chapel Hill: University of North Carolina Press, 1944), pp. 312, 314, 315. Alienation and rebellion among Southern black youths were stressed in Allison Davis and John Dollard, *Children of Bondage: The Personality Development of Negro Youth in the Urban South* (Washington, D. C.: American Council on Education, 1940), pp. 244–246; Charles S. Johnson, *Growing Up in the Black Belt: Negro Youth in the Rural South* (Washington, D. C.: American Council on Education, 1941), pp. 294–299; and Hortense Powdermaker, *After Freedom: A Cultural Study in the Deep South* (New York: The Viking Press, 1939), pp. 331–334, 339.

25. MOWM held conventions and mass meetings through the summer of 1943. See Garfinkel, *When Negroes March*, pp. 125–147.

26. Charles S. Johnson, "Social Changes and Their Effects on Race Relations in the South," *Social Forces*, XXIII (March 1945), 343–348.

27. Norfolk *Journal and Guide*, October 3, 1947.

their twelve children, but they nurtured young Luther's curiosity about race. One biographer has stated that he always "wanted to know why . . . white teachers of the North . . . were willing to come to the South to teach Negro boys and girls." The search for an answer led him to Fisk University, where he studied Negro history and civilization under George Edmund Haynes, a noted black sociologist and author, who encouraged Negroes to become their own missionaries of learning. Graduating from Fisk in 1914, Jackson served on black college faculties in South Carolina and Kansas before earning the M.A. degree from Columbia University in 1922, the year he began his tenure at Virginia State College in Petersburg. A theorist and realist, he combined research and action. Chairman of the Virginia chapter of the Association for the Study of Negro Life and History, secretary of the all black State Teachers Association, organizer of the Petersburg Negro Business Association, and a door-to-door advocate of the ballot, Jackson practiced, in his own words, that "sense of social responsibility on the part of those who have gained advantages to those who have not been so fortunate." When he received the Ph.D. in history from the University of Chicago in 1937, he had already achieved statewide recognition for his works on Virginia Negroes.[28]

An activist à la Hancock, Jackson devoted himself to the development of black pride, self-help, and political clout. Although he lacked historian Carter G. Woodson's chauvinistic flair, he popularized Negro history and Negro History Week in Virginia's black schools and churches. The truth about slavery and emancipation, disfranchisement and accommodation, survival and upward striving in black history, Jackson thought, would foster a proud and intelligent Negro community. With cultural identity and group esteem, blacks could dispel the notion of inferiority, resist oppression, patronize their own enterprises,

28. Wilhelmina E. Hamlin, "Luther Porter Jackson—Historian," *Negro History Bulletin*, VI (November 1942), 34–35; James H. Johnston, "Luther Porter Jackson, 1892–1950," *ibid.*, XIII (June 1950), 195–197; "Biographical Sketch of Luther Porter Jackson," *Virginia Teachers Bulletin*, XX (May 1943), 3–4, 8; Luther P. Jackson, "The Early Strivings of the Negro in Virginia," *Journal of Negro History*, XXV (January 1940), 25. Dorothy B. Porter compiled Jackson's bibliography in *Negro History Bulletin*, XIII (June 1950), 213–215. His best known work is *Free Negro Labor and Property Holding in Virginia, 1830–1860* (New York: Appleton Century, 1942).

and vote.[29] Articulate blacks must lead the way, he said, particularly in uplifting the underprivileged. Describing the race's desperate plight to Fisk alumni, he challenged educated Negroes to "do some stepping down" and help the masses. Fundamentally, Jackson agreed with Hancock that the building of a black economic substructure and Federal enforcement of equal opportunity pointed the Negro's way out, but he went a step further. Government responded essentially to influence and power, Jackson believed, whether of classes, special interest groups, or individuals. If Negroes wanted government to act on their behalf, they would have to compel it "by voting, by organizing political parties, by maintaining pressure groups, by . . . the lobby, and by such common every day devices as the letter, the telegram, or the personal interview with office holders." [30]

To Jackson, the blame for an undemocratic political system rested squarely on the shoulders of prejudiced whites and apathetic Negroes. Complaining of resistance to equal pay for black teachers, he scorned white Virginians for regarding "the Negro only as an inferior and not as a person." Similarly, he rebuked the indifference of black teachers. If determined, they could brave literacy tests, pay poll taxes, and vote in the primaries, and thereby force county school boards to eliminate dual salaries.[31] He seldom commented on their fear of white intimidation and reprisal, which traditionally kept blacks out of politics. In 1940 Jackson stressed the point that, except for scattered cases, Negro Virginians were encountering few restrictions in registering. Hence Negro apathy and nonpayment of the poll tax explained most continued disfranchisement. Usually friendly persuasion or threatened

29. L. F. Palmer, "He Left a Lonesome Place," *Negro History Bulletin*, XIII (June 1950), 198, 214; Jackson, "The Work of the Association and the People," *Journal of Negro History*, XX (October 1935), 395–396; and his "Unexplored Fields in the History of the Negro in the United States," *Negro History Bulletin*, VIII (December 1944), 57–58, 65–67.

30. "The Call for the Highly Educated," Alumni Address by Luther P. Jackson at Fisk University, June 13, 1939, in *Virginia State College Gazette*, XLV (December 1939), 39–40; Jackson, "The Petersburg Negro Business Association," *ibid.*, XLIV (November 1938), 19–20; and his "Improving the Economic Status of the Negro through Governmental Participation," *Virginia Teachers Bulletin*, XVI (January 1939), 15.

31. Jackson, "The Work of the Association and the People," 395–396; and his "Citizenship and Government Participation," *Virginia State College Gazette*, XLIII (November 1937), 10–15.

court action were sufficient for handling stubborn registrars.[32] In 1941, Jackson founded the nonpartisan Virginia Voters League, which banded black civic groups throughout Virginia under a central head. Originally begun in eighty counties and twenty-four cities, the League rapidly covered the rest of the state. It encouraged blacks to pay poll taxes and then follow through by qualifying to vote. Also, it compiled statistics on the political status of Virginia Negroes and worked side by side with the NAACP in voter discrimination cases.[33]

During World War II, Jackson used his weekly column in the Norfolk *Journal and Guide* to advocate "the double *b*," bullets and ballots. "By the bullet our soldiers and civilians may help to win the present war against fascism, but a permanent democracy can only be achieved by the ballot." Jackson expected the war to stimulate racial adjustment and advancement, "but without attaining the ideal of complete democracy for which Negroes are supposedly fighting." To obtain the latter, Negroes would have to wage a relentless fight through the ballot box and the courts. "A voteless people is a hopeless people," he maintained. "Those who vote, rule. We must continue to use all available means to convince our voteless teachers and other professionals and those of the masses of these truths." Criticizing black lethargy and lack of interest, he insisted that politics was no longer just "the 'white folks' business." Negro preachers and teachers needed to wake up, therefore, and stop parroting such traditional ignorance. Going even further, Jackson asked Negro voters to ridicule, embarrass, and "give the non-voter no quarter," particularly the many nonvoting leaders in schools, churches, and mutual aid organizations.[34] Few persons knew more about the dearth of Negro voting in Virginia than Jackson. For example, he reported that in 1942 exactly 28,845 Virginia Negroes had paid their poll taxes to vote. For 1943 the number advanced to 32,504. Both figures were minuscule. Of Virginia's 365,717 Negroes of voting age for 1942 and 1943, then, only 7.9 and 9 per cent respectively were

32. Andrew Buni, *The Negro in Virginia Politics 1902–1965* (Charlottesville: University Press of Virginia, 1967), pp. 128–129; Ralph J. Bunche, *The Political Status of the Negro in the Age of FDR*, ed. by Dewey W. Grantham (Chicago: University of Chicago Press, 1973), pp. 438–446.

33. Buni, *The Negro in Virginia Politics*, p. 127.

34. Norfolk *Journal and Guide*, April 18, September 19, October 24, December 5, 1942, February 20, October 17, 1943.

qualified to vote. Expressed otherwise, 92.1 and 91 per cent of all potential Negro voters were ineligible for those two years "because they had not met the celebrated poll tax requirement." [35]

Provoked by his findings, Jackson called Virginia one of the most undemocratic states in the South. Not surprisingly, he joined the chorus of Southern blacks who demanded Federal abolition of the poll tax and the white primary, a strategy designed to make blacks voters and a powerful political bloc in elections. "That white Southerners will call this dangerous agitation is true. They will continue to say that Negroes are taking advantage of the war to press for 'racial equality,' " Jackson asserted. "But it is equally true that these whites are taking advantage of the war to prevent Negroes from carrying on legitimate endeavors to achieve a measure of democracy." To him, the most effective way to eradicate the poll tax was to have Negroes pay the tax and "thereby be ready to vote on the question of eliminating it." Yet, unless the white primary were abolished simultaneously, Negroes still could not vote in most Southern states.[36] By removing these stumbling blocks to political democracy, Jackson concluded, it would be far easier "to prepare, educate, and organize the Negro race for the problems of a war torn world." [37]

Plummer Bernard Young, born in Littleton, North Carolina, July 27, 1884, rose from poverty to become "the respected and admired 'Dean of the Negro Press.' " Little is known of his parents, Winfield and Sallie Adams Young, or of his siblings. But by 1898, at age fourteen, P. B. had

35. *Third Annual Report: The Voting Status of Negroes in Virginia* (Petersburg: Virginia Voters League, 1942), p. 3; *Fourth Annual Report* (1943), p. 5. At the end of World War II, despite Jackson's efforts, 88 per cent of all Negroes of voting age in Virginia remained disqualified because of the poll tax. See *Fifth Annual Report* (1945), p. 5. In "Citizenship Training—A Neglected Area in Adult Education," *Journal of Negro Education*, XIV (Summer 1945), 485, Jackson stated that the Virginia Voters League increased the number of Negro voters from 25,000 in 1941 to 50,000 in 1945.

36. Norfolk *Journal and Guide*, October 3, 17, 24, 31, November 14, 28, 1942. Several other parties campaigned against the poll tax, including the Southern Conference for Human Welfare, labor unions, farm groups, and women's clubs. Attempts to pass a law abolishing the poll tax in Federal elections were invariably filibustered. One partial victory came in 1944 when the United States Supreme Court struck down the Texas white primary in *Smith v. Allwright*.

37. Norfolk *Journal and Guide*, June 15, 1943.

moved to Raleigh and found work as a printer's devil in the offices of the *True Reformer*, a fraternal newspaper. After a four-year apprenticeship, he advanced to journeyman printer and, in 1904, became instructor in printing at local St. Augustine's College, where he also took some courses. In 1907, schooled in his craft and determined, he accepted the assistant editorship of the *Lodge Journal and Guide*, then published by the Knights of Gideon in Norfolk, Virginia. When fire destroyed the physical plant in 1910, Young secured a loan, purchased the paper, and converted it to a secular journal. Using his editorials to promote "full citizenship rights for proscribed and disadvantaged Negroes," he built the new *Journal and Guide*, between 1910 and 1930, from four pages and five hundred copies per week to twenty-four pages, with one of the largest circulations of any weekly, black or white, below the Mason-Dixon line. An entrepreneur, forceful in style, Young was preeminently the people's tribune. An incorporator of the Virginia Interracial Commission, he served as vice-president of the state Negro Organization Society, and a board member of the Anna T. Jeanes Foundation. He chaired the boards of Norfolk Community Hospital and the Redevelopment and Housing Authority, became a trustee of five black colleges, and "was called to public service on state commissions by four Governors of Virginia, the City Council of Norfolk, and a President of the United States, who named him to a path-finding Fair Employment Practices Commission."[38]

Before the war, Young editorialized against lynching, Jim Crow state appropriations, unequal education, slums and racial bigotry.[39] An impassioned orator, he also addressed audiences throughout the South

38. Thomas Yenser, ed., *Who's Who in Colored America* (New York: Who's Who in Colored America Corp., 1941–1944), pp. 590–591; "Biographical Sketch: Plummer Bernard Young, Sr.," 1962, Plummer Bernard Young Papers, Norfolk, Virginia; Richmond *Times-Dispatch*, June 23, 1940; Armstead S. Pride, "A Register and History of Negro Newspapers in the United States: 1827–1950" (Ph.D. Dissertation, Northwestern University, 1950), p. 161; Virginius Dabney, *Liberalism in the South* (Chapel Hill: University of North Carolina Press, 1932), p. 411; John Gunther, *Inside U.S.A.* (New York: Harper and Brothers, 1947), pp. 626–627; Roland E. Wolseley, *The Black Press, U.S.A.* (Ames: Iowa State University Press, 1971), pp. 51–52.

39. Norfolk *Journal and Guide*, February 8, 1930, August 22, 1931, February 10, 1934, July 3, 1937, January 8, 1938.

and nation. Although the political scientist Ralph Bunche classified him as a "radical type," [40] Young worked within the biracial system. Like Hancock and Jackson, he had a hand in almost every area concerning the betterment of Virginia Negroes. In his opinion, the race needed "tradesmen, artisans, skilled laborers—the brackets in which the world's money is earned and influence exerted." This black middle class or social foundation, in turn, would become a wedge for prying open the doors to civil, political, educational, and economic equality. Liberal whites were welcome to help, if they divested themselves of paternalism and respected black leadership. Believing that "intolerance and prejudice thrive on ignorance," Young asked white leaders to seek a "better understanding" of what Negroes were doing, saying, and thinking. For in a climate of interracial harmony, he told a white audience at North Carolina's Atlantic Christian College, lynchings decreased, per capita income increased, and justice prevailed. Such appeals to conscience notwithstanding, Young related black problems to black powerlessness. Negroes occupied a subnormal status, measured by any standard of democracy, he warned the State Teachers Association, admonishing its members to vote. Barred from political participation, Negroes received whatever "those who are in control give us as a matter of sufferance or sympathy." [41]

Young's latent disenchantment over the failure of the New Deal to end crippling black unemployment and underemployment made him adamant. Billions of dollars on public works and relief had "failed to substantially avert a repetition of the Hoover drought," he noted. Americans simply could not afford to be rescuing crumbling structures abroad. Yet, as war broke out in Europe and threatened to engulf America, he conceded that the disillusioned and oppressed Negro would probably fight. Behind the race's dark clouds of despair, he saw a ray of hope. In 1940, after the Federal Circuit Court of Appeals ruled

40. Ralph J. Bunche, "A Brief and Tentative Analysis of Negro Leadership" (September 1940), pp. 64, 67–68, in the Carnegie-Myrdal Study of the Negro in America, Duke University Library, Durham, North Carolina.

41. Norfolk *Journal and Guide*, January 25, 1930, July 11, 1931, November 16, 1936; P. B. Young, Sr., "The Extent and Quality of the Negro Press," *Southern Workman*, LXII (August 1933), 328–329; Young, "Diminishing Distances," *ibid.* (October 1933), 396–397; and his "Civics and Citizenship," *Virginia Teachers Bulletin*, XII (January 1935), 4.

in favor of equal salaries for Norfolk's black teachers, Young stated that Negroes were finally being vindicated in their quest for economic parity. Fearing white reprisals and looking ahead, however, he informed blacks to "keep cool, protest vigorously, apply pressure where it is advisable . . . and we will find our way out." Heartened by the March on Washington Movement's stand regarding defense employment and black involvement in the military, Young exulted that blacks were more united than ever before "concerning the impact of segregation on their lives."[42]

The *Journal and Guide* supported the war against the Axis, but not the manner in which the country was waging it. Virtually every issue publicized unfair hiring practices in the shipyards of Newport News and Norfolk, or how blacks in general were being insulted, deprived, lynched, and electrocuted. "What is more injurious," Young asked, "than to deny a whole race of people a chance to work and live?" Veering left, he repudiated the "go slow" attitude of Southern liberals. Writing to Virginius Dabney, who had criticized the militancy of the black press, Young accused the Richmond *Times-Dispatch* editor of "using erroneous statements" and failing to "see that the Negro is under tremendous pressure." As discrimination continued, he refused to push for closed ranks. "This is no time to be conservative; to stick to a middle-of-the road policy," he announced to the Negro's white friends. "Help us get some of the blessings of democracy here at home first before you jump on the free other people's band wagon and tell us to go forth and die in a foreign land."[43]

Gordon Blaine Hancock, the third triumvir, shared more than skin color with his two colleagues. All three men were mature in perspective. In 1941 Hancock and Young were both fifty-seven years old; Jackson forty-nine. They were born and reared in the caste-ridden South of the late nineteenth and early twentieth centuries and, having made the most of their opportunities, had entered active careers in

42. Young, "The Negro Press—Today and Tomorrow," *Opportunity*, XVII (October 1939), 205; Norfolk *Journal and Guide*, January 8, 1938, April 29, June 10, July 15, August 26, September 9, 16, 1939, June 20, December 28, 1940, November 7, 1942.

43. Norfolk *Journal and Guide*, March 23, 1940, March 1, April 12, July 11, December 13, 1941, April 25, 1942; Young to Dabney, January 20, 1942, Virginius Dabney Papers, University of Virginia Library, Charlottesville, Virginia.

Virginia. Almost from the time of arrival, they were involved in statewide race causes and, by chance or choice, emerged as molders of Negro thought. Educated, skilled, accomplished, and middle class, they were members of the race's "Talented Tenth." Well known among the black and white interracialists of Virginia, they were also acclaimed by Negroes in the streets.[44] More immediately, each had lived through the promises and betrayals of the twenties and thirties and now, during World War II, found himself more committed than ever to Negro advancement.

Hancock's reactions to the war paralleled those of Jackson and Young mainly in two ways. Like them, he became more militant in his pronouncements and experienced rising expectations. While Hancock did not advocate 100 per cent black loyalty, he encouraged Negroes to join the Army, ostensibly to help the "nation live down the awful curse of race prejudice." In a democracy Negroes would at least have some rights, he reasoned, whereas under Hitler they would have none. In reality, this was no ordinary plea for the Negro's right to die in segregated foxholes, but the rationale of a moral offensive at home. He told the white South that it must dispense with its "hellish traditions" of lynching, subjugation, "and believing that no Negro has rights any white man was bound to respect." Contrasting the wartime boon for white workers in the South and nation with the penury of Negroes, Hancock charged that blacks were "living even closer today to the ragged edge of existence than 50 years ago." Although opposed to violence, he cautioned that if the Federal government procrastinated much longer in ameliorating racial wrongs Negro resentment might get out of hand.[45]

On second thought, knowing well white America's capacity for genocide, Hancock implored blacks to channel their anger and rage along constructive lines. He realized, as J. Saunders Redding put it, "that in the game of violence here in America the Negro cannot win." Whites outnumbered blacks ten to one, had all the weapons, and long practice in using them. Common sense dictated that Negroes "should employ a strategy of survival," Hancock argued. "It is true that some-

44. Interview with William L. Ransome, June 23, 1974, Richmond, Virginia.

45. Norfolk *Journal and Guide*, September 7, 28, November 9, 1940, April 12, May 3, 31, December 27, 1941.

body must die for rights; it is also true that somebody must live for them." Inevitably, the war impelled him to dwell on the prospects for averting increased strife. More than either Jackson or Young, he feared that "bloody days are ahead for this country." So, out of the abyss of black protest, white hysteria, rumors and riots of a turbulent South, Hancock called upon levelheaded blacks and whites to bury the hatchet and save the day. In short, he believed there were black and white Southerners who could become equal partners in shaping a program whereby violence might be avoided and Negroes could enjoy the freedoms for which they were dying. "One of the weaknesses of the old interracial cooperation was its paternal nature," he explained. "The outbreak of riots . . . is calling for another type."[46] Hancock wanted interracial action.

Interestingly, Hancock had parted company with Southern liberals in the twilight of the New Deal, when it appeared that they were moving too slowly on issues like segregation and equal opportunities. Now, in the midst of war and heightened racial contradictions, he was again soliciting their support. Whether acting out of guarded optimism, a sense of dependency, or sheer desperation, he seemed to be pouring new wine in old bottles. Quite appropriately, late in 1941, Hancock set the stage for detente in an article entitled "Interracial Hypertension." Pointing to "the all-too-frequent riotous outbursts here and there about the country," he stated that black-white relations were definitely in a state of rupture. Race war lurked on the horizon and this ominous possibility posed an unprecedented challenge to "better class whites" and black leaders. "The future of both races," Hancock concluded, "is indissolubly bound up with the way this challenge is met."[47]

Alarmed by Hancock's dire prophecy, Jessie Daniel Ames, who most assuredly represented "better class whites," responded. The longtime Interracial Commission secretary requested a meeting with Hancock. He consented and in February 1942 she traveled to

46. Norfolk *Journal and Guide*, March 2, 1940, May 10, 1941.

47. Reprint of Hancock, "Interracial Hypertension" (Atlanta: Commission on Interracial Cooperation, July, 1942). Originally released to the Associated Negro Press sometime in December of 1941, although it cannot be found in any issue of the Norfolk *Journal and Guide* for that month, this article led directly to the founding of the Southern Regional Council. See Benjamin E. Mays, *Born to Rebel: An Autobiography* (New York: Charles Scribner's Sons, 1971), pp. 213–215.

Richmond, checked into a white hotel, and met him at the colored YMCA. They discussed deteriorating race relations and the feasibility of getting black and white leaders to take corrective steps. Although they adjourned before settling on a time table, they developed a fairly frank and open correspondence in the ensuing months.[48] In one letter Mrs. Ames solicited an article for *Southern Frontier*, the commission's monthly news sheet. She recalled Hancock's recent column about the Atlantic Charter, which inspired the thought that perhaps the South needed a similar charter, and wondered if he would enlarge upon it. She also commented on the urgency of having intelligent Southern Negroes speak out. Following these cues, Hancock wrote candidly, proclaiming that whites who were not afraid of being called "Nigger Lovers" and blacks who were not afraid of being called "Uncle Toms" must draft a Southern racial charter. Afterwards, while thanking him for his timely contribution, Mrs. Ames suggested that if he and other blacks proposed a program white progressives would certainly help to implement it. Should he accept this task, she noted, there was one demurrer. Her own involvement, at least in the first phase, had to be kept secret.[49]

Privately, Jessie Ames knew that blacks distrusted whites. A careful observer, she cringed at the militancy of the black press and the concomitant assertiveness of the black masses. Only if the voices of moderation prevailed, she thought, would black radicals and white bigots be discredited. Furthermore, she believed that the South's resistance to "the obvious minima of citizenship" for Negroes abetted Northern black "extremists." More and more, she feared, disenchanted black Southerners were looking North for leadership.[50] It was partly her desire to thwart this "outside" threat which prompted her actions. Similarly, she wished to save the dying Commission on Interracial Cooperation. Besides black disaffection, the Atlanta-based op-

48. Hancock, "Writing a 'New Charter of Southern Race Relations,'" 18; Hancock to Leslie W. Dunbar, January 24, April 25, 1963, Gordon B. Hancock File, Southern Regional Council Office, Atlanta, Georgia.

49. Ames to Hancock, March 12, April 7, 1942, Jessie Daniel Ames Papers, University of North Carolina Library, Chapel Hill, North Carolina; Hancock, "Needed . . . A Southern Charter for Race Relations," *Southern Frontier*, III (April 1942), i, 3.

50. Ames to Mark Ethridge, of the Louisville *Courier-Journal*, March 7, 1941, to Jonathan Daniels, of the Raleigh *News and Observer*, September 19, 1941, to Virginius Dabney, May 26, 1942, Ames Papers.

eration faced financial cutbacks, staff depletion, and great pressure to reorganize from academic liberals like sociologist Howard Odum, who considered the interracial approach inadequate and dated. They argued that race relations were integral to the whole corpus of the South's agricultural, industrial, and welfare problems, and could not be treated separately. Earlier, though unsuccessfully, they had tried to dissolve the Commission and set up a Council on Southern Regional Development.[51] By reestablishing black confidence in the commission, Mrs. Ames hoped to disprove the argument that interracialism was outmoded and thereby to weaken the hand of the regionalists and preserve the old commission. At the time, Hancock knew nothing of her scheme.

He, Jackson, and Young caucused at the *Journal and Guide* offices in mid-May, weighed the merits of Mrs. Ames's suggestion, and decided to poll their colleagues. Although Jessie Ames reiterated the importance of concealing white input, they published a "feeler" which did just the opposite. It indicated that a "concerned white Southerner" had challenged Negroes to meet and state "what they desire of the white South." In addition, it asked respondents whether they were interested in, looked with favor upon, or would attend such a meeting. Consistently favorable reactions poured in, among them replies from Charles S. Johnson, Horace Mann Bond, Benjamin E. Mays, James E. Shepard, and publisher Carter Wesley of the Houston *Informer*. So enthusiastic were the responses that Hancock started thinking about organizing blacks Southwide, a thought which Mrs. Ames quickly discouraged. "It was not in my mind that a new organization would be set up," she wrote, "merely a conference." Hancock did not like her defensive tone, but he tabled the question and convened a planning session of his supporters.[52]

Thirteen blacks gathered at Virginia Union on June 30, and made

51. Edward F. Burrows, "The Commission on Interracial Cooperation, 1919–1944: A Case Study in the History of the Interracial Movement in the South" (Ph.D. Dissertation, University of Wisconsin, 1954), pp. 266–276; Dykeman and Stokely, *Seeds of Southern Change*, pp. 282–283; Tindall, *The Emergence of the New South 1913–1945*, pp. 718–719.

52. Interview with Hancock, February 5, 1969, Richmond, Virginia; Norfolk *Journal and Guide*, May 24, 1942; Hancock to Ames, June 6, 1942, Ames to Hancock, June 11, 1942, Ames Papers.

themselves ad hoc sponsors of a Southern black leaders' conference. Hancock, Young, and Jackson were named temporary director, chairman, and secretary-treasurer respectively. Also participating were Presidents John M. Ellison of Virginia Union and J. Alvin Russell of St. Paul's; Acting President Luther H. Foster and President Emeritus John M. Gandy of Virginia State College; Dean R. O'Hara Lanier and Extension Director William M. Cooper of Hampton Institute; Principals L. F. Palmer of Huntington High School and W. M. Whitehead of the School for the Handicapped, Newport News; Professor Henry J. McGuinn of Union; and Executive Secretary Wiley A. Hall of the Richmond Urban League. Clearly, educators predominated.[53] The group agreed on the goal of presenting black demands to the white South and on holding the conclave in Durham, tentatively on October 20, but divided and almost disbanded over who should be invited. Jackson, McGuinn, and Hall were zealously in favor of extending invitations nationally. Hancock and a few others argued that only Southern Negroes should attend. Otherwise, they said, "the whites of the South would dismiss our urgent appeal as just a petition of Northern agitators." Young straddled the fence before finally siding with Hancock, and the matter rested. "Only Southern Negroes of influence" would be invited.[54]

Yet the compromise had polarized feelings within the Virginia committee precisely when it needed a united front. While many of the members saw the practical value of Hancock's position, they feared adverse criticism from Northern Negroes. McGuinn and Hall, largely because of this, soon faded out of the picture. Ellison, who became Virginia Union's first black president in 1941, looked at the whole project through jaundiced eyes. Although he and Hancock were both Baptist ministers and trained sociologists, they were never close. Wary of Hancock's popularity in the community and of his personal motives in this matter, Ellison refused to become deeply involved. Jackson

53. "Preliminary Conference on Race Relations," Virginia Union University, Richmond, Virginia, June 30, 1942, Hancock Papers. Also, see Norfolk *Journal and Guide*, October 24, 1942.

54. Hancock to Leslie W. Dunbar, January 24, 1963, Hancock File, Southern Regional Council Office; Hancock, "Writing a 'New Charter of Southern Race Relations,'" 18; interview with Henry J. McGuinn, June 26, 1974, Richmond, Virginia.

himself endorsed the idea of inviting "only Southern Negroes" reluctantly. However, he still gave the endeavor his full support. Young, who enjoyed a greater degree of acceptance among Northern black spokesmen than any other member of the group, rationalized his dilemma. Like Hancock, he honestly wanted Southern black leaders to speak out, and did not see the projected conference as either kowtowing to white liberals or dividing the Negro race. As long as they were outspoken and "take the position—with dignity—that something is wrong with the . . . system," Young confided to Hancock, the people would trust them. For their task was not to follow the "lead of Northern Negroes who are raising so much hell," he added, but to change the status of the Southern Negro "as a worker and a human being.[55]

Compared with subsequent acrimony, the foregoing statements were like the quiet before a storm. Hancock, while shouldering the burden of planning, became the whipping boy of the committee. Renewing its longstanding disapproval of Hancock, the Baltimore *Afro-American* scorned him for saying that it would be better if Negroes, instead of trying to force the race issue, bargained during the war. It contended that the white author Pearl Buck exhibited far more courage than the "timid" professor when she told Harvard University graduates not to yield for one moment to inequality. Hancock, in an open letter, repeated his allegedly misrepresented statement that Negroes could not withdraw from the war until their citizenship rights were fully recognized, but might press intelligently for them while fighting abroad. He admitted to being "a little timid about advising my people to take a course that will result in disaster, wherein the lowly Negro will do the suffering and dying, while the stall-fed Negro with his head in some jim-crow trough withdraws to his swivel-chaired retreat until the fires of persecution burn themselves out." Pearl Buck and the so-called Negro radicals were "indulging in pure piffle," he said, because people who were "bushwhacked, lynched and ku-kluxed into submission" must "wait, work, pray, make breaks and take them." Three weeks later, the *Afro-American* ridiculed the secrecy surrounding the forthcoming Durham meeting and caricatured Hancock as a

55. Interviews with McGuinn, June 26, 1974, and John M. Ellison, June 27, 1974, Richmond, Virginia; Young to Hancock, May 26, July 25, 1942, Hancock Papers.

stooge for Mark Ethridge and Virginius Dabney. In a personal letter to the editor, Hancock denied the allegation, declared his opposition to segregation, and demanded an end to the hate campaign.[56]

As the Virginia faithful prepared the roster and agenda for the October conference, the critics got louder. Chicago editor Arthur C. MacNeal called Hancock "one of the most dangerous betrayers of democracy, national unity and Americanism that has [sic] appeared on the interracial scene in the past 20 years." President Joseph J. Rhoads of Bishop College, Marshall, Texas, apparently angered by not being invited to Durham, considered Hancock "superfluous and impertinent." Rhoads also repudiated him for advocating appeasement, which did "serious injustice to the Negro." Hancock ignored both attacks, and more than thirty black leaders wrote letters backing his efforts to unify Southern Negroes.[57] Puzzled by all the jealousy and mudslinging, Jessie Ames sighed: "I have felt for some time that many Negroes look upon the Commission as a possible danger and if a Negro seems to be cooperating with us he gets into trouble." Not greatly comforted by her concern, Hancock replied: "The bare fact remains that with a large sector of Negroes the Interracial Commission has lost caste somewhat. It has been accused of inertness." The strain of the enterprise was beginning to tell, but Hancock did not give way. "It will make I believe the first time that the Negroes of the South have spoken in concert," he informed Atlanta University professor W. E. B. Du Bois in September. "Your willingness to join us would be highly gratifying."[58]

Du Bois, however, declined the opportunity to attend the conference, which convened on the morning of October 20 at North Carolina College in Durham. Of the 80 Negro leaders invited, 59 showed up, 5

56. Baltimore *Afro-American*, June 27, July 4, August 1, 1942; Hancock to Carl J. Murphy, August 4, 1942, Hancock Papers.

57. Clipping of A. C. MacNeal, "Criticism of Men and Conditions Which Make or Mar the Future of a Race," n.d., Joseph J. Rhoads to Robert B. Eleazer, Educational Director of the Interracial Commission, July 27, 1942, clipping of "Bishop Prexy Hits Dean Hancock's Race Views As 'Dangerous Philosophy,'" Associated Negro Press, n.d., and "Comments on the Pamphlet—'Interracial Hypertension,'" August 4, 1942, all in the Robert B. Eleazer portion of the Commission on Interracial Cooperation Papers, Atlanta University Library, Atlanta, Georgia.

58. Ames to Hancock, August 7, 1942, Hancock to Ames, August 11, 1942, Ames Papers; Hancock to Du Bois, September 12, 1942, Hancock Papers.

wrote letters, and 16 sent telegrams. The entire group, except 2, lived and worked in the South. Virginia had 14 representatives; the Carolinas, 11 each; Georgia, 7; Alabama, 5; Tennessee, Louisiana, Texas, and Florida, 2 apiece; Arkansas, Maryland, and Washington, D. C., 1 each. Uniformly, the participants were professionals: 34 educators, 3 ministers, 1 editor-publisher, 3 physicians, 2 businessmen, 2 social workers, 1 Federal bureaucrat, 8 labor union officials, and staff persons from the Urban League, National Negro Business League, Associated Negro Press, Commission on Interracial Cooperation, and Southern Negro Youth Congress.[59] Primarily, they were shapers of thought and opinion, though many represented substantial black constituencies.

Moreover, they constituted an interesting blend of youth and age, for whom the memories of World War I were indeed real. Based on a random sampling of 15, 1 person was in his thirties, 6 were in their forties, 4 in their fifties, 3 in their sixties, and 1 in his seventies.[60] In this case, also, their aggregate achievements were impressive: 15 bachelor's, 13 master's, 2 divinity, and 6 Ph.D. degrees; 19 published books, 112 articles, and 3 pamphlets; and successful Negro newspaper and insurance enterprises. Only 5 women took part in the proceedings, 2 accompanying their husbands and 3 as bona fide participants. At least 23 of those present were former members of the Interracial Commission, and, while their presence in Durham reflected disenchantment with its "inertness," they knew the kind of statement which might appeal to Southern liberals. Collectively, the conferees were middle-

---

59. Burrows, "The Commission on Interracial Cooperation, 1919–1944," pp. 277–279; *The Durham Statement, The Atlanta Statement, The Richmond Statement* (Atlanta: Commission on Interracial Cooperation, 1943), pp. 8–9.

60. Horace Mann Bond, thirty-eight; Robert P. Daniel, forty; Frederick D. Patterson, President, Tuskegee Institute, forty-one; Rufus E. Clement, President, Atlanta University; forty-two; Benjamin E. Mays and William M. Cooper, forty-seven; Charles S. Johnson, forty-nine; Luther P. Jackson, fifty; Gordon B. Hancock and P. B. Young, fifty-eight; Jessie O. Thomas, Staff Assistant for War Bonds and Stamps, fifty-nine; Charlotte Hawkins Brown, sixty; James E. Shepard, sixty-seven; C. C. Spaulding, President, North Carolina Mutual Life Insurance Company, sixty-eight; and John M. Gandy, seventy-two. Also, see Yenser, *Who's Who in Colored America*, pp. 59–60, 79–80, 124, 134, 145, 197, 282, 285, 361–362, 396, 461, 479, 509.

class moderates who assumed the right to speak for all Southern Negroes—regardless of class.[61]

A solemn mood pervaded the opening session. The conferees officially organized themselves as the Southern Conference on Race Relations and unanimously named Hancock, Young, and Jackson permanent director, chairman, and secretary-treasurer. In a statement of purpose, Hancock maintained that they "need not cringe and crawl, tremble or truckle or even tip-toe" in face of Northern black opposition. Southern blacks were not seceding from Negroes of other sections, he explained, but asserting themselves in their own region. By setting forth "just what the Negro wants and is expecting of the postwar South and nation," they hoped to stimulate the constructive cooperation of the concerned white South. The delicate task before them required a toughness of spirit, he stated. "May God help us to acquit ourselves like men."[62]

Afterwards, the assemblage divided into discussion groups under the headings submitted by the Virginia sponsors: political and civil rights, industry and labor, service occupations, education, agriculture, armed forces, social welfare and health. Discussants were asked to prepare reports outlining complaints and remedies in each area. When these came in at the close of the day's deliberations, Benjamin Mays spoke in favor of writing a conference statement "commensurate with the possibilities of the occasion." He asked for the appointment of an editorial subcommittee, and the body concurred. Charles S. Johnson was made chairman.[63]

In taking more time to draft their charter, the Durham leaders acted wisely. For through it, perhaps, they would represent themselves well before the public and silence their enemies.[64] Although the dialogue at North Carolina College yielded no clear-cut consensus on segregation

61. Pamphlet, *Southern Conference on Race Relations, Durham, N. C., October 20, 1942*, n.p., pp. 12–13, Hancock Papers; interview with Benjamin E. Mays, June 19, 1974, Atlanta, Georgia.

62. "Statement of Purpose," in *Southern Conference on Race Relations*, pp. 3–5.

63. Hancock, "Writing a 'New Charter of Southern Race Relations,' " 19. The other subcommittee members were Hancock; Patterson; Mays; Clement; Bond; Cooper; Young; Ernest Delpit of the Carpenters' Local Union, New Orleans; and James E. Jackson of the Southern Negro Youth Congress.

64. Hancock to Ames, October 24, 1942, Hancock Papers.

or Southern black strategy, committeemen were not widely divergent in their feelings. To the man, they accepted the democratic framework, subscribed to the philosophy of intelligent protest and legal redress, and looked toward integration. Also, from experience, they knew that change in race relations came slowly and grudgingly. In the crunch, therefore, they were prepared to be pragmatic.

When the chairman summoned meetings in Atlanta and Richmond, November 9 and 26, at least three points of view emerged. Observing wartime repression, Horace Mann Bond and Benjamin Mays contended for a full, unequivocal denunciation of forced racial separation, particularly in education.[65] Hancock thought this might salvage their self-respect or even please their bitterest opponents. Yet, if they frightened off white liberals, they would only end up getting something said rather than something done. Consequently, Hancock favored adopting a position that opposed Jim Crow, but one that allowed some room for compromise. Again, Young found himself agreeing with Hancock and, simultaneously, recommending strong emphasis on economic opportunity. The chief evil of segregation, said Young, lay in denying the Negro an equal chance to earn a decent living.[66] In the final analysis, it fell upon Charles S. Johnson, whose coolness and detachment sometimes troubled the others,[67] to synthesize their views. On December 15, 1942, he issued the subcommittee's report to the press.

This document, commonly called the Durham manifesto, noted that the war had sharpened racial tensions and aggressions, particularly in the South. Segregation, discrimination, minority rights, and democratic freedom were at last open issues, it said, but white prejudice blocked even common-sense consideration for improving the Negro's status. It pledged black loyalty to America's worldwide struggle, which, of course, did not preclude attacking the problems of Negro inequality at home. While recognizing the strength and age of the South's peculiar racial customs, the report declared: "We are funda-

65. Bond to Charles Johnson, November 17, 1942, Charles Johnson to Bond, December 2, 1942, Horace Mann Bond Papers, Atlanta University Library, Atlanta, Georgia; Mays, *Born to Rebel*, pp. 218–219.

66. Interview with Hancock, February 5, 1969; Hancock to Ames, November 22, 1942, Young to Ames, November 20, 1942, Ames Papers.

67. Interviews with Mays, June 19, 1974; Young to Ames, November 27, 1942, Ames Papers.

mentally opposed to the principle and practice of compulsory segregation in our American society, whether of races or classes or creeds, however, we regard it as both sensible and timely to address ourselves now to the current problems of racial discrimination and neglect." In brief, rather than committing themselves to a knock-down-drag-out battle against segregation, which would likely cost them white support, Southern black leaders opted to end it gradually. "It is possible to evolve in the South a way of life, consistent with the principles for which we . . . are fighting throughout the world," the signers commented, "that will free us all, white and Negro alike, from want, and from throttling fears."[68]

The remainder of the statement specified reforms in the categories discussed at the Durham conference. Most changes were sought on grounds of justice or beneficial results, including Negro police and the use of qualified Negroes by the emergency rationing, wage, and rent control programs. As matters of legal and constitutional right, the document demanded the abolition of the poll tax, the white primary, voter intimidation, and jury discrimination. It advocated Federal antilynching laws and endorsed FEPC. Partly to demonstrate that they were not Federal partisans, the signers criticized the War Manpower Commission's wage and job freezing order, which militated against black economic advancement. They urged open membership in labor unions; Social Security benefits for black service workers; equalization of teachers' pay, equal public facilities, graduate and professional training opportunities, and Negro representation on school boards; equitable assistance to Negro farmers; racial integration in the military; mandatory provisions that a proportion of every public hospital be available to Negro patients; better slum clearance and low-cost housing. "The correction of these problems is not only a moral matter," the writers concluded, "but a practical necessity in winning the war and in winning the peace."[69]

The Durham conferees, Benjamin Mays recalled, were like "men walking on thin ice, so explosive they thought the race problem."[70]

68. "A Basis for Interracial Cooperation and Development in the South: A Statement by Southern Negroes," in *Southern Conference on Race Relations*, pp. 5–6.
69. *Ibid.*, pp. 6–11.
70. Mays, *Born to Rebel*, p. 219.

Judged in terms of the contemporary milieu, rather than by present-day ideologies, they wrought well. Never before in Southern history had black people made such a comprehensive and lucid declaration of what they expected from white people. Despite its purposeful ambiguity on segregation, the statement indicated that Southern Negro leaders were not mere accommodationists. They were dead set against the status quo. As one variation on the theme of rising racial aspirations during World War II, the Durham statement projected a vision of equality and projected the changing mind of the black South.

Noting the wide editorial comment about the document in the Virginia press, Jackson wrote to Hancock. "You are to be commended most highly for [your part in] our magnificent effort. In all probability our statement of interracial cooperation will go down as one of the most significant efforts of Negroes in our history." Impressed by the top billing from the national wire services, Young exulted: "Our manifesto seems to be turning out to be another 'shot at Concord' that was heard around the world. You really started something brother!" Although he had borne the major responsibility of coordination and the brunt of scathing criticism, Hancock gave the real credit to Jessie Ames, P. B. Young, Luther P. Jackson, and Charles S. Johnson. The entire episode, he said, was "the most constructive departure in race relations since the emancipation of the Negro."[71] He anxiously awaited the next round.

71. Jackson to Hancock, December 19, 1942, Young to Hancock, December 18, 1942, Hancock to Ames, December 16, 1942, Hancock Papers; Hancock, "Writing a 'New Charter of Southern Race Relations,'" 19; and his "Race Relations in the United States: A Summary," in Logan, ed., *What the Negro Wants*, p. 237.

VI. Dialogue Off-Key

The Durham manifesto, a Southern black declaration of independence, demanded specific changes in language which sounded neither florid nor chauvinistic. It put forth a black agenda and provoked uneasy discussion between its critics, defenders, and white sympathizers. For Hancock and his cohorts, it initiated a continuing but vacillating dialogue with Southern liberals. The latter responded favorably to the statement, but did not wage an offensive against institutionalized racism. The two groups founded a regional organization designed to solve the South's economic, political, social and racial problems, yet it failed to oppose segregation. Disillusioned by the whites' hesitation, the blacks pushed for official repudiation of Jim Crow. When this inside pressure and the NAACP's postwar assault on the *Plessy* doctrine finally drove the liberals to disavow forced separation of the races, the *Brown* decision was imminent.[1]

Following the Durham meeting, Jessie Ames congratulated Hancock "on a difficult job well begun!" She expressed amazement that his arrangements for the program had required such a long time and that he had nevertheless been able to keep word of the conference out of the press. This, of course, was not exactly true. Bits of information leaked out in the planning stage which stirred up damaging rumors and unfair remarks. Hancock, whom several people tried to discredit personally, remarked in September 1942 that "the opposition though subtle is nevertheless strong." Again, in late November, he asked the conferees

1. In *Plessy v. Ferguson* (1896) the United States Supreme Court ruled that a Louisiana statute providing "equal but separate accommodations for the white and colored races" in railway travel constituted a reasonable regulation within the meaning of the Fourteenth Amendment. This ruling became the keystone of racial segregation in America, which straitjacketed the Negro for almost sixty years. The reversal came in *Brown v. the Board of Education* (1954), when the Court, by declaring that "segregation of white and colored children in public schools has a detrimental effect upon the colored children," demolished racial separation as a standing principle of constitutional law and removed the legal props from segregated schools. See Robert H. Brisbane, *The Black Vanguard: Origins of the Negro Social Revolution 1900–1960* (Valley Forge, Pa.: Judson Press, 1970), pp. 27–28, 239–244.

to watch out for their enemies' machinations. "There are those lying in wait to pounce upon us and rend us and the whole enterprise," he warned. In short, Hancock knew there were objections to the conference from its inception. These became more pronounced after it had met and the subcommittee had released its report.[2]

Certain black newspapers prejudged the whole affair. At the end of August, doubtless conducting one last editorial foray against "the gloomy Virginian," the Baltimore *Afro-American* dubbed Hancock and his supporters the "hush-hush boys." They lacked manhood, it charged, and were too fearful of whites. In the wake of the October conclave the denunciations continued. The Oklahoma City *Black-Dispatch* criticized the meeting's exclusively Negro constituency, which obviously negated the interracial principle. The Negroes were speaking from a Jim Crow corner, stated the weekly, because the Southern Conference for Human Welfare had already demonstrated that segregated proceedings were no longer necessary or respectable. The Pittsburgh *Courier* fumed: "Apparently this is an attempt to appease the reactionary South and gain some minor concessions by formulating a program free from the 'taint' of Northern Negro radicalism."[3]

Once the conference statement appeared, the opposition and the defense squared off. Editor Carter Wesley of the Houston *Informer* called it an "historical achievement destined to play a large part in bringing about adjustments" and a blueprint of Negro rights to which the race everywhere could adhere. Roscoe Dunjee, editor of the *Black-Dispatch*, roundly condemned the Texan's unbounded optimism. Talmadge, Dixon, Bilbo, and their political cronies were thumping their chests and shouting "nigger" during the 1942 summer campaigns, said Dunjee, producing much "synthetic" racial tension. The Durham leaders purported "to tone down this temporary unrest," he concluded, "and they were unwise in the methods adopted."[4] Literary critic J. Saunders Redding, however, rejected the argument

2. Ames to Hancock, October 27, 1942, Hancock to Ames, September 8, November 22, 1942, Jessie Daniel Ames File, Southern Regional Council Office, Atlanta, Georgia.

3. Baltimore *Afro-American*, August 27, 1942; Oklahoma City *Black-Dispatch*, November 7, 1942; Pittsburgh *Courier*, November 14, 1942.

4. Houston *Informer*, April 2, 1943; Oklahoma City *Black-Dispatch*, April 17, 1943.

that the Durham signatories were appeasers. "Ten years ago this declared opposition to custom would have been impossible," he wrote. "The declaration must have sounded treasonable to the South. None of the old shibboleths here, no truckling to expediency. . . . This statement of policy runs sharply counter to any based on the maintenance of a concept of inferior and superior races." Writing three months later, historian Carter G. Woodson overlooked Redding's observation entirely. He referred to the Durham spokesmen as Daniels', Dabney's, and Graves' lackeys, who "seceded from the aggressive leadership of the race." These "slaves," Woodson reacted, "offered no program toward liberty and freedom, and they placed themselves in the position of defending segregation, the very antithesis of democracy."[5]

Luckily, many key black opinion makers eschewed emotional and divisive rhetoric like Woodson's. Some came out in support of the Durham statement, including NAACP chief Walter White and President Mordecai Johnson of Howard University. Claude A. Barnett, director of the Associated Negro Press, termed it "forceful, sane, practical and realistic." William H. Hastie, dean of Howard University Law School and civilian aide to the Secretary of War, said the "detailed and carefully worked-out statement shows the fundamental agreement of Negroes throughout the country upon the next steps which must be taken toward complete emancipation." W. E. B. Du Bois commended the signers for attempting to guide the future of the Negro in America. "On the whole the Durham program is a pretty good document," the veteran Negro ideologue announced. "I should have written it a little differently myself, but I would not be unwilling to sign it."[6]

Negro responses to the Durham movement and statement, then, ran the gamut from sneers to praise. They consisted of a decidedly mixed bag of sectionally partisan, personal, and ideological pronouncements which revealed fundamental schisms within the black world. Easily, segregation dominated the debate. Yet opponents were content only to

5. J. Saunders Redding, "A Negro Speaks for His People," *Atlantic Monthly* CLXXI (March 1943), 62; Carter G. Woodson, "Negroes Not United for Democracy," *Negro History Bulletin*, VI (May 1943), 177.

6. The endorsements of Barnett, Hastie, and Du Bois were printed in *Southern Conference on Race Relations, Durham, N. C., October 20, 1942*, n.p., pp. 14–15; Hancock to Ames, n.d., William H. Hastie to P. B. Young, January 6, 1943, Gordon Blaine Hancock Papers, Richmond, Virginia.

chide Southern blacks for accepting it and proponents, too often, simply denied that any other approach would work in the South. Still, the Durham leaders faced a gnawing dilemma in this battle of words. They acted autonomously in formulating a charter for the South, while insisting that blacks all over the country shared a common struggle.

P. B. Young thought Southern blacks were "confronted with a situation which cannot be handled by persons outside the region." Therefore, they "must assume leadership." If whites surmised that the more vocal Northern blacks expected something different, they were wrong. For the Southern Negro, said Young, also wanted a chance to work at any job for which his training and ability qualified him, to become a member of a union, to vote and participate in government, to serve his country in war as a civilian and soldier, and to have "the stigma of implacable Jim Crowism in its barbarous impact upon every phase of his life removed."[7] Young believed that the geographical divisions of the race, while united by the goal of first-class citizenship, should work independently on their aspects of the problem. However, when Virginius Dabney published an article in *Atlantic Monthly* attacking Northern Negro leaders and white rabble-rousers for pushing the nation toward a racial blood bath, Young perceived it as a dividing wedge. Referring to Northern Negroes, he replied to Dabney: "The Durham conference did not . . . declare a break with them. We just did not invite them."[8]

Jackson and Hancock addressed their rebuttals mainly to the thorny question of segregation. The roots of biracialism extended deep into American social history, said Jackson, and it persisted despite the nation's democratic creed. "The sixty or more Negroes who comprise this body detest segregation," he wrote, "but they are willing to begin now 'to evolve in the South a way of life, consistent with the principle for which we . . . are fighting throughout the world.' "[9] According to Hancock, "the real bone of contention . . . was that the Southern

7. Young to Ames, October 1, 1942, Jessie Daniel Ames Papers, University of North Carolina Library, Chapel Hill, North Carolina; Norfolk *Journal and Guide*, October 17, 1942.

8. See Virginius Dabney, "Nearer and Nearer the Precipice," *Atlantic Monthly*, CLXXI (January 1943), 94–100; Young to Dabney, January 12, 1943, Virginius Dabney Papers, University of Virginia Library, Charlottesville, Virginia.

9. Norfolk *Journal and Guide*, March 27, 1943.

Negroes stepped out of their own free will and accord and attempted to take things into their own hands." Steadfast in the conviction that the Durham conference had done the right thing, he stated his points succinctly. "We have asked for everything that the Northern Negro could have asked for and in as pointed language," he said. "If our reference to segregation is the weakest point in the document we certainly have wrought a great work for the cause. . . . We are not going to be denied." [10]

For a while, indeed, it seemed that the Durham vanguard definitely would not be denied. In general, the liberal Southern press commented favorably upon their handiwork, whether owing to an implied willingness to tolerate the dual system or the statement's factual tone. The Norfolk *Virginian-Pilot* said that the proposed changes could be made without having Negroes invade the fields posted against trespass, while its local rival, the *Ledger-Dispatch*, reported that "it deserves, if it does not demand, reflection and study on the part of the white South— far more of both than is possible in an hour or two." [11] The Richmond *Times-Dispatch* praised the absence of "denunciatory harangues," and the *News Leader* considered 75 per cent of the report acceptable to whites. The latter did not specify the 25 per cent that they might reject.[12] By far the most sympathetic evaluation came from editor Ralph McGill of the Atlanta *Constitution*. Relieved that the statement did not exacerbate the segregation issue, McGill said Negroes were making steady progress toward winning equal rights. If whites refused to discuss Negroes' stated grievances "calmly and intelligently," he added, it would be unfortunate. "If Southern Negro leaders, asking for the cooperation of the majority race, do not receive encouragement," McGill ended, "then the South will have failed the first effort by Southern Negro leadership along realistic lines." [13]

From the beginning of World War II, the newspapers were not nearly so reassuring to blacks, and Southern liberals, a label applied loosely to

10. Hancock to Carter Wesley, April 1, 1943, Hancock Papers.
11. Norfolk *Virginian-Pilot*, December 11, 1942, and *Ledger-Dispatch*, December 16, 1942.
12. Richmond *Times-Dispatch*, December 18, 1942, and *News Leader*, December 16, 1942.
13. Atlanta *Constitution*, December 18, 1942.

the minority of whites who urged fairer and saner treatment of blacks,[14] frequently assumed a defensive posture. Witnessing violent clashes and hearing strident protests, they exhibited a sense of collective alarm over the ever-widening racial chasm. To sociologist Howard W. Odum, there were indications in the abundance of rumors, tensions, and conflicts that the white South and the Negro, in the early 1940's, faced the most dangerous racial confrontation since Reconstruction. Unwilling to storm an entrenched position, however, Odum blamed the chaos on "the new Negro leadership . . . militantly advocating a radical and revolutionary change in the Southern way of life." Writer David L. Cohn extended Odum's reasoning. "Let them beware," he said of militant black leaders. "He who attempts to change the mores of a people . . . runs risks of incalculable gravity."[15]

White liberalism seemingly was calling for caution and gradualism. John Temple Graves of the Birmingham *Age-Herald* felt the war gave Southerners the chance to bury their guilt and do something to save the region from "a mess of Communism and Ku Kluxery." Nonetheless, he wanted it understood that segregation was "not an argument in the South" but "a major premise."[16] James E. Chappell of the Birmingham *News* supported his colleague from the Steel City. "After all, we can move only as fast as the slow, tough prejudices of our people permit," he explained. "We cannot force progress; we cannot compel convictions; we can only try to lead and influence public thought."[17] Mark Ethridge, editor of the Louisville *Courier-Journal* and the first chairman of FEPC, spoke adamantly. "There is no power in the world . . . which could now force the Southern white people to the abandonment of the principle of social segregation," he maintained. "It is a cruel disillusionment bearing the germs of strife and perhaps tragedy

14. See William H. Leary, "Race Relations in Turmoil: Southern Liberals and World War II" (M.A. Thesis, University of Virginia, 1967), pp. 1–10.

15. Howard W. Odum, *Race and Rumors of Race: Challenge to American Crisis* (Chapel Hill: University of North Carolina Press, 1943), pp. 4, 44; David L. Cohn, "How the South Feels," *Atlantic Monthly*, CLXXIII (January 1944), 50.

16. John Temple Graves, "The Fighting South," *Virginia Quarterly Review*, XVII (Winter 1942), 71; his "The Southern Negro and the War Crisis," *ibid.* (Autumn 1942), 512; and his *The Fighting South* (New York: G. P. Putnam's Sons, 1943), p. 120.

17. Newspapers and the Race Problem" (Atlanta: Commission on Interracial Cooperation, 1942), p. 1.

. . . to tell them [Negroes] that they can expect it, or that they can exact it as the price of their participation in the war."[18] Such men were going to move slowly, if at all.

At the same time, though, there were individuals whose thinking reflected more optimism about the race problem. Former Interracial Commission director Will W. Alexander, then of the Julius Rosenwald Fund, stated that the Four Freedoms and the impetus of a burgeoning defense effort had clarified the need for well-meaning white people to confront segregation. He asked interracialists to break the habit of paternalism and work with Negroes as equals. President Clark Foreman of the Southern Conference for Human Welfare, unlike many in the liberal camp, admitted that ugly stories of Negro-baiting in the South were true. Lillian E. Smith of Clayton, Georgia, co-editor of *South Today*, viewed Jim Crow customs as the cornerstones of a tragic way of life in the South, one characterized by humiliation, complacency, fear, arrogance, hate, ignorance, blindness, and willful hypocrisy. "Somehow we must realize that in keeping the black man in his place," she lamented, "we white Southerners are lynching the spirit of every one of our children."[19] Few of her fellows were as open-minded.

Virginius Dabney, the most conspicuous friend of the Negro in Virginia, neither defended the old order outright nor strongly condemned oppression in the new. He found the middle ground apropos. Prior to FEPC, for example, he wrote several editorials on blacks and national defense. "In Virginia unfair discrimination against skilled Negro workers is hampering the arming of America," he pointed out. "In a Commonwealth with some 700,000 Negro citizens it is only right and proper that such a large element be given an adequate share." The following year, notwithstanding, Dabney accused the NAACP of inciting Negroes "to demand the complete wiping out of racial differences overnight." Like Jessie Ames, he saw agitation and militancy as con-

---

18. Quoted in Graves, *The Fighting South*, pp. 125–126.

19. Wilma Dykeman and James Stokely, *Seeds of Southern Change: The Life of Will Alexander* (Chicago: University of Chicago Press, 1962), pp. 249, 253–254; Clark Foreman, "Race Tension in the South," *New Republic*, CVII (September 21, 1942), 340–342; Lillian E. Smith, "Growing into Freedom," *Common Ground*, IV (Autumn 1943), 47, 51–52.

stant dangers. Convinced that black and white "extremists" were fomenting race war, which would certainly hurt blacks more than whites, he stated that "if the disturbing elements on both sides of the color line can somehow be muzzled . . . the slow but certain processes of evolutionary progress can function." [20] Irritated by this advice, Charles Thompson of Howard University confessed: "Liberals such as Mr. Dabney are an enigma to me. There has always seemed to me to be too much of the attitude of Santa Claus about them." Continuing, Thompson said: "What they bring to the Negro, or any other downtrodden group, is given because he has been a good boy. Thus when Negroes misbehave, they are threatened with 'Santa Claus won't come' or with something worse." [21]

Santa Clauses or not, Southern liberals faced the challenge of responding constructively to the Durham statement. Very soon after its issuance, P. B. Young reminded Mrs. Ames of her promise to organize a white follow-up meeting. [22] This would be a trying experience for her, but she wanted to make good her pledge. On the advice of editors James E. Chappell, Mark Ethridge, and Virginius Dabney, and with the assistance of Josephine Wilkins of the Interracial Commission, she secured a number of representative whites to sign a letter inviting others to attend a conference in Atlanta. Thirteen signatures of prominent Atlantans were affixed to the call, placed alphabetically: C. H. Gillman, regional director, CIO; George L. Googe, regional director, AFL; M. Ashby Jones, minister, Ponce De Leon Baptist Church; Ryland Knight, minister, Second Ponce De Leon Baptist Church; David Marx, rabbi, The Temple; Arthur J. Moore, Methodist Bishop; Ralph McGill, editor, Atlanta *Constitution*; Stuart R. Oglesby, minister, Central Presbyterian Church; Gerald P. O'Hara, Catholic Bishop; Dean S. Paden, president, King Hardware Company; J. McDowell Richards, president, Columbia Theological Seminary, Decatur, Georgia; John Moore

20. Richmond *Times-Dispatch*, January 18, 19, 1941, April 10, 1942; Dabney, "Nearer and Nearer the Precipice," 100. Also, see his *Below the Potomac: A Book about the New South* (New York: Appleton-Century, 1942), pp. 300–303.

21. Charles H. Thompson, "Mr. Dabney and the 'Precipice,' " *Journal of Negro Education*, XII (Spring 1943), 143.

22. Young to Ames, December 24, 1942, Ames Papers.

Walker, Protestant Episcopal Bishop; and Goodrich C. White, president, Emory University.[23]

Recognizing the seriousness of their task, these people acted deliberately. The original date of the conference was February 9, 1943, but because of their wish to include President Preston Arkwright of Georgia Power Company among those signing the invitation they changed it to February 24. However, when several indicated that the latter date was inconvenient and "the question arose as to how much the signers are going to be responsible for the conduct of the conference in the outcome," they decided to discuss procedure and objectives at length.[24] Some "were feeling resistance to any sort of interracial scheme and were not therefore eager to move fast."[25]

From Mrs. Ames's point of view, practical considerations undergirded these delays. She informed Young that members of the steering committee did not "seem inclined to agree" on mechanics and long-range goals. Also, many were fearful of adverse publicity, which might "precipitate controversy before the fact and intimidate persons who would otherwise attend." The political situation entered the picture too. Writing to Dabney, she mentioned the "articulate Talmadgites" in the Georgia legislature, then convened in Atlanta, who were exploiting the race issue. "We do not propose to add any fuel to the smoldering fire that is certainly present over in the Capitol," she stated. When the callers reached a consensus, therefore, they set the conference for April 8, a time when the General Assembly would not be in session. They further planned to limit the proceedings to one day, issue a statement replying to Negro demands, and appoint a collaboration committee to meet later, and in another city, with the blacks.[26]

Meanwhile, Hancock wondered if enough whites were interested to implement the plan successfully. Sensing his creeping pessimism, Jessie Ames wrote to him: "We are going to have the conference—of that there is no doubt—because these people who have signed . . . view it

23. Josephine Wilkins, "An Answer When Negro Southerners Spoke," *New South*, XIX (January 1964), 24.

24. Ames to Young, January 22, 26, February 1, 1943, Ames Papers.

25. Henry P. Houser, "The Southern Regional Council" (M. A. Thesis, University of North Carolina, 1950), p. 30.

26. Ames to Young, January 22, February 1, 1943, Ames to Dabney, February 2, 1943, Ames Papers.

as something we in the South have got to do. So there is no fear of the conference not being called." [27] Actually, even while she was being so reassuring, dark clouds were forming on the Negro side. P. B. Young, worried almost sick, told her that the whites must work faster. "A North Carolina group, headed by Dr. James E. Shepard, is calling a conference in April, to which will be invited Negroes from North, South, East, and West, to 'write a charter' that is satisfactory to all Negroes," Young lamented. "*This is unfortunate.*" He feared that Shepard would only "create a lot of confusion and give the impression that the Southern Negro group is divided." [28]

News about Shepard came first to Hancock when Fred M. Alexander, Virginia Supervisor of Negro Education, sent him two of Shepard's letters. Hancock and Young, in turn, got J. Alvin Russell, president of St. Paul's Institute and Shepard's personal friend, to do some dissuading. "To hold another conference and issue another statement before our Southern white group has had opportunity to act on the statement of the October conference would, I fear, greatly muddy the waters," Russell said to his esteemed colleague, "and I know that this is not your desire." [29] In reality, few people knew what Shepard's real motives were. Having supported the Durham conference, even hosting it at North Carolina College, he suddenly acted in a way that seemed odd to his erstwhile colleagues. Many thought he might have been overly sensitive to Northern black criticism. One Negro official, Harold L. Trigg of the North Carolina Department of Education, said on good authority that Shepard "was looking for preferment with the Republican party." Whatever the case, Young soundly rebuked him. "It is your intention to say tacitly that we failed and that you are going to do a better job," Young wrote. "If that is your intention you will certainly stir up a lot of resentment and bitterness. . . . I suggest that you meet with Dr. Hancock and me sometime in the near future for the purpose of arriving at an understanding." [30]

27. Hancock to Ames, January 28, 1943, Ames to Hancock, February 2, 1943, Hancock Papers.

28. Young to Ames, December 31, 1942, February 4, 1943, Hancock Papers.

29. Copies of James E. Shepard to Fred M. Alexander, December 9, 28, 1942, J. Alvin Russell to Shepard, March 1, 1943, Hancock Papers.

30. Houser, "The Southern Regional Council," p. 31; Young to Shepard, March 9, 1943, Hancock Papers.

That meeting never took place, but Shepard called off his venture.

Within the shadow of their deadline, the whites were still soliciting signers. Somewhat anxiously, Mrs. Ames wrote to Rabbi Marx asking him to do what he could to get Preston Arkwright's cooperation. The effort failed, as did other attempts to corral business support. A barrage of personal letters to industrialists and manufacturers yielded mostly negative replies. A leading businessman from Alabama, J. Handley Wright, indicated that he would not confer with labor people under any conditions, much less Negroes. The president of the Nashville, Chattanooga, and St. Louis Railway refused, among other reasons, because he felt that somebody like Alabama Governor Frank Dixon, who believed that race troubles stemmed from "the meddlers and carpetbaggers from the North," needed to be present.[31] Amid such indifference, although a total of 553 invitations went out, the organizers hardly expected crowning success. The handful of businessmen willing to go along wanted nothing said of the Negro's economic status.[32]

On April 8, 1943, 113 Southern white leaders gathered at the Piedmont Hotel in Atlanta. They constituted approximately 20 per cent of those invited and represented the press, education, religion, and civic organizations, with very few from business and labor. Most were members of the Interracial Commission, and it appeared as though the commission were facing en masse the crisis of the hour. Chairman Ralph McGill asked the delegates to "arrive at certain affirmations of good will and justice as they relate to the Negro race." After the morning discussions and noon recess, a committee was appointed to review the statement "prepared in advance." Carlyle Fraser, president of the Atlanta Chamber of Commerce, argued for a stronger endorsement of segregation and, in order to sell it to whites, an equally strong denial of social equality. McGill pointed out that this dominative approach would not be sympathetic with nor found agreeable by Negro leaders. Jessie Ames, Josephine Wilkins, Bishop Moore, and

31. Ames to Rabbi Marx, January 22, 1943, J. Handley Wright, executive vice-president, Associated Industries of Alabama, to Ralph McGill, March 23, 1943, Fitzgerald Hall to McGill, March 26, 1943, Ames Papers.

32. Ames to Hancock, February 10, 1943, Ames Papers; Houser, "The Southern Regional Council," pp. 32, 34.

M. Ashby Jones backed McGill's view.[33] Apparently Fraser was convinced.

The statement—approved, signed, and given to the press that afternoon—praised Negro leaders for being frank, courageous, unthreatening, and exemplars of good will. White people were not answering every question raised or offering solutions for all the vexing problems, it stated, but pledging their desire to cooperate in "any sound program aimed at the improvement of race relations." It admitted that Negroes were victims of deprivation and dependent upon the will of the majority group, conditions which violated the spirit of democracy and abrogated equal rights and opportunities. Poverty and slow economic development complicated color prejudice in the South, the statement continued, while maintaining that "the only justification offered for those laws which have for their purpose the separation of the races is that they are intended to minister to the welfare and integrity of both races." The document's chief complaint was that "those laws" were being unfairly administered in the allocation of school funds, educational facilities, and teacher salaries; travel; legal justice; safety and comfort; and in the distribution of public utilities and benefits such as sewers, water, housing, street and sidewalk paving, playgrounds, health and hospital services. The remaining sections deplored police brutality, job discrimination, land tenancy, and "the poison of racial antagonism," each of which affected Negro life. "Evolutionary methods" rather than "ill-founded revolutionary movements," it warned, would pave the way to solving the race problem. In conclusion, it agreed that Negroes' struggles to correct obvious wrongs were not efforts to invade the privacy of white family life or to sow seeds of disunity during the war, but justifiable attempts to gain the elementary principles of American life.[34]

The Atlanta statement received wide exposure. Eventually, more than three hundred whites signed it, including Governor Colgate W.

33. Wilkins, "An Answer When Negro Southerners Spoke," 24–25; Houser, "The Southern Regional Council," p. 35.

34. *The Durham Statement, the Atlanta Statement, the Richmond Statement* (Atlanta: Commission on Interracial Cooperation, 1943), pp. 10–11.

Darden, Jr. of Virginia.[35] Through it Southern liberals publicly acknowledged the legitimacy of the Durham demands without opposing segregation or the "separate but equal" principle. They committed themselves to nothing except cultivating an atmosphere of understanding, cooperation, and mutual respect. Unquestionably, these qualities were surely missing in the South and the group did brave the bigotry of the times to be concerned at all. Yet they were probably too fearful of taking advanced steps and defended the dual system. If black leaders pragmatically tolerated biracialism, they had also proposed to work gradually toward its demise. The white leaders seldom, if ever, envisioned a desegregated South.

That difference in perspective strained subsequent dialogue. For instance, several days after the Atlanta conference Hancock wired Mrs. Ames, applauding her vision, faith, and sense of righteous endeavor. In his column, moreover, he described the white statement as "heartening" and "courageous." Covertly, however, he was disappointed. Calling on Dabney at the *Times-Dispatch* building, Hancock said the whites had demonstrated too little moral courage on segregation. They should have repudiated it in principle, he felt, even if they were constrained to accept it in practice. Writing in turn to Young, Dabney expressed shock over Hancock's attitude. "Many white people are fearful that such movements as this have the destruction of segregation as an ultimate objective," he reported. In replying, Young reminded him that Hancock spoke for the Durham signers, who were "fundamentally opposed" to compulsory segregation. "Segregation means far more than keeping Negroes and whites in separate schools, separate churches, separate in public conveyances, and separated in places of public assembly," Young explained. "It means the separation of the Negro from a decent chance to make a respectable living."[36] When the leading liberals were made privy to this correspondence, they became lukewarm about the forthcoming collaborative meeting.

The respective chairmen, McGill and Young, appointed committees of thirty-seven members each for a joint conference in Richmond on

35. Virginius Dabney, "The South Marches On," *Survey Graphic*, XXXII (November 1943), 442.

36. Telegram, April 12, 1943, Ames Papers; Norfolk *Journal and Guide*, April 13, 1943; Dabney to Young, April 17, 1943, Young to Dabney, April 20, 1943, Dabney Papers.

June 16. The blacks soon enlarged theirs to forty-two, and they consented to having neutral observers present. Preparations devolved largely upon the shoulders of Jessie Ames and the blacks. McGill declined the chance to preside and, instead, scheduled a June trip to Cuba. Besides, he thought it would be better if the blacks prepared the agenda. Dabney entertained no desire to take up the gauntlet either. Earlier, he had rejected the opportunity to chair the Atlanta conference, pleading that he was a poor parliamentarian and had a speaking engagement elsewhere in Georgia the next day. Finally, Mrs. Ames got Young to preside and Hancock to give the keynote speech in Richmond. If the blacks were in charge, she presumed, they could best determine how to implement their manifesto. Yet she also wanted to head off Howard Odum and other proponents of the Council on Southern Regional Development. It did not make her happy that they would be in attendance.[37]

Jessie Ames must have seen the handwriting on the wall. "I am attending the conference in Richmond," she wrote to a friend, "but I do not feel now that I am any longer solely responsible for what may come of it." In brief, she felt outnumbered.[38] The proceedings of the Atlanta conference were hardly over when McGill received a letter from Will Alexander criticizing the old commission's church, academic, and social work constituency. He recommended a fresh approach "with much broader support, particularly from business, professional and labor leaders." Unmistakably disagreeing, Mrs. Ames told Odum that Alexander had grossly underestimated its influence among churchmen, laymen, and the press. "In these troublous times we cannot wipe out an organization with the history back of it that the Commission has and establish overnight a new organization with the same purposes and program of the old one," she argued. "From the inception of the Durham conference . . . I have seen in this whole movement

37. Ames to Young, April 28, June 14, 1943, Young to Ames, May 7, 1943, Ames to Theodore F. Adams, minister of First Baptist Church in Richmond, June 7, 1943, Ames Papers; Houser, "The Southern Regional Council," p. 39; Edward F. Burrows, "The Commission on Interracial Cooperation, 1919–1944: A Case Study in the History of the Interracial Movement in the South" (Ph.D. Dissertation, University of Wisconsin, 1955), pp. 274–275.

38. Ames to Mrs. Hamilton, June 10, 1943, Ames File, Southern Regional Council Office.

an opportunity to strengthen and revitalize the Interracial Commission."[39] Odum, however, remained committed to instituting the regional idea, whereby the focus would be shifted from race to the problems of agriculture, labor, industry, and health that affected the entire South.[40]

Odum's immediate intentions were known only among the white inner circle. The blacks did not have a similar plan, save Hancock's notion of state and local Negro councils to serve as adjuncts to the commission's work. Preoccupied with segregation, they never really assessed the advantages and disadvantages of regionalism as a way of attaining racial equality in the South. Meanwhile, having rejected Jim Crow and white paternalism, they were headed to Richmond seeking action without specific mechanisms of implementation in mind. They wanted something different from and better than the Interracial Commission;[41] hence they considered their own body, the Southern Conference on Race Relations, necessary. During its fourteen months existence, the Southern Conference nurtured their esprit de corps. In March, 1943, secretary-treasurer Luther P. Jackson reported an active membership of forty-three. These had contributed a total of $228.25, from which typing, correspondence and traveling expenses of $212.35 were paid. Besides memoranda from Hancock and Young, the members received copies of the *Southern Vision*, the official organ from April through December, 1943. The first issue dramatically portrayed the slogan "Men Must Be Brotherized or They Will Be Brutalized," featured a black-white handshake, and highlighted the feats in Durham and Atlanta.[42] Occasionally, sensitive matters abounded. James

39. Alexander to McGill, April 13, 1943, Ames to Odum, June 12, 1943, Ames File, Southern Regional Council Office.

40. Burrows, "The Commission on Interracial Cooperation, 1919–1944," pp. 268–272. For Odum's conception of regionalism and the race problem, see "The Position of the Negro in the American Social Order in 1950," *Journal of Negro Education*, VIII (July 1939), 587–594.

41. Houser, "The Southern Regional Council," p. 39; Hancock to McGill, June 3, 1943, Hancock Papers. "We need an organ of expression," Hancock said. "I would like to see the South organized by states and counties in Race Relations Councils to carry out the spirit of our laudable enterprise. It is going to take a lot of time and money but it will be worth it. This matter of course could be taken up by our promotion Committee."

42. Jackson to Hancock, December 19, 1942, March 13, 1943, Hancock, "What is Your Pleasure?" February 10, 1943, P. B. Young memorandum, February 25, 1943,

Shepard's attempt to hold a meeting of blacks from all sections provided one case in point. Another concerned the Pittsburgh *Courier's* national black statement, which the Southern Conference refused to endorse because it was designed to overshadow the Durham program. The openness of the approaching collaboration conference also troubled the waters. In a frank letter to Mrs. Ames, Hancock suggested that the groups convene in a church or wherever integrated seating could be obtained. This would spare blacks the insult "that always comes of these interracial gatherings." After learning that many of the whites were apprehensive over the matter, Young told her: "Our group cannot of course retreat from the position taken at Durham. But I believe a way can be found to deal with this question in a manner that will not irritate either side." [43]

Developments at the Richmond Collaboration Conference belied Young's fondest hope. Although he, Hancock, and Jessie Ames met the night before and hastily put together a satisfactory agenda, tensions were high on both sides. On the morning of June 16, 1943, 60 people gathered in the main sanctuary of Richmond's Grace Covenant Church, 33 of them black. Only 17 of the whites were official representatives; 10 were visitors or observers. Even though seating arrangements were unrestricted, the delegations sat apart. P. B. Young presided, and Hancock opened with a searching keynote address. He said that those present "occupied an eminence of moral grandeur unparalleled in our war torn world," and, for Negroes, "the clock of destiny is striking a mighty hour pervaded by a now or never feeling." Black leaders were weary of "counseling patience and the elusive consolations of social evolution," he stated, while urging "a more advanced policy of the white South toward its Negroes." Southern black leadership could "be strangled or strengthened," Hancock warned, and just which one it would be depended upon the vision and statesmanship of the collaborators. If the South resented interference from "outside elements" then it needed greater liberalism within; and interracialism must not be synonymous with " 'a motion to lay on the table' every

financial reports, March 2, 13, April 15, 1943, Hancock to coworkers, March 25, 1943, copy of the *Southern Vision*, I (April 1943), 1–2, Hancock Papers.

43. P. L. Prattis, editor of the Pittsburgh *Courier* to Young, May 7, 1943, Hancock Papers; Hancock to Ames, February 8, 1943, Young to Ames, May 4, 1943, Ames Papers.

proposal for social and economic advance." In conclusion, Hancock noted the dangers facing the conclave, "namely, the danger of going too fast—a danger the white South fears, and the danger of going too slow—a danger the Negro fears." [44]

Hancock's insistent message upset the whites. He was hardly seated when Atlanta clergyman M. Ashby Jones took the floor, denounced him "for going too far," and lectured the blacks "somewhat in the old Southern way." Feelings escalated, various people shouted at one another, and the conference fell into chaos. A white woman from Tennessee demanded, in the middle of the morning, that everybody stop for prayer. The blacks probably would have walked out if Odum had not taken the rostrum and refuted Jones's position. [45] With calm restored and the Negroes apparently grateful for his timely intervention, Odum proceeded to sell his concept of a regional council. Given the tense atmosphere, there was virtually no room for critical reflection. In haste, the participants adopted resolutions directing that a "continuing committee . . . be charged with the responsibility for working out methods and practical means of approach" to Odum's program. Without affirmative action, they noted, "we shall fall far short of our hopes and possibilities." [46]

Judging from the reactions, there was more confrontation than collaboration in Richmond. The blacks were angry. "With all due respect to our friend who followed you, he made no contribution," wrote a perturbed Benjamin Mays to Hancock. "It is unfortunate." Hancock himself resented what happened. "A man of Dr. Jones' mind has a place in our scheme of things," he told Mrs. Ames, "but I doubt if that place is in such a meeting as we held in Richmond." P. B. Young, undoubtedly, felt the same way. "It is my intention to write Mrs. Ames and tell her in a nice way how, inadvertently perhaps, the Atlanta group permitted old brother Jones to throw a wet blanket over the Richmond

44. Houser, "The Southern Regional Council," p. 40; Ames to Hancock, June 21, 1943, Copy of "The South's Greatest Vision," An Address delivered by Gordon B. Hancock before the Collaboration Conference in Richmond, Virginia, June 16, 1943, Hancock Papers. Also, see the *Southern Vision*, I (June 1943), 1, 4.

45. Details of what happened were recapitulated in Odum to Jackson Davis of the General Education Board, June 19, 1943, Hancock Papers.

46. *The Durham Statement, the Atlanta Statement, the Richmond Statement*, pp. 15–16.

conference," he said. "I don't think they ought to go on without knowing . . . that this sort of thing is no longer acceptable. In my estimation, Dr. Jones is dead and ought to be buried and forgotten." Young also accused the whites of being scared, noting that "Mr. Dabney was rather frantic . . . in the fear that it would be published that he was chairman of the continuation committee of the white group." [47]

Generally, the whites were defensive. "So far as I know, not one of the earlier leaders that were considered liberal is willing to go along," Odum confided to an associate, explaining his own actions. McGill did not say one word about backing them or what should be done, he reported, whereas Mark Ethridge and Goodrich White were simply "too busy" to come. He sighed: "I am convinced, even if I were not sincere in it, that the immediate obligation of the white South was to say that we understand, appreciate, and are going along with the Negro leadership of this best type." Yet Odum wished to go no farther than launching a regional council, an idea which Negro leaders readily supported.[48] Jessie Ames, who assumed a low profile in Richmond and allowed Odum a free hand, let Hancock know explicitly that the state committees of the Interracial Commission were capable of carrying out the Durham program. In response, Hancock said if they were not going "to build an organization that would afford standing room" for blacks and whites committed to racial equality then they might as well call the whole thing off. Only Odum's initiative, he admitted, had saved the Richmond meeting from "dismal failure." [49]

Somewhat shaken, Mrs. Ames wrote back, saying that she never thought he or Young expected "anything more than a conference of Southern white people." If the commission was not "sufficiently aggressive," any number of existing agencies could answer the Durham demands, she noted. These included the Southern Conference for Human Welfare, the Southern Negro Youth Congress, the NAACP, the National Urban League, and the churches. As for Odum's "masterly statement" in Richmond, she mocked: "It was prepared before he got there. It was what the white man thought should come out of that

47. Mays to Hancock, June 9, 1943, Hancock to Ames, June 25, 1943, Young to Hancock, June 30, 1943, Hancock Papers.

48. Odum to Jackson Davis, June 19, 1943, Hancock Papers.

49. Ames to Hancock, June 21, 1943, Hancock to Ames, June 25, 1943, Ames Papers.

meeting and it is what came out of the meeting." In closing, however, she promised that if the continuing committee decided upon a new organization, "I am the last person who would raise my finger to block it." Sensing her irritation, Hancock simply informed her that the blacks were lining up behind Odum's plan, which he thought would work.[50] Dabney remained noncommittal. "I find his [Hancock's] discouragement somewhat puzzling," he wrote to Jessie Ames. "Is it your understanding that he feels that a South wide organization . . . ought to be set up in addition to the Interracial Commission?" Her reply was almost caustic. "Frankly the Negroes have the jitters," she said. "From remarks dropped by Dr. Mays and Dr. Clement, and letters from Mr. Young and Mr. Hancock, I have about concluded that in defending their action in the meeting at Durham they have committed the white South to a more aggressive action than we appear to be going to take. . . . I cannot go along with them."[51]

To Mrs. Ames's regret, however, the continuing committee met at Atlanta University on August 4–5 and authorized the creation of a new organization. Odum presided and won approval of his regional proposal, receiving strong endorsement from Hancock, Jackson, Young, Charles S. Johnson, Benjamin Mays, and Rufus E. Clement. "To the end that there will be actual realistic accomplishments rather than mere words. . . ," the minutes read, "we urge the South to pool its efforts and set up a strong, unified Southern Regional Council, constituted of representatives of both races and of private and public groups."[52] At another meeting in November, which Jessie Ames did not attend, the committee voted that as of January 1, 1944, the Interracial Commission "ceases to function" and "the personnel and good features of the Commission will be incorporated in the Council." Howard Odum and Charles S. Johnson were made temporary co-chairmen; and plans were adopted to appoint a staff, board of directors, and national advisory committee. The Council's purpose was to improve "economic, civic and racial conditions in the South . . . [and] to attain through research and action programs the ideals and practices of equal opportunity."[53]

50. Ames to Hancock, July 1, 1943, Hancock to Ames, July 5, 1943, Ames Papers.
51. Dabney to Ames, July 2, 1943, Ames to Dabney, July 16, 1943, Dabney Papers.
52. Minutes of the Continuing Committee, Atlanta, Georgia, August 5, 1943, Hancock Papers; "Resolution Launching the Southern Regional Council," *Southern Frontier*, IV (August 1943), 1.
53. Minutes of the Continuing Committee, Atlanta, Georgia, November 27, 1943,

Paralleling this beginning was an attempt by Virginius Dabney to have segregation ended on common carriers in Virginia, a move which surprised blacks and heightened the Richmonder's image in their eyes. Writing to William M. Cooper of Hampton Institute in early November, Dabney suggested that black and white leaders "ought to get busy right away in an effort to abolish Jim Crow laws in street cars and buses." In his judgment these comprised "the one great irritant which can be done away with without public outcry." [54] Within a week the *Times-Dispatch* said that crowded conditions aboard streetcars and buses at rush hours made separate seating of the races impractical, wounded the feelings of Negroes, and increased friction. The same editorial called for repeal of the state segregation ordinance. Encouraged by initial replies, Dabney continued. Unrestricted travel, he said, would constitute a minor concession which black leaders could present to their followers as tangible evidence of white good will. Otherwise, Northern black radicals might usurp the loyalty of the Southern black masses. Lest anyone thought differently, Dabney further pointed out that he was "not advocating the repeal of any of these laws except those covering urban streetcars and buses." The whole problem of segregated transportation, he concluded, "is the most pressing one now confronting the people of Virginia." [55] Not surprisingly, the campaign failed completely. Not a single politician in the legislature dared risk being labeled a "Nigger Lover." By the same token, although hundreds of letters-to-the-editor favored his stand 3 to 1, every Southern white newspaper except the Kinston, North Carolina *Free Press* ignored Dabney's plea.[56] The black press, including the Norfolk *Journal and Guide*, enthusiastically approved.[57]

Significantly, Dabney's campaign raised black expectations of the

Copy of "Highlights of the Conference at Atlanta, November 27, 1943," Hancock Papers.

54. Dabney to Cooper, November 8, 1943, Dabney Papers.

55. Richmond *Times-Dispatch*, November 13, 21, 27, 30, 1943.

56. Nancy Armstrong, *The Study of an Attempt Made in 1943 to Abolish Segregation of the Races on Common Carriers in the State of Virginia*, Phelps-Stokes Fellowship Paper No. 17 (Charlottesville: University of Virginia, 1950), pp. 47–58; Barbara B. Bartle, "Virginius Dabney: Southern Liberal in the Era of Roosevelt" (M.A. Thesis, University of Virginia, 1968), pp. 58–76; Virginius Dabney, *Virginia: The New Dominion* (New York: Doubleday and Co., 1971), p. 514; Charles E. Wynes, "The Evolution of Jim Crow Laws in Twentieth Century Virginia," *Phylon*, XXVIII (Winter 1967), 421–423.

57. See Norfolk *Journal and Guide*, November 20, 27, 1943.

Council, which began formal operations in January 1944. All participants in the Durham-Atlanta-Richmond Conferences, together with the constituencies of the Interracial Commission and Southern Conference on Race Relations, became charter members. University of North Carolina sociologist Guy B. Johnson, whom Odum privately described as "a conservative who will not be stirring up strife," was named executive director. Blacks were more visible than they were in the old commission. Ira DeA. Reid, professor of sociology in Atlanta University, took over as associate executive director. P. B. Young and Carter Wesley were vice-presidents. Rufus E. Clement, Charles S. Johnson, and Gordon B. Hancock were elected to the seven member executive committee. Horace Mann Bond, Charlotte Hawkins Brown, Luther P. Jackson, and Benjamin Mays, among others, served on the board of directors.[58]

Despite the urgency of the segregation issue during World War II, the Southern Regional Council refrained from making a declaration opposing it. Critics considered this inexcusable, and they embroiled the council in a controversy that cast shadows over its early years. The ensuing debate split the liberals' ranks, spread doubt among black spokesmen, and exposed the racial limitations of regionalism.

It was an independent, resolute white woman from Georgia who first rocked the boat. Declining membership in the council, Lillian Smith told Guy B. Johnson that she could not feel comfortable in any organization working for racial democracy which did not take a firm public stand against segregation and in defense of human equality. To remain silent while the bigots and fascists loudly proclaimed the Negro's inferiority, she declared, would be traitorous. "I believe the time has come when we must make our stand."[59] In an article for *New Republic* Miss Smith augmented her dissent. She indicated that "we have looked at the 'Negro problem' long enough." The time had come to study the white man: "the deep-rooted needs that have caused him to seek those

58. "The Southern Regional Council," *Southern Frontier*, V (March 1944), 1, 4. Burrows, "The Commission on Interracial Cooperation, 1919–1944," pp. 285–287; Odum to McGill, January 4, 1944, Howard W. Odum File, Southern Regional Council Office, Atlanta, Georgia.

59. Lillian Smith to Guy B. Johnson, June 12, 1944, Lillian Smith File, Southern Regional Council Office, Atlanta, Georgia.

strange, regressive satisfactions that are derived from worshipping his own skin color." These irrational, prejudiced feelings underlay the myth of white supremacy. She also added, "I cannot endure the idea so many liberals hold that segregation must change slowly. I believe it can change as rapidly as each of us can change his own heart." [60]

If nobody got the message then, it certainly came through loud and clear when J. Saunders Redding and Lillian Smith made a dual assault on the Southern Regional Council in *Common Ground*. Redding, the longtime nemesis of white liberals who had earlier applauded the Durham signers, dismissed the notion that the council was combating racism. He charged it with being "a duplicating action" because the former leaders of the Interracial Commission were its "directing forces," or "worn gears in what is at best a reconditioned machine." Worse still, they proposed to do a new job with an old, conservative ideology. Enslaved by segregationist attitudes, they also avowed "to solve sectionally a problem that is admittedly national," a delineation which he regarded as "potentially more harmful than beneficial." In his opinion, it would be far better "to push ahead, to storm and defend advanced positions against segregation . . . so that when the forces of the native enemy . . . counterattack, no retreat will be made beyond the lines now—in the spring of 1944—held." [61] Miss Smith said that human equality and forced racial separation were incompatible. The council could not pretend to be the answer to the Durham manifesto, she observed, unless it acknowledged openly that "segregation is injuring us on every level of life." She raised disturbing questions. "Do we want the tangled race skein completely unraveled? Or don't we?" she asked. "Are we merely trying to avoid . . . more 'tensions' which embarrass white folks, or are we trying to secure for the Negro his full human rights?" [62]

In a formal reply Guy B. Johnson tried to clear the air. Making only slight references to Miss Smith, he quarreled mainly with Redding for alleged misstatement of facts, unfair interpretations, and naïveté on

60. Lillian Smith, "Addressed to White Liberals," *New Republic*, CXI (September 18, 1944), 331–332.

61. J. Saunders Redding, "Southern Defensive I," *Common Ground*, IV (Spring 1944), 36, 38–39, 42.

62. Lillian Smith, "Southern Defensive II," *ibid.*, IV, 43–45.

strategy. Johnson denied that the Council's "chief purpose is 'solving the race problem.'" Its members were "ordinary people who do not believe in miracles," representing "the combined efforts of . . . both races to do their best to give democracy a chance in the South." They would have to use the old methods of propaganda, conference and personal pressure, he conceded, but in so doing there was ample room for cleverness, insight, and realism. For the present, in the South anyway, they deemed it wiser to capture the foothills than merely to point out the distant peaks. Moreover, the council apologized to no one for being a "sectional" organization, for it posted no "'keep out' signs," attacked no Northern groups, and had even announced its eagerness to cooperate with other bodies—state, regional, or national. "We are striving to improve the social, civic, and economic life of our region in spite of a deep-seated and undemocratic pattern of segregation," Johnson pled. "This pattern, we think, will be with us for a long, long time regardless of what any of us might think or say or do, and we believe that someone has to do the very things that we are doing before the dissolution of this pattern can even enter the realm of possibility." [63]

Many of the whites, while remaining uncomfortably silent, were pleased by Johnson's defense of the gradualist philosophy. Some, like Jessie Ames and Virginius Dabney, quietly retreated from the whole discussion. John Temple Graves did not think whites would ever let go of segregation. For it, he asserted, "the Southern white . . . is willing to filibuster, fight, play foul or fair, risk another Civil War." [64] An infuriated Howard Odum declared: "*Common Ground*, like a good many of the others, seems to think that when they set up an argument and get people to split among themselves, they are doing something liberal." He straddled the fence. "Our lovely Lillian Smith is of course right in saying that it is the white people we want to study," Odum assured Hancock. "Of course it is and of course they are the ones to blame. We are saying this over and over. . . . Now where do we go from here?" [65]

63. Guy B. Johnson, "Southern Offensive," *Common Ground*, IV (Summer 1944), 87, 89–92.

64. John Temple Graves, "The Chance Taking South," *Virginia Quarterly Review*, XXI (Spring 1945), 168.

65. Odum to Guy B. Johnson, June 20, 1944, Odum File, Southern Regional Council Office; Odum to Hancock, September 19, 1944, Hancock Papers.

Expatriate Will Alexander answered Odum's question. Writing for *Harper's Magazine*, Alexander rejected the time-honored clichés and benign simplicity of liberal apologists. Only the "abandonment of the old patterns of segregation" would affirm the nation's democratic creed, he argued, and it was time for Southern whites to realize it.[66]

The blacks moderated their denunciation of segregation in the Durham statement because they did not wish to forfeit white cooperation. Now they found themselves trapped by having gained some semblance of support and, simultaneously, the reassertion that segregation "will be with us for a long, long time." Indefinite gradualism, subtle resignation, and quiet endorsement of the status quo, however, taxed their patience. "The 'Southern Offensive,' as Dr. Johnson calls it, has been launched with much caution," Carter Wesley wrote to P. B. Young, "and I agree with you that the SRC does not seem to be following vigorously the Durham statement."[67] To be certain, the blacks detested segregation. Having invited fourteen Negro leaders, including Hancock, to write *What the Negro Wants*, W. T. Couch of the University of North Carolina Press cushioned the shock of revelation with a publisher's introduction. "If complete elimination of segregation could be accomplished overnight—as many of the authors of this volume assume it ought to be," Couch stated, "the consequences would be disastrous for everyone and more so for the Negro than the white man."[68] The Council's black adherents hardly thought this "could be accomplished overnight," but they definitely wanted a desegregation plank in the organization's platform. Most agreed with Charles S. Johnson that the Negro's increased self-awareness made him "less . . . satisfied with the inferior position involved in enforced segregation and the discrimination which is invariably associated with segregation."[69]

66. Will Alexander, "Our Conflicting Racial Policies," *Harper's Magazine*, CXC (January 1945), 177–179.

67. Wesley to Young, January 28, 1944, Hancock Papers.

68. Rayford W. Logan, ed., *What the Negro Wants* (Chapel Hill: University of North Carolina Press, 1944), p. xx.

69. Charles S. Johnson, "The Present Status of Race Relations in the South," *Social Forces*, XXIII (October 1944), 31.

President J. E. Blanton of Voorhees Institute in South Carolina wrote to Hancock about the unsettling state of affairs in Atlanta. Contrary to what people thought, he reported, Charles S. Johnson, Ira DeA. Reid, Rufus E. Clement, Mary McLeod Bethune, Charlotte Hawkins Brown, and Frederick D. Patterson were not really pushing the council. "Don't put too much stock in Southern Regional Council," he warned, "I hear that all is not going as we expected." Personally, Blanton frowned upon its racial hypocrisy, and he felt "that Dr. Alexander is going to control Dr. Guy Johnson . . . and we are heading for another era of talk." Hancock thanked him for the confidential information and tried to assuage him. "Like you, I am opposed to further research, and like you I am looking and pressing for action," Hancock maintained. "And, if the Southern Regional Council cannot give this action, like you I want to see it pass. However, let's give it a good chance." [70]

In face of black suspicion and white procrastination, Hancock became worried and disillusioned. He oscillated between defending the Council and doubting the sincerity of Southern liberals. Forced into the twilight zone of racial frustration, he strove to stave off complete hopelessness. "You addressed yourselves to the question of segregation in Durham, even if you felt obliged to qualify," M. Margaret Anderson, editor of *Common Ground*, wrote to P. B. Young. "None of the statements since then—of the Atlanta or Richmond groups—has come to grips with it at all. I have no hope for any movement, North or South, that does not come clean on this." Responding on behalf of the blacks, Hancock cynically asked Miss Anderson for an airtight plan of Negro advancement, if she knew of one. "As I see it," he retorted, "the biggest difference between you, Mr. Redding, and Miss Smith and the sponsors of the Southern Regional Council is you are mainly concerned with getting something said and we are mainly concerned with getting something done." [71]

Writing similarly to Lillian Smith, Hancock expressed "super-admiration" for her frankness and indicated that he, too, was "bitterly

70. Blanton to Hancock, June 7, 1944, Hancock to Blanton, June 14, 1944, Hancock Papers.

71. Anderson to Young, February 4, 1944, Hancock to Anderson, May 6, 1944, Hancock Papers.

and unalterably opposed to segregation." Yet mere denunciation of this diabolical practice would not suffice, he said. Something had to be done about it. "You seem to overlook the major fact that segregation is a manifestation of racial prejudice," Hancock continued, "and as such becomes incidental while race prejudice is fundamental." He suggested that if a fraction of the time spent denouncing segregation were utilized in finding ways and means of eradicating prejudice the cause would be immeasurably advanced. The Southern Regional Council, he concluded, "seeks to destroy race prejudice by getting after the roots of prejudice many of which are rooted in misunderstanding." [72]

Hancock's defense of the council, however, still left him wondering. Why, indeed, should individuals of Miss Smith's convictions stand aloof from it? What if J. Saunders Redding and Lillian Smith were justified in condemning the enterprise? Might the blacks be deceiving themselves in thinking that the whites were at heart committed to racial equality? Harboring these questions, he remained sensitive and touchy about the whole matter. Clinging tenaciously to high principles, he would not disavow his philosophy of trying to change the hearts and minds of people in dealing with segregation, even when more direct methods of eliminating it were desirable. So, finding himself torn between pragmatism and pessimism, Hancock was indecisive about when and under what conditions to be militant. For better or worse, the battle lines were drawn. Even if he understood the whites' ambivalence, he knew that blacks were dissatisfied. Turning to Jessie Ames, now "withdrawn from professional activities in the field of race relations with no regrets," [73] Hancock vented his criticisms of the Council.

At one point, Hancock felt Negro leaders were being slighted and overlooked by the white hierarchy, which foreshadowed, in his opinion, the eclipse of black policy-making influence. In short, they did not enjoy equal status. "I cannot bear the thought that you will be shunted aside as I have been," Mrs. Ames said sympathetically. "I am merely an individual . . . but you and the other Negroes are a symbol and it would hurt to have this symbol tarnished or belittled or covered up. I

72. Hancock to Lillian Smith, June 24, 1944, Hancock Papers.
73. Ames to Hancock, February 26, 1944, Ames Papers.

153

hope this will not happen."[74] Hancock also complained about the Council's strategy of slow change and its failure to take advanced positions. This puzzled Jessie Ames. "You have talked about a more aggressive attitude," she sighed. "I have not been able to get from you any clear understanding of what you mean. . . . I have felt at times that my inability to grasp your ideas were [sic] altogether a limitation in vision on my part."[75] Unwittingly, although she really knew that he was suggesting offensives against segregation, Mrs. Ames had isolated the most complicated factor in the interracial equation—the difference in vision.

From the beginning, Hancock reminded her, the blacks, disturbed about race relations and the plight of their people, had wanted an action-oriented organization, one dedicated to achieving racial democracy in the South. Unfortunately, he lamented, the council's broad, regional focus diluted the emphasis upon solving race problems and, instead, gave priority to fact-finding and publication. Jolted by these observations, and imploring Hancock to keep "my identity well concealed," Jessie Ames, in a lengthy reply, opened the whites' closet. She agreed that the blacks were "'on the outside looking in.'" To her, this proved that the Southern Regional Council "is getting as far away from the Durham statement as it can and as quickly as it can." Reviewing events between September 1942 and August 1943, she said "certain leaders of the Commission," who did not favor either the Durham or Atlanta meetings, "came in and took over the two subsequent meetings." Too easily, the newcomers converted the blacks to their way of thinking. "It is not important that they took a new name but it is that they pacified the Durham Negroes," she asserted. "It is in effect the same organization under a new name and under the same leaders." Somewhat solicitously, she ended: "I am sick . . . over the failure of the Negroes to get what they believed they were entitled to and to which I believe they were entitled."[76]

Jessie Ames's major grievance stemmed from the dismantling of the

74. Interview with Gordon B. Hancock, March 5, 1969, Richmond, Virginia; Ames to Hancock, February 14, 1944, Ames Papers.
75. Ames to Hancock, February 26, 1944, Ames Papers.
76. Ames to Hancock, August 7, 1945, Ames Papers.

Interracial Commission, and, like a frustrated Cassandra, she simply pointed the finger of blame at Will Alexander, Howard Odum, and company. Still, her revelations to Hancock were not misleading. In fact, they shed light upon white attitudes and ideology in the formation of the council, as well as why whites would not come to grips with the race issue. "I acknowledge that I thought you wanted something different from the Interracial Commission," Mrs. Ames goaded Hancock again. Although she carefully avoided mentioning her own position on segregation, she suggested that he "re-read" Redding's article. "Some thought his statements indicated peevishness," she admitted. "They may have but he had, wittingly or otherwise, struck at the roots of the matter." [77]

Notwithstanding his despair, Hancock stayed on the council's board of directors and executive committee. In short, he accepted Luther P. Jackson's assertion that "Negro Southerners may strike blows at the segregation laws forever, but final victory can never come until white Southerners unite with them." [78] Considering the relative powerlessness of blacks and the vulnerability of black leaders, Hancock believed that cooperation was, after all, the wisest course to follow. Charles S. Johnson, in his typology of Negro responses to segregation, called this the strategy of "indirect or deflected hostility." He identified it mainly with middle-class Southern blacks whose sense of dignity and fear of white retaliation forced them to reject the other three tactics: "acceptance, avoidance, direct hostility and aggression." By resorting to subtle, covert attacks upon race prejudice and discrimination, Johnson observed, they could control their anger "toward the oppressor." [79]

Blacks chose to walk the narrow pathway of restraint, but segregation hung over the council like the sword of Damocles. The *Southern Frontier*, the official organ until January 1946, devoted very few pages to a serious discussion of it. There was one brief report—without comment—on the Supreme Court's decision ordering Missouri to provide equal education for Negroes. While the priorities for "Building

77. Ames to Hancock, October 16, 1945, Hancock Papers.
78. See Norfolk *Journal and Guide*, January 8, 1944.
79. Charles S. Johnson, *Patterns of Negro Segregation* (New York: Harper and Brothers Publishers, 1943), pp. 243, 302–310.

a Post-War South" never broached the subject, the "Program for 1945" included a study of segregation in the South.[80] When Ira DeA. Reid estimated in the board meeting that a comprehensive inquiry would take two years and cost $68,000, Hancock objected. The Southern Regional Council, he said, should spend its time and money changing Jim Crow laws rather than fruitlessly studying them. Only Charles S. Johnson's suggestion, that "it would be tremendously valuable, not simply to the student, but to the practical man of affairs who wants to know . . . what next step to take," enabled the measure to pass. "We've got to dispose of the segregation dilemma as soon as possible," Guy B. Johnson reminded Odum, "or it will keep on blocking the future of the Council."[81]

Regrettably, most white liberals remained inflexible and the vexatious problem lingered, as evidenced by two articles in the *Southern Frontier*. In one, historian Broadus Mitchell and Virginius Dabney debated whether Phi Beta Kappa "should deny charters to colleges which do not admit Negro students." Mitchell argued that the society, before issuing a charter, ought to require a pledge of nondiscrimination on account of race, creed, color, or national origin. Dabney thought that such a policy "would be unwise." If given time and left alone, he stated, white Southerners were going to settle the horribly complex business of segregation to the mutual benefit of both races. "As far as the South is concerned, the worst way to promote a fair deal for the Negro . . . is through the application of drastic pressure from outside the South," Dabney maintained. "This may seem silly and even outrageous to those who are unfamiliar with the situation, but it is indisputable."[82] Meanwhile, Rufus E. Clement attributed much of the white South's resistance to ending legalized caste to the scare of amalgamation. Among Negroes "there is no deep-seated desire for intermarriage with the non-Negro," he explained, adding that "Ne-

80. "Will Missouri University Admit Negro Students?" *Southern Frontier*, V (February 1944), 3; "Building a Post-War South," *ibid.*, V (October 1944), 3; "Program for 1945," *ibid.*, V (December 1944), 2.

81. Houser, "The Southern Regional Council," pp. 54–55; Guy B. Johnson to Odum, January 9, 1945, Odum File, Southern Regional Council Office.

82. "Phi Beta Kappa Members Debate Action on Segregated Schools," *Southern Frontier*, VI (October 1945), 2.

groes want to eat in the restaurant where the white person eats because Negroes are hungry." [83]

Black contributors to *New South*, which became the council's mouthpiece in 1946, advocated desegregation.[84] Writing in 1948, Luther P. Jackson reviewed the history of Negro protest during World War II, the struggle for civil rights, and the postwar assault on the poll tax, literacy test, and white primary. Although he saw a continuing need to arouse Negroes' "voting consciousness" and to allay their fear of overt intimidation, economic reprisal, and mob violence, Jackson blamed white Southerners for the appalling lack of democracy in the region. Unless color barriers were removed in all phases of public life, not just politics, the Negro could not move "toward a fuller citizenship." He concluded that "it would . . . require a stretch of the imagination for anyone to assert that white supremacy is threatened by the present size of the Negro electorate; for the developments of the 1940 decade represent not a fulfillment of political equality, but only a beginning toward its realization." [85]

Undeniably, the blacks were forging ahead. When Virginius Dabney, in an editorial about the presidential election of 1948, deprecated Harry Truman's pro-civil rights stand, Hancock sternly rebuked him and other liberals for double talk. "If Truman's and the Federal actions are repulsive to the proud Southerners, what are they offering in the premise?" he asked. "Or are they willing to grudgingly grant the Negro citizens of the South the basic essentials of citizenship?" [86] Dabney answered: "I am considerably hurt by your letter. . . . I did not think you would impute to me the base motives and lack of intellectual integrity which your language seems to imply." Hancock then attacked directly. Southern blacks were being forced into the courts "to sue for everything," he fulminated, which meant "that underneath some fine

83. Rufus E. Clement, "Black GI Joe Comes Home," *ibid.*, pp. 3–4.

84. See Ira DeA. Reid, "The White Primary Problem Must Be Solved to Strengthen Democracy," *New South*, I (January 1946), 7; Charles S. Johnson, "The Will and the Way," *ibid.*, II (May 1947), 1–5, 8; Harold L. Trigg, "SRC and Southern Progress," *ibid.*, II (November 1947), 7–8.

85. Jackson, "Race and Suffrage in the South since 1940," *New South*, III (June–July 1948), 1–26.

86. Richmond *Times-Dispatch*, November 4, 1948; Hancock to Dabney, November 15, 1948, Hancock Papers.

gestures there is the determination to eternalize the subjugation and domination of the Negroes." Eager to "go much farther and much faster," Hancock also accused Dabney of having made "a 'strategic retreat' " from his earlier position opposing segregation aboard common carriers. This "definitely discouraged" blacks, as did all the hostility toward Truman's racial liberalism. As for the Southern Regional Council, it was "about to disprove everything we went to Durham to prove, that is, there was a sufficient number of whites who were sufficiently humanely inclined to make an organization like ours live and prosper." Hancock ended: "The Northern Negroes who told us we were dupes had something. I hate it to say the least. I put so much in it and when it fails I fail." [87]

The council did not collapse, but it came to terms with segregation. Needing enthusiastic support from blacks and whites committed to equality, swept along by the rushing tide of enlightened race thought, the organization slowly threw off the old onus. In 1949 the executive committee sent a letter to the thirteen Southern governors requesting Negro appointments "to positions upon policy-making boards," a step which only North Carolina had taken. The *New South*, the same year, noted that "the 'separate but equal' doctrine is under heavy attack" and called attention to court suits in education, transportation, and public accommodations which were "challenging the view that equality is possible within a segregated system." [88] Somewhat encouraged, Hancock commented: "World opinion is helping to drive the segregationist to cover. It has forced him to the defensive and tomorrow has yet to come." [89] By 1951, when the *New South* reviewed the majority and dissenting opinions in a Clarendon County, South Carolina, school case, the latter of which stated that "segregation must go," the Council decided to make its stand. The annual conference adopted a statement pledging to build "a South where the measure of a man will be his ability, not his race; where . . . segregation will be

87. Dabney to Hancock, November 9, 1948, Hancock to Dabney, November 15, 1948, Hancock Papers.

88. "A Recommendation for Action by the Southern Governors," *New South*, IV (May–June 1949), 1–2; "The Supreme Court Considers Segregation," *ibid.*, IV (November–December 1949), 4–6.

89. New York *Amsterdam News*, January 5, 1949.

recognized as a cruel and needless penalty on the human spirit, and will no longer be imposed."[90]

This step might have been too little and too late, but the new policy provided a psychological lift for the blacks. Naturally, the council joined them in their vigil on the Supreme Court. Looking at the NAACP's suits against segregated schools in Clarendon County, South Carolina, Prince Edward County, Virginia, Topeka, Kansas, and Wilmington, Delaware, it asked: "How long can a court of equity condone inequality—albeit gradually diminishing?" At another point, and in anticipation of a decision overturning *Plessy v. Ferguson*, it forewarned thoughtful Southerners "to repudiate the false leaders and irresponsible citizens who threaten drastic or violent action."[91] Benjamin Mays, speaking on behalf of black leadership, hailed the forthcoming ruling as the cardinal test of America's morality. He queried: "Can the United States afford to say to a billion colored peoples in Asia, millions of colored peoples in Africa, the Middle East, South America, and the European democracies, that we believe in second class citizenship for 15,000,000 people—solely because their race is Negro and their complexion colored?"[92]

In *Brown v. Board of Education of Topeka*, handed down on May 17, 1954, the Supreme Court unanimously declared that racial segregation in public education denied the Negro group the equal protection of the laws. "In the field of public education the doctrine of 'separate but equal' has no place," said the Court. "Separate educational facilities are inherently unequal."[93] Most white Southerners were shocked; black Southerners were jubilant; and the curtain was raised for the Second Reconstruction.[94] P. B. Young did not mind seeing "Southern

90. "Two Opinions on School Segregation," *New South*, VI (July 1951), 7–11; "Toward the South of the Future: A Statement of Policy and Aims of the Southern Regional Council," *ibid.*, VI (December 1951), 1–2.

91. "On the Southern Scene," *New South*, VII (May 1952), 7; "Supreme Court Considers Segregation," *ibid.*, VII (December 1952), 5.

92. Benjamin E. Mays, "We are Unnecessarily Excited," *ibid.*, IX (February 1954), 1.

93. 347 U.S. 483 (1954); NAACP, *Forty-Sixth Annual Report* (New York: National Office of the NAACP, 1955), p. 84.

94. Leary, "Race Relations in Turmoil," pp. 56–58.

Negroes, who were most adversely affected by segregation," rejoice. Yet, he cautioned—"Let it be remembered in this great hour of triumph: 'He conquers twice who upon the verge of victory overcomes himself.' "[95]

For Hancock and the other black spokesmen, the road from the Durham conference to the *Brown* decision was rough. Unable to bargain with white liberals from a position of strength, frequently perplexed by their inability to force the issues, they nonetheless refused to give up. Amid the chorus of dissident black and white voices in the postwar South, they insisted upon affirmative action and abolition of Jim Crow. As the age of segregation passed and the civil rights ovement emerged, however, these older leaders declined in influence. Although many remained active professionals, some, like Hancock, were relegated to unmerited obscurity.

95. Norfolk *Journal and Guide*, May 22, 1954.

VII. Age and Isolation

Sociologist Horace Cayton, discussing the generation of blacks before *Brown*, wrote in *Long Old Road*: "Frustrated by their isolation from the mainstream of American life and out of their impotence to control their fate decisively, Negroes developed the notion of a race man, an individual who was proud of his race and always tried to uphold it whether it was good or bad, right or wrong." He saw everything in terms of race and interpreted all events in terms of how they affected the Negro. He not only resented white supremacists but disapproved of black sycophants, mass indifference, social disorganization, and all who refused to become involved in the struggle for human dignity. As a leader, he differed significantly from the Uncle Tom and the Racial Diplomat types. Whereas the Tom accepted segregation without question and begged crumbs from the white man's table, and the Diplomat separated himself from poor blacks and guarded the special interests of the middle class, the race man considered biracialism ethically and legally inconsistent with true democracy. Though he worked realistically within the dual system, he pushed toward first-class citizenship and total black participation in the society. Yet because he was constantly pulled between blackness and black desire to integrate, the race man seldom escaped being a marginal man—living on the edge of two worlds. This dilemma, according to Gunnar Myrdal, especially characterized Southern Negro leadership.[1]

1. Horace R. Cayton, *Long Old Road* (New York: Trident Press, 1965), p. 250; Robert Johnson, "Negro Reactions to Minority Group Status," in Milton L. Barron, ed., *American Minorities* (New York: Alfred A. Knopf, 1957), pp. 207–208; Daniel C. Thompson, *The Negro Leadership Class* (Englewood Cliffs, N. J.: Prentice-Hall, Inc., 1963), pp. 74–79; Ralph J. Bunche, "A Brief and Tentative Analysis of Negro Leadership" (September 1940), pp. 34–35, in the Carnegie-Myrdal Study of the Negro in America, Duke University Library, Durham, North Carolina; J. Saunders Redding, *On Being Negro in America* (Indianapolis: Bobbs-Merrill, 1951), pp. 25–27; Everett V. Stonequist, *The Marginal Man: A Study in Personality and Culture Conflict* (New York: Charles Scribner's Sons, 1937), pp. 106–119; Bernard Eisenberg, "Kelly Miller: The Negro Leader as a Marginal Man," *Journal of Negro History*, XLV (July 1960), 182–185; Gunnar Myrdal, *An American Dilemma: The Negro Problem and Modern Democracy* (New York: Harper and Row Publishers, 1944), pp. 774–775.

During the 1950's and 1960's, the final years, Hancock was an aged race man whose longstanding ideas on black solidarity and self-help and interracial cooperation were very much alive. While he had relied upon conferences, moral suasion, restrained protest and the good will of white liberals, younger spokesmen resorted to nonviolent direct action, politics, and radical demands for black power. Moreover, with race relations dramatically removed from cloistered meeting places into the streets, only those black leaders acclaimed by television and the press were deemed important. Hancock did not achieve such recognition, and he was dwarfed by the changes for which he had labored throughout his career. Belonging to a declining breed of old-timers, drawn to and repelled by various features of the civil rights and black power movements, he played the role of a Socratic gadfly who stung and warned and pleaded. Although he strove to vindicate his philosophy and to win greater recognition from blacks and whites, Hancock died an unsung hero and a marginal man.

If Hancock entertained notions of growing old gracefully, these were quickly dispelled by an unexpected termination of tenure in Virginia Union University. Early in 1952, at age sixty-seven, he received a notice from President John M. Ellison that he would become professor emeritus in June. This news surprised, shocked, and saddened Hancock so much that he broke down physically. Hospitalized for several weeks, which depleted his savings, he was never again the same.[2] Since 1921, teaching, preaching, and writing had formed an inseparable triangle in Hancock's work, and Union, despite past complications, held a unique place in his heart. Now, he would have to adjust to Richmond without Union, a dreaded task. Because the school maintained no mandatory retirement policy and favored septuagenarians like former president William J. Clark were permitted to retain faculty status, he felt rejected and cheated. As he and Marie moved from their campus residence to an apartment in the city, and subsequently to a spacious home on Noble Avenue affectionately called "The Julianna,"

2. Shreveport *Sun*, June 21, 1952; interview with Marie D. Hancock, September 23, 1972, Richmond, Virginia.

Hancock could not help thinking that Ellison had finally evened a personal score.[3]

In 1948, Hancock and Ellison had feuded over rank and salary. Under new guidelines, all teachers were extended appointments in one of five categories: part-time, instructor, assistant professor, associate professor, and professor. Hancock summarily objected to being named an associate professor, charging that his classroom performance, scholarship, and twenty-six years of service to the University merited a full professorship. Furthermore, at $3,600 per year, he considered himself grossly underpaid. Miffed by these complaints, Ellison told him that because he did not hold the doctorate and spent a great deal of time in "outside matters," including Moore Street Church, the arrangements were final.[4] For Hancock, this was the biggest slap in the face since Clark overlooked him and named "Pat" McGuinn divisional director of social sciences back in 1935. Humiliated, he still refused to resign. Unlike the dissatisfied Arthur P. Davis, who abandoned Union for a lucrative post at Howard University,[5] Hancock realized that his own chances to move were practically nil. Negro colleges, as well as Negro organizations, preferred younger men and women.

Wounded feelings from the Hancock-Ellison encounter congealed, and not a little gossip lingered. In it, Hancock donned the face of the faithful academician and race servant whose manifold labors were unrequited, while Ellison became a pedagogical tyrant who ruled his kingdom by punishing enemies and rewarding friends. Although both images were exaggerated, there was a tragicomic rivalry between two aging men.[6] When Ellison took over as Virginia Union's first black president in 1941, he knew that the trustees had selected him almost last. After Charles S. Johnson of Fisk and then Robert P. Daniel of Shaw had declined the position, Miles W. Connor, Ellison, and Hancock were approached. All those interviewed were Unionites except

3. Hancock to Ellison, April 3, 1951; "Autobiographical Reflections," Gordon Blaine Hancock Papers, Richmond, Virginia. The house was named for Hancock's paternal grandmother, Julia, and his mother, Anna.
4. Hancock to Ellison, October 16, 1948, Hancock Papers; interview with Hancock, February 5, 1969, Richmond, Virginia.
5. Interview with Arthur P. Davis, July 11, 1974, Washington, D. C.
6. Interview with Clarissa Kyles Dillard, June 27, 1974, Richmond, Virginia.

Hancock, yet the board members thought his wide reputation and community influence were fund-raising assets that gave him a slight edge over Connor and Ellison. For "personal reasons," though, Hancock dropped out of the running. Ellison, virtually unknown, got the job.[7] Of course, he remained somewhat suspicious of Hancock and cool toward faculty opponents of his administration. In spite of Hancock's attempt to include Ellison in the Durham-Atlanta-Richmond developments and his generally complimentary attitude toward the new president, genuine affection eluded them.[8] Consequently, Hancock did not doubt that Ellison had used retirement as a pretext to dump him.

Hancock lifted anchor and moved on, but ripples of influence were left behind. Every loyal Unionite knew the fabled "Harvard scholar." Whether caricatured as the "Gloomy Dean" or the callous professor whose courses in the final analysis were always about race, he occupied a pedestal of esteem in Union's oral traditions. "'Doc' was a dynamic personality," one former student recalled. "He won you with his voice."[9] Another said that he performed poorly in the classroom, but in racial advocacy, consciousness raising, and practical economics Hancock had few peers.[10] Emma Wesley Brown, Class of '30, remembered the famous Logan-Hancock chapel debates. If Hancock seemed more accommodating, he preached a realistic philosophy of race relations shaped by the folkways of the rural South, she said. Logan's tendencies were definitely non-Southern.[11] Even Hancock's archcritic Arthur P. Davis paid him a subtle compliment. Casting him in the mold of a latter-day Washingtonian, Davis submitted that "Dr. Hancock's reputation and following went far beyond Virginia Union."[12]

7. Interview with Ellison, June 27, 1974, Richmond, Virginia.
8. *Ibid.* Ellison said, "We clashed because Dr. Hancock always wanted Union to do something for Hancock. He even had the nerve to ask the board for an honorary degree." In 1955, Ellison, then sixty-six, gave up the office of president and continued indefinitely as chancellor of Virginia Union and professor in the School of Religion. See *V.U.B.*, Centennial Issue, 40–41.
9. Interview with the Reverend Gilbert C. Campbell, December 13, 1974, Richmond, Virginia.
10. Interview with President Allix Bledsoe James of Virginia Union University, June 12, 1974, Richmond, Virginia.
11. Interview with Dr. Emma Wesley Brown, June 12, 1974, Richmond, Virginia.
12. Interview with Davis, July 11, 1974.

Whatever the case, Hancock's world changed. As longtime associates died or dropped out of view and his infirmities worsened, he became isolated. Luther P. Jackson was already dead, expiring suddenly, April 13, 1950.[13] Hancock and Young, along with blacks from all over the South and nation, attended the funeral at Virginia State College. Solemnly, they eulogized Jackson "as the man who, on his own initiative, did more than any other of his day and age to awaken his people to the dangers of political apathy, and to the importance of an intelligent use of the ballot."[14] In October 1956 Charles S. Johnson, soft-spoken Virginia native, distinguished sociologist and "dean of 'professional Negro race leaders,' " succumbed "enroute from the Fall meeting of the Fisk Board of Trust in New York."[15] Meanwhile, veteran journalist P. B. Young, plagued by sickness, turned the *Journal and Guide* over to his children. Hancock, also ailing, managed only two trips to Norfolk before Young himself died, October 9, 1962.[16] Bereaved, Hancock underwent surgery for a malignant tumor and probably would have given up, too, if it had not been for Marie, Benjamin Mays, and William M. Brewer, editor of the *Journal of Negro History*. Periodic visits from Mays and Brewer raised his sagging spirits.[17]

Locally, Hancock turned to George W. Watkins and Thomas H. Henderson, who cared for their enfeebled mentor with the fidelity of sons. Watkins, a Union-trained Baptist minister, advised him in personal and business matters, persuading Hancock to retire from the pastorate of Moore Street in 1963, the same year that Virginia Union, acting upon the recommendation of Dr. Thomas H. Henderson, awarded Hancock an honorary D.D. degree.[18] Born at Newport News, January 31, 1910, Henderson graduated from Union in 1929 and earned the M.A. and Ph.D. degrees from the University of Chicago. In 1960,

13. Norfolk *Journal and Guide*, April 15, 1950.
14. Norfolk *Journal and Guide*, April 22, 1950.
15. "Personal," *Journal of Negro History*, XLII (January 1957), 86.
16. Norfolk *Journal and Guide*, October 13, 1962; "Historical News," *Journal of Negro History*, XLVIII (January 1963), 68.
17. Interviews with Mrs. Hancock, September 23, 1972; and Benjamin E. Mays, June 19, 1974, Atlanta, Georgia. William M. Brewer to the author, March 15, 1968.
18. Interview with Mrs. Hancock, September 23, 1972; Gordon B. Hancock, "Back to Benedict—An Abbreviated Account of My Stewardship," n.d., Hancock Papers.

when Dr. Samuel D. Proctor resigned to head North Carolina A. & T. College, Henderson became the third alumnus and first layman to serve as president of the university.[19] An admirer of Hancock, he almost single-handedly mended the old man's broken ties with the institution.

Unwittingly, Henderson provided Hancock with a platform for self-vindication. When the Centennial Historical Committee, under the direction and editorship of Ellison and McGuinn, released its history of Virginia Union,[20] Hancock issued a rebuttal which created an uproar among the alumni. Bluntly, he indicated that the Ellison-McGuinn narrative minimized the role of the early white administrations and of the young black scholars—Hancock, Maloney, Connor, Fisher, and Logan—who were responsible for bringing the school academic distinction in the late 1920's. He said the document also glossed over the work in race relations initiated through the Torrance School, which easily was one of the constructive departures in Negro education for that day. While Virginia Union's contribution to the founding of the Southern Regional Council received only passing mention, Hancock concluded, far too much space went to the presidency of John M. Ellison.[21] To some, this seemed like ego tripping or getting old adversaries told,[22] but Hancock claimed that he just wanted to set the record straight.

Occasionally, with Henderson's permission, Hancock appeared on campus to promote his interest in Negro songs. With religious fervor, he developed a compelling concern for the collection, preservation, and popularization of black spirituals.[23] By organizing "the National Negro Music Association," he suggested, Virginia Union could spearhead and pioneer in this worthwhile endeavor. To one audience, he presented an elaborate treatise on the beauty of traditional black musical forms. "What good purpose can be served by digging up that quaint old music, quaintly rendered by former generations?" Hancock

19. *V.U.B.*, Centennial Issue, 43–44.
20. *Ibid.*, p. 107.
21. Hancock, *Supplementary Facts Pertaining to the Centennial Issue of the Virginia Union Bulletin* (Richmond: Virginia Union University, 1966).
22. Interview with Henry J. McGuinn, June 26, 1974, Richmond, Virginia.
23. See Atlanta *Daily World*, December 5, 1959; Louisville *Defender*, December 3, 1959.

asked rhetorically. "All history is a continuity and a great today can only be explained by an humble yesterday and Negro music in its current stage of sophistication is unintelligible without acquaintance with Negro music in the raw."[24] Although he never got Union to sponsor his project, Hancock published two songs and a poem, which highlighted themes of adversity, sorrow, and ultimate victory. For example, he wrote: "As long as human hearts are brave / And mock Misfortune's cruel bond, / So long must struggling mortals crave / Some Great Beyond."[25]

Hancock's cultural proselytizing and intense spirituality were perhaps signs of that craving. Never before had he whooped and swooned when preaching, but, according to eyewitnesses, these became standard features of his sermons. "If the current generation of young Negroes with education could cast aside certain petty sophistications and preach the gospel in its power they could move the world," he once declared. Hancock further called upon black churchgoers to forget academic degrees, seek Pentecostal power, and sing with the rhythm, plaintiveness, pathos, and melodic sweetness of their forebears. For it would take the old-time religion, as practiced in the village and country churches along the Savannah River, to endure sorrow, tribulation, heartache, disappointment and humiliation—the Negro's lot. Indeed, Hancock no longer seemed to be the dignified, restrained minister who rejected undue emotionalism or shouting in worship. To many people, he was a curiosity, an anachronism.[26]

Ideologically, Hancock was a race man for all seasons. A molder of black thought in Virginia and the South for over thirty years, he wore the mantle of experience freely during the 1950's and 1960's. Until declining health forced him into silence, he spoke out through hundreds of releases to the Associated Negro Press. If he sounded like the "Gloomy Dean" of depression days or the ardent interracialist or the

24. Hancock, "A Dialogue Pertaining to 'Negro Songs in the Raw,'" n.d., p. 4, Hancock Papers.

25. *Two Homeward Songs: My Journey Home* [and] *Our Long Home*, words and music by Gordon B. Hancock, arranged by Pearl H. Wood, 1965; "Plus Ultra," A Poem Dedicated to Moore Street's Year of Jubilation, 1963, Hancock Papers.

26. Interviews with Allix Bledsoe James, June 12, 1974; and George B. Winston, June 26, 1974, Richmond, Virginia; Raleigh *Carolinian*, November 20, 1954; Lima *Post*, May 13, 1955, Indianapolis *Recorder*, August 20, 1955; Kansas City *Call*, December 4, 1959.

wartime black organizer or the representative of a now elderly vanguard, he always knew whose side he was on. Unable to resolve the dilemma of black self-determination and black-white integration, however, he was frequently inconsistent. This problem, which left him on the margin between the black and white worlds, might be illustrated by examining Hancock's thinking on five major topics: general race relations; desegregation; political-economic developments; international affairs; black leadership and civil rights strategy.

General race relations elicited mixed comments, good and bad. At the time of the historic *Brown* decision, Hancock hailed the advent of a long awaited emancipation. When eight white professors could walk out of the University of the South at Sewanee in protest against segregation, it indicated that Negrophobes like Jimmy Byrnes of South Carolina were selling the South short on decency. "Right is winning," he announced. "Our case is being tried in the Supreme Court of world opinion." Moreover, given steady advance in racial tolerance, the "Solid South" was fast becoming the "Liquid South," quietly urging compliance with the law of the land. The traditions of mules, subservient blacks, and cotton were "passing into the shadows of checkered memories." In 1955, when he refused to move out of the "white only" berth aboard trains in Washington, D. C. and Charlotte, North Carolina, Hancock mockingly reported that Jim Crow's lungs were collapsing. The Southern Regional Council, the Catholic Church, individual white liberals, and insistent blacks were ushering in a "New South," he said, one where the separate would be discarded and the equal retained.[27]

These prophecies were belied by subsequent events, including the Little Rock, Arkansas, school crisis, Virginia's massive resistance, the lynchings of Emmett Till and Mack Parker in Mississippi, and the rapid proliferation of White Citizens Councils. Unhappily, the "Old South" was not dead, and Hancock abandoned his optimism. "The forces of righteousness are taking an awful beating," he mourned. "The situa-

27. Dallas *Express*, July 14, 1951; West Palm Beach *Florida News*, January 24, 1953; Lima *Post*, October 2, 1954; Raleigh *Carolinian*, April 2, 1955. Undated releases: "Thy Kingdom Come"; "Right Is Winning"; "Catholics in South Lead in Desegregating Schools"; "Moral Courage Pays Off"; "Stand Taken by Christian Whites Heartening Aspect"; "The New South"; and "The Two Souths—Part II," Hancock Papers.

tion is confused but not hopeless." He said that blacks and their allies could either abdicate or fight back. Choosing the latter, he categorically condemned white intransigence, once calling editors James J. Kilpatrick of the Richmond *News Leader* and Thomas R. Waring of the Charleston *News and Courier* two of the most "rabid segregationists" in Southern history. He chided the Baptist World Alliance and the Southern Baptist Convention for not "stressing the dangers of race prejudice." He also criticized the move among writers to use the term human relations instead of race relations. "There is no need for the Negro to try to forget race unless the white man does," Hancock argued. "Changing from race relations to human relations does not solve anything." Proud of being a Negro, wary of hatemongering and increased violence, he concluded in 1960 that grudgingly little progress had been made toward interracial justice. Rebuffed and disappointed, he retreated to the shores of black pride.[28]

The tenaciousness of segregation deepened Hancock's apprehensions. Easily the Negro's number one priority and the most volatile issue in the South, desegregation ultimately depended upon the whites' consent. If forced to accept blacks, they would surely retaliate. If forced to do so by Federal authorities, they might ignore blacks completely. So, where possible, black leaders had to find a way to abolish segregation and insure equality without increasing racial polarization or compromising black dignity. This was indeed a stupendous task, but Hancock wrestled with it.

On the one hand, he described Southern rebelliousness and feared that the white supremacists would prevail. "We shudder at the thought that, in their efforts to disqualify the Supreme Court, the segregationists lost by one vote," Hancock stated. "There will be other

28. Lima *Post*, May 28, 1954; Raleigh *Carolinian*, February 5, August 6, 1955; Philadelphia *Tribune*, October 19, 1957; Dallas *Star Post*, February 1, 1958; Savannah *Tribune*, November 21, 1959; Westchester County *Press*, December 5, 1959; Louisville *Defender*, December 17, 1959; Indianapolis *Recorder*, February 13, 1960; Saint Louis *Argus*, February 26, 1960; Houston *Informer*, February 27, 1960. Undated releases: "Race Prejudice Threat to America's Existence," "Interracial Tensions Interpreted," "Liberal Groups Serve as 'Bumper' for Race Prejudice," "The Tragedy of Interracial Understanding," "Judge Lynch Returns to the Bench," "Divided We Fall," "Nation Suffers When Negro Is Denied Opportunity," and "Shall We Go Home?" Hancock Papers.

contests and other countings of votes and the segregationists . . . are like the jockey on the inside rail. He has an astounding advantage." With the infamous film *The Birth of a Nation* in the process of resurrection, the renaissance of Ku Kluxism inevitable, the appeal of the Dixiecrats axiomatic and terrorism in the offing, Hancock remarked: "The gravest question before the Negroes of this country is, can they take it?" In effect, he was admitting that further ruptures and tensions were unavoidable. It would be up to blacks themselves to overcome the odds.[29]

Repeatedly Hancock exhorted blacks to resist "the tyranny of segregation," saying that if they did not they would be recreant to the mandate passed on to them by the slaves, by the victims of the Phoenix Riot in 1898, and by those who gathered "that dark day down at Durham" during World War II. He welcomed the peaceful demonstrations against Jim Crow not only as extensions of America's protest tradition but as actions which encouraged the inarticulate masses. Martin Luther King, Jr., leader of the Montgomery bus boycott and founder of the Southern Christian Leadership Conference, embodied the collective hope of blacks. Perhaps more than any other contemporary figure, King symbolized black indignation, Christian morality, nonviolence, and racial brotherhood. Alluding to Christ, Gandhi and King, Hancock wrote: "The power of the passive resistance ideology is moral. . . . Keep the sit-down movement nonviolent, and be prepared physically to pay the price!"[30]

Drawing comparisons, Hancock also claimed that the Negro revolt validated his double-duty-dollar theory. "The current sit-downs are attempts to emphasize the possibilities in making the dollar do double duty, by using it as a weapon against segregation and as a protest against restricted economic opportunities." In addition, if he con-

29. Florida *Sentinel*, January 1, 1955; Miami *Times*, January 3, 1953, October 26, 1957; Kansas City *Call*, February 14, March 21, 1958; Philadelphia *Tribune*, March 21, April 26, 1958, November 14, 1959. Undated releases: "A Tragedy in the Making," "Die-Hardism in the South," "The South's Militant Minority," "Troublesome Struggle Seen in Desegregation Move," and "Propaganda Potential of the Segregationist South," Hancock Papers.

30. Raleigh *Carolinian*, October 23, 1954, May 7, 28, 1955; Louisville *Defender*, August 6, 1959; Savannah *Tribune*, March 5, 26, 1960; Westchester County *Press*, March 26, 1960.

sidered integration an imperative backed by legal decrees, he thought superior achievement, Christian character, thrift, and group solidarity were necessary accompaniments. These were tried-and-true racial theses, connecting links between age and youth, and a foundation upon which to continue building even if desegregation were still a long way off. Ever the skeptic, though, he cautioned: "Ne'er think the victory won!"[31] Thus, while eager and determined to live in an open society, Hancock remained doubtful and hesitant over whether such a society would ever come about. Hope and doubt existed side by side.

Political-economic developments, to Hancock, were inseparable from race. As an observer of issues and personalities in American politics, he seldom deviated from this assumption. In his view, politicians like Virginia's Harry Byrd, Ohio's Robert Taft, and South Carolina's Jimmy Byrnes were not statesmen, but "scullions, de-funnies, snipers, congressional bullies, bumpkins, and moral Lilliputians." Such men would eternalize the Negro's subjugation and ignore the public good. By contrast, Harry Truman, whose administration provided strong backing for civil rights, was a "hero of the first magnitude." In 1952, although he termed Adlai Stevenson "the most potent and penetrating voice crying in the wilderness of our confused and turbulent times," Hancock disdained party allegiances. Dwight Eisenhower was a "sorry spectacle," he said, and black voters must either "decide to stick by the Democratic devil or swap him for the Republican witch." Indeed, Eisenhower's indifference to segregation, lynching, voting restrictions, and the Southern defiance of desegregation, as well as the scandalous custom of rushing blacks to the front in time of war and to the rear in time of peace, alienated the black community. It took the martyred John F. Kennedy and his successor, Lyndon B. Johnson, to revive White House concern for the Negro. "In the nature of things, the Negro must be a political opportunist," Hancock explained. "He must support the political party that supports his aspirations to full equality in this country." Moreover, if Hancock reminded Negroes that demonstrations without votes were like tinkling cymbals and sounding brass, he was also convinced that ballots alone

31. Atlanta *Daily World*, December 10, 1959; Westchester County *Press*, March 26, 1960.

were insufficient to guarantee racial equality.[32] Somehow, this flexible position seemed natural for the marginal man.

Hancock's economic analyses were as unroseate as they had been in the 1930's. He still contended that the chief problems in world economy were not population explosions or scarce food supplies, but inequitable distribution of wealth and human exploitation. Rejecting birth control as the panacea for overpopulation, he sincerely believed that white supremacists supported its use as a means of controlling the colored populations of the world and checking the growth of black people and poor people in American society. He said that in America racial oppression and, to a lesser extent, class discrimination combined to produce disproportionate poverty, disease, illiteracy, and unemployment among minority groups. If racial prejudice and segregation were methods of keeping blacks in economic captivity, it followed that tolerance and desegregation could facilitate their making a decent living. In the final analysis, Hancock argued, there would be no effective integration without equality of opportunity. Also, he suggested that fair employment practices would do more to settle urban unrest than useless surveys.

Characteristically, he told blacks that there were no virtues in being moneyless and propertyless in a dollar-oriented and highly propertied society. Not surprisingly, he revived his programs of the double-duty-dollar, job holding, and black-consumer solidarity, together with instructions on frugality, sacrifice, and hard work. "It is all right for the Negroes to press for their rights. . . ," he maintained, "but unless the Negro can somehow strengthen his economic position in the nation and world his full citizenship will be indefinitely postponed." Although he placed the major burden of changing the system upon its black victims, he most assuredly thought they would not succeed without white help.[33]

32. Florida *Star*, July 9, 1951; Tampa *Bulletin*, July 5, 1952; Houston *Informer*, July 15, 1952; California *Sun Reporter*, April 18, 1953; Miami *Times*, April 6, October 15, 1955; Dallas *Star Post*, February 15, 1958; Philadelphia *Tribune*, April 5, 1958; Kansas City *Call*, January 9, 1960; Birmingham *World*, February 27, 1960. Undated releases: "Harry Truman a Moral Hero," "Is It Time for a Change?" "Senator Taft a Political Tragedy," and "Political Parties Different Only in Degrees," Hancock Papers.

33. Tampa *Bulletin*, April 11, 1953; Miami *Times*, December 11, 1954; Raleigh *Carolinian*, February 19, 1955; Kansas City *Call*, May 9, 1958; Pittsburgh *Courier*, November

International affairs, more than any other subject, catapulted Hancock into the conflicting roles of patriot and critic. Oscillating between the foreign and domestic scenes, while discussing Korea, Kenya, Formosa, Vietnam, race prejudice or propaganda warfare, he exposed American hypocrisy and greed. The United States' support of colonialist and imperialist regimes in Africa, Asia, and Latin America perpetuated the degradation and misery of the colored peoples, doing irreparable damage to her position in the Cold War. Similarly, the "blatant and blistering" practices of color prejudice and segregation were causing a ground-swell of anti-Americanism abroad. "The question keeps pressing for an answer," Hancock said: "what does it profit the nation to yield to the current anti-Negro forces and refuse to let the Negro go, and lose out in the international race for power and prestige?" Eastlandism, Talmadgism, and Negrophobia were handing the country over to Russia on a platter, probably much faster than real or imaginary subversives ever could.[34]

Accordingly, democracy had become "government by investigation," beset by creeping inflation, appalling national indebtedness, materialism, Communism, and racism. Witch hunts and security psychoses, of which Hancock disapproved, were symptoms of this malaise. "McCarthyism is not paying off," he related, "but is leaving a nation torn by suspicions and internecine strife." To wit, "although all Negroes knew Dr. Du Bois was not a Communist, they were afraid to defend him and left him to bear his cross alone." Hancock noted that while blacks were on the side of democracy in the contest for men's minds they refused to remain silent about its shortcomings. Frankly, however, he said they preferred fighting for their freedom in a sick democracy to living under atheistic Communism, also cursed by color-phobia. To help refurbish America's tarnished image, he demanded the

14, 1959; Westchester County *Press*, January 9, 1960. Undated releases: "Fair Employment Would Relieve Urban Troubles," "Financial Fumbling," "Integration and the Dollar," "Negro Enterprises Sorely in Need of Resurgent Interest," and "The Mighty Dollar," Hancock Papers.

34. Tampa *Bulletin*, April 25, 1953; Raleigh *Carolinian*, July 10, 1954, February 12, 1955; Miami *Times*, December 28, 1957; Kansas City *Call*, April 18, 1958; Oklahoma *Eagle*, December 17, 1959; Chicago *Negro Voice*, January 19, 1960. Undated releases: "Business at Bandung," "Dawn or Dusk!" and "Our Size No Longer Impressive," Hancock Papers.

appointment of black emissaries to nonwhite countries. This count-us-in attitude came across even clearer during Russian premier Nikita Krushchev's state visit. "If we would show Krushchev something to write home about show him Negro Atlanta," Hancock said.[35] He would have the nation's black minority exhibit its middle class as a testimony on behalf of the American system, one which relegated all blacks to an undemocratic existence.

Black leadership and civil rights strategy, like the previous topics, provoked multiple responses from Hancock. Consistently, as if grop-ing for personal vindication, he mourned the passing of the old race men. "There were giants in those days," he said nostalgically, while eulogizing C. C. Spaulding of North Carolina Mutual Life Insurance Company. He considered Spaulding "one of the greatest men of his times and the chiefest disciple of the lamented, but not unhonored, Booker T. Washington, who saw 50 years ago as we all see today, that learning without economic support is hollow and frustrating." The deceased publisher Joseph E. Mitchell was "a man of stalwart charac-ter" whose "constructive genius is immortalized in the growth of the St. Louis *Argus* which rates high among the best progressive journals of the country." The fallen Bishop Charles M. "Daddy" Grace, Han-cock wrote, "built one of the most powerful religious organizations to be found in this country." For Grace's five hundred houses of worship, four million members, and real estate holdings conservatively esti-mated at $25,000,000 certainly "placed him above the cult level and in the class of great achievers."

Hancock was unstinted in eulogies to others. He called Walter F. White of the NAACP the modern Moses of freedom's fight because, although his light complexion gave him an entrée into the white world, he chose to suffer affliction "with the segregated, suppressed, op-pressed, distressed Negro race." In 1963, when the expatriated Du Bois died in Ghana, Hancock hailed him as "the paragon of Negro fighters . . . who designed the pattern of attack we are currently making on the citadel of bigotry and race prejudice." Similarly, in 1964,

35. Kansas City *Call*, June 19, 1959; Louisville *Defender*, September 17, 1959. Un-dated releases: "Government by Investigation," "I Was Afraid," "Later Than We Thought," "Our Seriously Beset Nation," "Peaceful Co-Existence with Russia Impos-sible," and "The Greater Battle Raging," Hancock Papers.

Hancock wrote a defense and vindication of Booker T. Washington, pointing out that black and white Southerners, despite token strides forward, were still one like the hand "in things economic" and as separate as the fingers "in things social." Unlike many young civil rights activists, Hancock argued, Washington understood that blacks must have something to eat while struggling for full citizenship. He operated on the assumption that " 'who has the dollar' is a far more powerful question than 'who is going to marry whose daughter?' " Because Washington grasped bread-and-butter issues in a way which current black leaders would not, the Tuskegeean stood "out in bold relief like the towering Alps, snow-capped and majestic." [36]

Rarely were such accolades extended to the new crop of highly vocal militants, who, in Hancock's view, lacked the wisdom, restraint, character, and race consciousness of their elders. Regrettably, the younger men and women were long on protest and short on unity. Hancock saw a lamentable void of true leadership, too much resentment and too little building. On one occasion he recommended that black leaders become less vitriolic and more levelheaded. "The forces that would thwart integration are alert and resourceful; and above all law entrenched," he warned. "It is going to take great patience and courage and ingenuity to bring in integration. . . . But it can and will be done!" Deploring the feud between Negro Congressmen Adam Clayton Powell of New York and William L. Dawson of Chicago, cringing at the warfare being waged by newer organizations against the established NAACP and Urban League, Hancock charged that blacks were "too far behind to squabble and call names." To clean up the big mess and end the unhealthy competition, Hancock reproposed Kelly Miller's "Negro Sanhedrin," which would be the national clearinghouse for black advancement. "A scattered leadership might have been sufficient in the early years of our struggles," he added, "but today we need a unified leadership." [37]

36. New York *Amsterdam News*, March 6, 1954; Chicago *Negro Voice*, February 8, 1960. Undated releases: "C. C. Spaulding: A Moral Giant," "Joseph Everett Mitchell," "A Modern Moses Passes," and "W. E. B. Du Bois: Moral Titan," Hancock Papers. Hancock, "Booker T. Washington: His Defense and Vindication," *Negro Digest*, XIII (May 1964), 5–10.

37. Raleigh *Carolinian*, November 13, 1954; Philadelphia *Tribune*, May 3, 1958; Saint Louis *Argus*, November 6, 1959, April 1, 1960; Chicago *Negro Voice*, November 10,

Among the field of contenders, there was one who possessed enough charisma to unify the black freedom movement. Said Hancock: "Not since the rise of Booker T. Washington and W. E. B. Du Bois has there appeared on the horizon a personal leader with the potentialities of a Martin Luther King." As a spokesman, King not only carried forward the ideals set forth in the Durham conference, but, through nonviolence, spiritually elevated the cause. Even so, Hancock found a weakness in nonviolent passive resistance. "Today we are in urgent need of an economic Martin Luther King, someone to advise the Negro on ways and means of self-help," he observed. "It is not enough for the Negro to be taught to be resentful of discrimination and segregation." Yet, when King demanded that America pull out of the Vietnam War in the interest of eradicating poverty and economic oppression, Hancock blurted: "Dr. King, our hero, blunders badly!" If America pulled out, Hancock believed, it would mean "abject surrender" to Russia and Communism, "and slavery for us all." To Hancock, solutions to poverty and segregation hinged upon "the security and survival of our nation." Similarly, when Floyd McKissick, head of the Congress on Racial Equality, secured a Federal grant to build Soul City in Warren County, North Carolina, Hancock rejected the project as a step towards dangerous black self-sufficiency. "The price of our government's investment in a Soul City is strengthened bonds of segregation against which the NAACP has fought lo these many years," he stated. Besides, if blacks developed the habit of accepting handouts they would get "Heart Cities, Head Cities, Hand Cities, Finger Cities, Big Toe Cities and so on"—anything but full integration.[38]

Ambivalent, simultaneously advocating and repudiating integration and self-help, Hancock insisted upon moderation in black lifestyle and strategy. The Negro's troubles stemmed both from white oppression and his own callousness, Hancock maintained, and probably more of the latter than admitted. He praised President Henderson of Virginia Union for giving the students "straight talk," warning them "not to

1959, February 8, 1960. Undated releases: "Era of Weak Leadership Endangers United States," and "Our Murder Habit," Hancock Papers; Eisenberg, "Kelly Miller: The Negro Leader as a Marginal Man," 186–188.

38. Philadelphia *Tribune*, May 3, 1958. Undated releases: "Dr. King's Second Great Blunder," and "The High Cost of Handout," Hancock Papers.

overreact and turn humorless and rude and boorish in their efforts to prove themselves no Uncle Toms." Furthermore, blacks needed to know that marching, singing, demonstrating and demanding were useless without work and sacrifice. "If the Negro does considerable advancing he must do so by hard 'working in' and saving his money or spending his earnings wisely," Hancock advised. Frequently, in their attempt to keep up with the white Joneses, educated blacks indulged in conspicuous consumption. "Negroes are rushing for Cadillacs when Fords and Chevrolets are more geared to their economic underpinning," he suggested. "In other words we as Negroes have champagne tastes with coca cola pocketbooks." [39]

Hancock worried about black youths, too. Justifiably frustrated with white racism, they either adopted the dubious methods of would-be revolutionaries or, like the whites, burned draft cards and fled to Canada. Having rejected the nonviolent philosophy and saturated themselves in the teachings of former Black Muslim minister Malcolm X, they were seeking a power confrontation with white America which could easily spell disaster. Curiously, Hancock noted, those who cried "black power" were also begging for white handouts, and the slogan of "Burn, baby, burn" had become a tragedy for black neighborhoods and businesses rather than white ones. "There is a great army of young Negroes who have resolved to steal, rob, rape and riot but not work," Hancock reacted. "When these get through preying on . . . Negro business it is greatly to be feared that but little will be left." Meanwhile, almost in a last-ditch effort to avert the kind of violence which swept the country in 1967, Hancock called upon black leaders—Randolph, Wilkins, Powell, King, Young, McKissick, Carmichael and Meredith—to overcome "the oratory complex" and project "a program of deliverance for the Negro masses." [40]

39. Saint Louis *Argus*, March 18, 1955; Kansas City *Call*, May 16, 1958; Philadelphia *Tribune*, March 28, 1959. Undated releases: "Conscience-Made Cowards," "Courting Failure," and "Time for Straight Talk," Hancock Papers.

40. Undated releases: "The Negro's Lamentable Leadership," and "Team-Work the Answer," Hancock Papers. A Philip Randolph; Roy Wilkins, executive secretary of the NAACP; Adam Clayton Powell; Martin Luther King, Jr.; Whitney M. Young, Jr., executive director of the National Urban League; Floyd McKissick; Stokely Carmichael, national chairman of the Student Nonviolent Coordinating Committee; and James Meredith, the first black graduate of the University of Mississippi.

Despite the many pronouncements and protestations, Hancock could not break the bonds of a certain obscurity. Although he spoke to a national black newspaper audience, he could not goose step with young black activists, radicals, or revolutionaries. In fact, he did not wish to keep up with these "nihilists and anarchists and arsonists,"[41] and he held tenaciously to the values which shaped the social outlook of his generation. Fortunately, he made the ideological adjustment from the age of segregation to the era of civil rights and black power, but not without being shocked by the incredible explosion in black expectations and popular notions of violent encounter. Aged, infirm, and no longer in the limelight, he tried desperately to exert influence from the sidelines. Whether cheering the moderates or warning the militants, he felt the "twoness" of which Du Bois wrote in 1903, "an American, a Negro; two souls, two thoughts, two unreconciled strivings; two warring ideals in one dark body, whose dogged strength alone keeps it from being torn asunder."[42] A cultural pluralist who chauvinistically celebrated black culture, an interracialist who sometimes doubted the feasibility of integration, a self-help advocate who dismissed schemes promoting black economic independence as segregationist, and a critic of American democracy who patriotically defended it against Communism, Hancock remained a marginal man.

After being hospitalized for terminal cancer in 1968, Hancock lived nearly two years in intermittent pain. He turned in his pen as a columnist, but two of his final releases were prophetic. One pictured the election of president Richard Nixon as a bad omen for blacks. "The amount that the anti-Negro elements spent to put Nixon over . . . indicates how determined are the forces that would keep the Negro in the bondage of second-class citizenship," the old warrior commented. "The probabilities are that little by little the gains Negroes had made under Roosevelt, Kennedy and Johnson will be whittled away and this writer gets considerable assurance that he will not be alive . . . to see what is happening to the hapless Negro." The second release deplored the racial polarization which followed the assassination of Martin

41. "Conscience-Made Cowards," Hancock Papers.

42. W. E. B. Du Bois, *The Souls of Black Folk: Essays and Sketches* (Chicago: A. C. McClurg and Co., 1903), p. 3.

Luther King, Jr. One day blacks and whites were going to live as equals and in peace, Hancock predicted. He ended with an earnest plea, "Let's be brothers!"[43]

Few visitors stopped at "The Julianna" during those final agonizing months. "My eighty-five years are bearing down upon me and heavily it would seem. Rolls-Royces finally hit the dump . . . and so must we all," Hancock wrote in 1969. "There is something always behind us trying to catch up with us and when it catches up with us it gives us a terrible beating."[44] Of course, when President Bartlett of Colgate University visited after Colgate had conferred upon him the LL.D., his fifth honorary degree, Hancock had a brief respite from suffering. Colgate cited him as "a man whose life has been a serious and sustained effort to do something about race relations in the United States during a time when the atmosphere and environment required the utmost in courage, wisdom and faith."[45] Such words might well have been his epitaph. Hancock lingered on less than a year and died, with Marie at his bedside, July 24, 1970.

43. "A Double Calamity," November 9, 1968; and "Let's be Brothers!" December 23, 1968, Hancock Papers.

44. Hancock to the author, September 4, 1969.

45. Hancock received the D.D. degree from Benedict College in 1925; LL.D., Shaw University, 1952; LL.D., Benedict College, 1952; and D.D., Virginia Union University, 1963; "A Facsimile of the Citation as read at Colgate University in Convocation Assembled, September 25, 1969," Hancock Papers.

VIII. An Evaluation

Hancock's body lay in state at Moore Street Baptist Church where for thirty-eight years he had preached and served his race. As hundreds of mourners from Jackson Ward, Northside, and Virginia Union signed the register, perhaps only the old ones knew that he had been fighting prejudice and uplifting blacks long before the *Brown* decision and the civil rights movement. Young people paid their respects, too, but they remembered him as the aged philosopher who deprecated militancy and counseled moderation. The funeral services, held July 28, 1970, attracted a large crowd. Old and young, black and white, many of whom stood outside, were there. Appropriately, the program included several works by Hancock: a poem, "Plus Ultra," a prayer, "Contrition," and two spirituals, "My Journey Home" and "Our Long Home." In the memorial meditation, Moore Street pastor Gilbert G. Campbell said that Hancock lived a constructive life, one dedicated to being his brother's keeper and to unselfish leadership in the crusade for social justice. Later that afternoon, under the warm Virginia sun, Hancock was laid to rest in Roselawn Memory Gardens.[1]

Shortly afterward, journalist Thomas L. Dabney, writing for the Norfolk *Journal and Guide*, summed up Hancock's career. Hancock was "an unusual educator and Baptist minister by any concept of human worth and achievement . . . a keen observer of contemporary history and a faithful student of the problems of the black man." Better than most men in his day, he saw that racial prejudice and segregation threatened the Negro's social and economic survival. He believed that through interracial good will and black solidarity, rather than hate and violence, Negroes could counteract oppression, pull themselves out of the "economic vicious circle," and win first-class citizenship. Disturbed over the plight of black workers, dubbed "Gloomy Dean" by his critics, Hancock wrote and lectured extensively, emphasizing frugality

1. Program, *Memorial Service for Dr. Gordon B. Hancock, Pastor Emeritus, Moore Street Baptist Church*, July 28, 1970, Richmond, Virginia; interview with George B. Winston, June 26, 1974, Richmond, Virginia.

and the double-duty-dollar, "'Spend your money where you can work.'" That theme, Dabney commented, "holds as true today as it did a half century ago." Hancock and a handful of courageous colleagues advocated "equality and justice for black men" in the 1920's, 1930's, and 1940's, braving white reprisals, personal threats, and, frequently, black indifference. "And Dr. Hancock waged his battle in the South—down where the action was," Dabney concluded. "That was where it was nice and legal to put black men and women in jail if they did not bow obediently to racial segregation—for that was the law of the land." [2]

An article in the *New South* appraised Hancock's place in Negro thought and role in founding the Southern Regional Council. Born in late nineteenth-century South Carolina into a family that idealized education and Christian service, schooled in hardship and sacrifice, Hancock emerged during the Negro renaissance of the 1920's. Historically, therefore, he belonged to a cadre of Southern black professionals who, in face of the racial deterioration following World War I, rallied to the Negro's cause. Associated with white liberals, either in the Interracial Commission or related organizations, they appealed to the conscience of the white South. To their credit, they sustained black hope. In the wake of World War II, Gordon B. Hancock, Luther P. Jackson, P. B. Young, Charles S. Johnson, Benjamin E. Mays, Horace Mann Bond, and others drafted the Durham manifesto, which led to the establishment of the council. Significantly, these blacks helped to incorporate the ideals of freedom and equal opportunity into the South's postwar agenda. As chief black spokesman, Hancock was a catalyst in the whole enterprise and "a precursor of the more militant leadership of the 1950's which reached its zenith in Martin Luther King, Jr." [3]

According to one historian, men like Robert R. Moton, Charles S. Johnson, Frederick D. Patterson, Gordon B. Hancock, and P. B. Young vied for Southern black leadership in "the period from the death of Booker T. Washington to the beginning of the King era." Although this kind of assertion calls special attention to intraracial competition

2. Norfolk *Journal and Guide*, August 8, 1970.
3. Raymond Gavins, "Gordon Hancock: An Appraisal," *New South*, XXV (Fall 1970), 36–43.

among the leaders,[4] it is true that after Washington died patterns of Negro leadership changed in the South. The idea or notion of the "One Great Negro Leader" gradually died out and many new personalities filled the presumed void. The latter were usually middle-class professionals, lesser known, and molders of black thought in education, religion, politics, and race relations.[5] Hancock operated within the context of this diversity and specialized competence, and he affected the people around him.

Judging from the testimony of contemporary supporters, opponents, and others who knew him well, Hancock achieved critical distinction. "The entire race is indebted to you. You have had great opposition in the advocacy of your principles for racial betterment; now it must bring you great satisfaction that after battling for twenty years your ideas are being accepted," Luther P. Jackson once told him. "I take off my hat to any man who holds to his principles in the face of stinging criticism." Likewise, Sandy F. Ray, a distinguished black minister, confided: "I personally consider you a major prophet of this generation, and I trust you will find it convenient to share your exceptional training, experience, and sound philosophy with Christian thinkers through the writing of a book."[6] While Hancock never published a book, he did write several scholarly articles and, between 1929 and 1968, more than two thousand columns for the Associated Negro Press.[7]

Reflecting on the 1920's, William L. Ransome, longtime dean of Richmond's black clergy, remembered Hancock as one of the most colorful men in the city, modern, theologically radical, and race con-

4. Patrick J. Gilpin, "Charles S. Johnson: An Intellectual Biography" (Ph.D. Dissertation, Vanderbilt University, 1973), pp. 638–639.

5. See Carl Stanley Matthews, "After Booker T. Washington: The Search for a New Negro Leadership, 1915–1925" (Ph.D. Dissertation, University of Virginia, 1971), pp. 1–5; and Horace Mann Bond, "Negro Leadership since Washington," *South Atlantic Quarterly*, XXIV (April 1925), 115–130; and Ralph J. Bunche, "A Brief and Tentative Analysis of Negro Leadership" (September 1940), pp. 23–24, 64–68, 153–154, in the Carnegie-Myrdal Study of the Negro in America, Duke University Library, Durham, North Carolina.

6. Jackson to Hancock, December 9, 1943; Ray to Hancock, August 29, 1947, Gordon Blaine Hancock Papers, Richmond, Virginia.

7. Gordon B. Hancock, "Back to Benedict—An Abbreviated Account of My Stewardship," n.d., Hancock Papers.

scious. "Nobody took him cheaply," Ransome recalled. "He and Miles Mark Fisher were highly respected, if not feared, by every Negro preacher in town."[8] Retired attorney Clarence M. Maloney, who considered Hancock "his closest colleague and friend at Union," agreed that he was popular. Yet Maloney confessed that Hancock probably put too much stock in religious platitudes, appeals to human decency, and personal diplomacy.[9] Clarissa Kyles Dillard of Virginia Union and a member of Moore Street described Hancock as being "contradictory and withdrawn, but an effective pastor and community leader even in those days."[10]

Hancock inspired his students. Distinguished educator Henry Allen Bullock, a 1929 graduate of Virginia Union and the first black professor at the University of Texas, affectionately credited "Gordon Blaine Hancock, our 'Gloomy Dean' of economics" with helping to inculcate his lifelong faith in "the doctrine that the Negro college was to develop the leadership for the emancipation of the Negro American as a person." Pearl M. Mankins, current chairperson of the Virginia Union history department, said that when she sat in Hancock's class in the 1940's, "I could not appreciate fully his emphasis upon self-help and organization of black labor power as I do now." Although not a meticulous teacher, she reported, "he introduced me to the real world of depression, Communism and competing ideologies, war, Afro-Asian independence movements, and civil rights." Preeminently, he was a "race model."[11] Both President Allix B. James of Virginia Union and Gilbert G. Campbell, pastor of Moore Street, derived their sense of professional purpose from Hancock's sociology classes, where service to the race and self-expression were infinitely more important than textbooks.[12] Historian Emma Wesley Brown studied under Hancock and Logan, whose chapel debates motivated her to achieve, but she

8. Interview with William L. Ransome, June 26, 1974, Richmond, Virginia.
9. Interview with Clarence M. Maloney, September 13, 1974, Lynchburg, Virginia.
10. Interview with Clarissa Kyles Dillard, June 27, 1974, Richmond, Virginia.
11. Henry A. Bullock, *A History of Negro Education in the South from 1619 to the Present* (Cambridge, Mass.: Harvard University Press, 1967), pp. vii–viii; interview with Pearl M. Mankins, June 12, 1974, Richmond, Virginia.
12. Interviews with Allix B. James, June 12, 1974, and Gilbert G. Campbell, December 13, 1974, Richmond, Virginia.

recollected being particularly impressed by Hancock's dictum that moral character must never be sacrificed for degrees.[13] Herman H. Bozeman, Thomas L. Dabney, Wendell P. Russell, and David Shannon, all Virginia Union graduates, reported that Hancock was an important influence in their choice of careers.[14]

Hancock's former adversaries judge him cautiously. "Hancock was a man with a marvelous mind," commented John M. Ellison, "but he was very artificial and overcome by the idea of his bigness." Of course, the great recognition he achieved outside the college, Ellison admitted, enhanced Union's community relations. "He was outstanding as a Negro spokesman, and I hope he will be remembered."[15] Rayford W. Logan, mellowed by the years, said: "I had a personal prejudice against Hancock. I thought he was a poseur." Being a young zealous follower of Du Bois, Logan said that he harshly criticized Hancock's teachings concerning character, thrift, and necessary accommodation to segregation. What started out as an ideological debate deteriorated into personal conflict. Overall, Logan guessed, Hancock's impact would have been greater if he had earned the Ph.D. and published like Charles S. Johnson and Ira DeA. Reid. Otherwise, he must be rated "a minor figure whose 'Back to the Farm' and 'Double Duty Dollar' slogans brought him temporary acclaim in the South." Hancock, Logan added, "did not make a record as a scholar or intellectual, but he did aspire to be a Negro leader."[16]

Literary critic Arthur P. Davis warned that he "was no great admirer of Hancock," but he rendered a balanced assessment of Hancock's personality. Davis separated the private man from his public image. Sensitive, introverted, seemingly self-sufficient, always talking to and not with others, "Hancock built a wall between himself and the world." Paradoxically, however, Hancock captured the hearts of

13. Interview with Emma Wesley Brown, June 12, 1974, Richmond, Virginia.

14. Interview with Dr. Robert Greene, vice-president for academic affairs, Virginia Union University, June 12, 1974, Richmond, Virginia; and individual evaluation forms in the author's possession. Dr. Herman H. Bozeman is professor of education at Norfolk State College; Mr. Thomas L. Dabney is a retired journalist; Dr. Wendell P. Russell is president of Federal City College; and Dr. David Shannon is dean of the seminary at the University of Pittsburgh.

15. Interview with John M. Ellison, June 12, 1974, Richmond, Virginia.

16. Interview with Rayford W. Logan, July 11, 1974, Washington, D. C.

common people with his folksy ways, boasted a black and white following, and "looked like somebody." Furthermore, he dressed stylishly, had wit and a sense of humor. Hancock interchanged these faces with consummate skill. Hancock the black spokesman was more interested in courting white liberals than in solving problems of the Negro community, Davis believed. Nevertheless, his popularity in white colleges and interracial circles strengthened his claims to black leadership and brought much-needed publicity to Virginia Union. In writing for the Negro press, Hancock cultivated a moving metaphoric style which made him one of the best known black columnists of the day, probably on a par with Kelly Miller, William Pickens, and George Schuyler. If in intellect and raw genius "Hancock is not to be compared with the likes of Abram L. Harris, Ralph J. Bunche, Paul Robeson, Charles S. Johnson, or W. E. B. Du Bois," Davis conceded that "the man deserves serious study as a Southern racial propagandist and a phenomenon of his times."[17]

Unlike Logan and Davis, Henry J. McGuinn looked at Hancock in a context broader than scholarship and letters. Avoiding any mention of the tensions between himself and Hancock, McGuinn saw great merit in his old colleague's works. To him Hancock was not simply an erudite sociologist on the order of Charles S. Johnson or Allison Davis, but a practical humanist whose major concerns were ordinary people and their daily problems. Hence Hancock made his mark in advocacy, not in empirical research. McGuinn said that Hancock's course in race relations, which stressed Negro interactions with whites and other minorities, was the first of its kind offered by any Negro college. Moreover, the short-lived Torrance School of Race Relations in Virginia Union University provided the blueprint for Johnson's Institute of Race Relations at Fisk. Because of Hancock, Virginia Union's students were never allowed to forget the realities of race prejudice and fear. McGuinn thought Hancock's key weaknesses were a reluctance to forgive anyone who wronged him, a tendency to romanticize white liberals, and an unwillingness to force the race issue.[18]

Benjamin E. Mays, former president of Morehouse College, put

17. Arthur P. Davis to the author, June 24, 1974; interview with Davis, July 11, 1974, Washington, D. C.

18. Interviews with Henry J. McGuinn, June 12, 26, 1974, Richmond, Virginia.

Hancock on a high pedestal. "Gordon Hancock was not a radical, but he was forthright in his writing and speaking," Mays observed. "His impact was greatest in Virginia where he lived and worked. For the most part, he had a good press, as well as black and white support." Mays said the effective leader was one who could instill high aspirations and a strong degree of morale among the following in accomplishing worthwhile goals. By this definition, he stated, Hancock must be judged "effective." In fact, Mays continued, Hancock showed that he had the seeds of greatness—"humanistic ideals and unselfish devotion to the cause of racial betterment." When asked if he might not be overstating his point, Mays replied: "I felt that way about Hancock, Wesley, Johnson, and Du Bois." [19]

William H. Leary has written that "Hancock saw himself in the role of a prophet, leading his people along the true path to the promised land of interracial cooperation." [20] If somewhat facetious, this characterization captures the aura of religiosity which surrounded Hancock. He vigorously looked toward the maxims of Christianity, democracy, human brotherhood, and morality for solutions to race problems. Simultaneously, he felt that such ideals were meaningless unless implemented by concrete political, economic, and cultural changes. Hancock's dual perspective was shaped by black religion, the theological liberalism of Colgate, environmentalist approaches to economics and sociology at Harvard, and the racial ideologies of Washington and Du Bois. Significant individuals, either as advisers or colleagues, also influenced him, including his wife, P. B. Young, Luther P. Jackson, and Jessie Daniel Ames.

A number of subtleties permeated Hancock's thinking about race. Like many black ideologues in his day, he believed that while blacks were deserving of first-class citizenship most whites were not prepared to accept them as equals. Therefore he expected racial equality to come gradually rather than suddenly. Still, he insisted upon immediate action toward that end. Though identified by education and social station with the black elite of professors, ministers, lawyers, physicians, and businessmen, he focused consistently on the "hardpressed

19. Interview with Benjamin E. Mays, June 19, 1974, Atlanta, Georgia.
20. William H. Leary, "Race Relations in Turmoil: Southern Liberals and World War II" (M.A. Thesis, University of Virginia, 1967), p. 36.

masses," rejecting all pretensions to class status. Consciously black, wedded to the race chauvinism of the generation of the 1920's, Hancock nonetheless considered white cooperation necessary in a viable strategy for black advancement. At the same time, he contended that the "lowly Negro" could help himself by cultivating middle-class habits of sobriety and thrift. Programs to promote these habits, together with timely exhortations to manhood and solidarity, formed the nucleus of Hancock's national role in Omega Psi Phi Fraternity and in Sigma Pi Phi, the latter being the oldest black Greek-letter organization in the United States.[21]

Hancock's shifting and sometimes agonizing position on segregation, doubtless the major issue of his times, reflected the narrow range of options for blacks and black leaders in the South. Proceeding from the assumption that blacks must survive economically and gain acceptance from white society, he saw segregation as a practical blessing and a racial curse. Until the late 1930's, that is before the NAACP launched its attack against the "separate but equal" doctrine, Hancock maintained that Negroes must make the most of the dual system, even contending that they should create an economy within the Negro community to provide jobs and opportunities for their own people. By the time America entered World War II, he realized that the inference of inferiority and other handicaps which Jim Crow imposed upon black opportunities to learn and earn far outweighed possible gains from a separate black economy. In the era of *Brown* and after, when integration became the major goal of Afro-Americans, Hancock's opposition to segregation crested. During the racially troubled 1960's, he rejected white segregationists and black nationalists, the former because they were obviously racist and the latter because their too radical methods could trigger a blood bath in the South and nation.

Unable to accept the increasingly revolutionary tactics of the black movement, Hancock spent his last years in ideological isolation, cut off from many young blacks who felt no allegiance to his kind of leadership. He had relied upon moral suasion, interracial dialogue, and

21. See Robert L. Gill, *The Omega Psi Phi Fraternity and the Men Who Made Its History: A Concise History* (Washington, D. C.: Omega Psi Phi Fraternity, Inc., 1963), and Charles H. Wesley, *History of Sigma Pi Phi: First of the Negro-American Greek-Letter Fraternities* (Washington, D. C.: Sigma Pi Phi, 1954).

legalism at a time when Southern whites were less rational about race relations and more likely to brutalize black dissenters. By precept and example, he helped to set in motion the changing expectations and demands which left him behind. Unacknowledged, if not forgotten, he symbolized the historical linkage between an oppressive past and a stormy present.

To be certain, there was much in the civil rights and black power movements to support the content of Hancock's ideology. The drive toward integration fulfilled his prophecy of 1938 at Randolph-Macon College that Negro survival hinged upon the elimination of segregation. Black power restated his time-honored pronouncements on black self-help and solidarity. Economist Frank G. Davis's recent proposals for black community development, which include a scheme to consolidate black purchasing power, logically extend the double-duty-dollar program. Ironically, a new book entitled *Still a Dream* systematically details conditions among blacks whose exposure once earned Hancock the dubious distinction of "Gloomy Dean,"—high unemployment, low wages, unequal education, poor housing, inadequate health care, rising dependency, crime, and family break-up.[22]

Hancock belonged to an earlier era and must be evaluated in the context of his times. For many years, in the South and throughout the nation, contemporaries regarded him as a mouthpiece for the Negro cause. Educator Walter G. Daniel of Howard University, an observer of the men and movements of that day, has rated Hancock an influential black leader. Similarly, Wyatt T. Walker, pastor of Canaan Baptist Church in New York and former executive-secretary of the Southern Christian Leadership Conference, noted that Hancock achieved Southwide recognition and was one who had a special influence on him.[23] Hancock's present obscurity is undeserved. The same may be said of Luther P. Jackson, P. B. Young, Charles S. Johnson, Horace Mann Bond, Benjamin E. Mays, and others.

22. Frank G. Davis, *The Economics of Black Community Development: An Analysis and Program for Autonomous Growth and Development* (Chicago: Markham Publishing Co., 1972), pp. 176–180; and Sar A. Levitan, William B. Johnston, Robert Taggart, *Still a Dream: The Changing Status of Blacks since 1960* (Cambridge, Mass.: Harvard University Press, 1975), pp. 185–204, 351–355.

23. Individual evaluation forms in the author's possession.

The black history explosion which accompanied the black revolt of the 1960's stimulated an abundance of writing on slavery, racial oppression, and black nationalism. Very little has been done on Southern black ideologies and strategies in the age of segregation. Blacks and the interracial movement, black responses to segregation and movements for change, and the role of blacks in initiating the Second Reconstruction still beckon to enterprising students of Southern and Afro-American history. In these neglected years, Hancock and his brethren comprised the South's black vanguard. They never won the plaudits showered upon nationally known giants like Washington and Du Bois. Black histories and biographies and race relations monographs frequently omit them altogether. Collectively, however, they were the most important black spokesmen in the South during the 1915–1955 interregnum between Washington and King. Hancock is significant not only for his individual contributions but because he is a microcosm of the group.

Hancock infused a sense of urgency and immediacy into Southern racial dialogue in his day. Like many of his contemporaries, he saw integration as the goal of black struggle and believed that democracy and justice would ultimately triumph over the forces of oppression. Working within the system, he had to appeal to white sympathy and the white sense of decency and fairness. Sometimes forced to compromise, he lived with ambiguity. An early black sociologist, his perspectives on black welfare, education, migration, urbanization, labor, unemployment, and ethnic relations anticipated current black social research.[24] Moore Street Baptist Church and Richmond's Memorial Hospital, Community Chest, and Urban League remain monumental, if forgotten, symbols of his indefatigable ministry and civic service.

By insisting that the church wage war against prejudice and work for racial uplift, Hancock actualized the social gospel and spaded valuable ground for the seeds of present day black theology. The double-duty-dollar philosophy, which he popularized in the Negro press, became a rallying cry for black economic solidarity in the three decades after

24. In 1973, acting upon the recommendation of President Allix B. James, Virginia Union established the Gordon Blaine Hancock Distinguished Professorship in Social Science.

World War I. It gave rise to the "Jobs for Negroes," "Don't Buy Where You Can't Work," and "Buy Black" campaigns of the 1930's.[25] A dynamic orator, he extolled the virtues of black self-help and interracial cooperation for fifty years. His position on segregation revealed the limitations of black leadership in the South, where the practice was pervasive and allies to fight it so few. He depended upon moral suasion, although the prerequisite for change was political power—an essential denied black Southerners at the time. A founder of the Southern Regional Council, he helped to engineer its transition from cooperation within the biracial framework to desegregation. It is today the leading interracial organization working for peaceful social change in the South. Neither an accommodator nor a radical, Hancock was a tough "race man" during a generation when pride and indomitable will enabled blacks to survive.

25. See John H. Bracey, Jr., "Black Nationalism since Garvey," in Nathan Huggins, Martin Kilson, and Daniel Fox, eds., *Key Issues in the Afro-American Experience* (New York: Harcourt Brace Jovanovich, 1971), II, 262–266.

190

Bibliography

Manuscript Collections

Ames, Jessie Daniel. University of North Carolina Library, Chapel Hill, North Carolina.

    Mrs. Ames was an outstanding Southern liberal between 1919 and 1944. Her papers contain numerous exchanges with Negro leaders, including Carter Wesley, P. B. Young, and Gordon B. Hancock.

Bond, Horace Mann. Atlanta University Library, Atlanta, Georgia.

    These consist of two boxes of speeches and statistical studies, primarily concerning Negro education, and a few letters to and from Charles S. Johnson regarding the stand which the Durham conferees should take on racial segregation.

Carnegie-Myrdal Study of the Negro in America. Duke University Library, Durham, North Carolina.

    Microfilm of the original forty-four working papers used in preparing *An American Dilemma: The Negro Problem and Modern Democracy,* published in 1944, this is one of the most extensive collections on black leadership and racial ideologies in existence.

Commission on Interracial Cooperation. Atlanta University Library, Atlanta, Georgia.

    Of major significance are the correspondence and state committees sections. Among the Southern blacks contributing to the work of the headquarters in Atlanta were Robert R. Moton, John M. Gandy, John Hope, Charles S. Johnson, Ira DeA. Reid, and Gordon B. Hancock. The materials on Virginia were disappointing.

Dabney, Virginius. University of Virginia Library, Charlottesville, Virginia.

    The Richmond *Times-Dispatch* editor corresponded regularly with Gordon B. Hancock and P. B. Young, who alternately praised and criticized his liberalism.

Hancock, Gordon Blaine. Richmond, Virginia.

    The most valuable and frequently used source for this book, the Hancock collection has now been moved from the old residence in Richmond to Detroit, Michigan, where Dr. Hancock's grandnephew lives. Consisting of eight large boxes of uncatalogued items, the papers comprise thousands of press clippings and releases; hundred of sermons, syllabi, and speeches; as well as lectures, photographs, citations, poems, songs, and other memorabilia. Besides copies of published articles, there are many, many letters to and from Luther P. Jackson, P. B. Young, Charles S. Johnson, Benjamin E. Mays, Horace Mann Bond, Carl J. Murphy, Carter Wesley,

Jessie Daniel Ames, L. R. Reynolds, Lucy Randolph Mason, Virginius Dabney, Howard W. Odum and Guy B. Johnson, and many others, from 1921 to 1954. The correspondence dwindles considerably after 1954, but Hancock's regular releases to the Associated Negro Press help to fill in his thinking for the last years.

North Carolina Commission on Interracial Cooperation. University of North Carolina Library, Chapel Hill, North Carolina.

The title is somewhat misleading. These are, to a great extent, records of the North Carolina and Virginia Commissions and include much information on black-white dialogue in both states during the 1930's.

Richmond Urban League Files. Richmond, Virginia.

These contain newspaper clippings, surveys, and sociological memoranda on Richmond Negroes in the 1920's, when William N. Colson, Ora Brown Stokes, J. Milton Sampson, Wiley A. Hall, and Gordon B. Hancock got the nascent Richmond Urban League off the ground.

Southern Regional Council Files. Southern Regional Council Office, Atlanta, Georgia.

The most helpful files were those of Jessie D. Ames, Gordon B. Hancock, Howard W. Odum, and Lillian E. Smith.

Young, Plummer Bernard. Norfolk, Virginia.

Except for many penetrating editorials, which were printed regularly in the Norfolk *Journal and Guide*, Young's exchanges with Hancock, Jackson, Dabney, and Mrs. Ames simply duplicate Hancock's papers. Other private correspondence was withheld.

Regrettably, this writer did not receive permission to use the Luther P. Jackson papers, which are housed in the Virginia State College Library, Petersburg, Virginia. Dr. Benjamin E. Mays's illness prevented use of his papers.

Documents and Reports

Annual Report: The Voting Status of Negroes in Virginia. Petersburg: Virginia Voters League, 1942–1945.

Armstrong, Nancy. *The Study of an Attempt Made in 1943 to Abolish Segregation of the Races on Common Carriers in the State of Virginia*. Phelps-Stokes Fellowship Paper No. 17. Charlottesville: University of Virginia, 1950.

Benedict College. *Catalogue and Announcements 1895–96*.

"Biographical Sketch of Reverend Robert Wiley Hancock, 1862–1902." In the possession of Mrs. Mae Hancock Garner, Greensboro, North Carolina.

Bunche, Ralph J. "A Brief and Tentative Analysis of Negro Leadership,"

September 1940. Carnegie-Myrdal Study of the Negro in America, Duke University Library, Durham, North Carolina.

_____. "The Programs, Ideologies, Tactics, and Achievements of Negro Betterment and Interracial Organizations," June 1940. Carnegie-Myrdal Study of the Negro in America, Duke University Library, Durham, North Carolina.

By Their Fruits. Richmond: Virginia Union University, 1939.

Chicago Commission on Race Relations. *The Negro in Chicago: A Study of Race Relations and a Race Riot*. Chicago: University of Chicago Press, 1922.

Columbia, South Carolina. *City Directory 1904–1905*.

"The Double Duty Dollar." An Address by Gordon B. Hancock on Educational Day, Tidewater Fair, Durham, North Carolina, October 20, 1933.

Durham, North Carolina. *City Directory 1921*.

The Durham Statement, The Atlanta Statement, The Richmond Statement. Atlanta: Commission on Interracial Cooperation, 1943.

Federal Writers' Program. *The Negro in Virginia*. Hampton: The Hampton Institute, 1940.

The Francis J. Torrance School of Race Relations in Virginia Union University. Richmond: Virginia Union University, n.d.

Furniss, W. Todd., ed. *American Universities and Colleges*. Washington, D. C.: American Council on Education, 1973.

The Future of Negroes on the Farm: Articles and Editorials Reprinted from the Journal and Guide. Norfolk: Association for the Advancement of Negro Country Life, n.d.

Guild, June Purcell. *Black Laws of Virginia: A Summary of the Legislative Acts of Virginia Concerning Negroes from the Earliest Times to the Present*. Richmond: Whittet and Shepperson, 1936.

Irwin, Mary., ed. *American Universities and Colleges*. Washington, D. C.: American Council on Education, 1952.

Johnson, Charles S., ed. *The Economic Status of Negroes*. Nashville: Fisk University Press, 1933.

Mason, Lucy Randolph. *Standards for Workers in Southern Industry*. New York: National Consumers' League, 1931.

Miller, Kelly. *Is Race Difference Fundamental, Eternal and Inescapable? An Open Letter to President Warren G. Harding, November 29, 1921*. Pamphlet Collection, Duke University Library, Durham, North Carolina.

National Association for the Advancement of Colored People. *Eighth and Ninth Annual Reports 1917 and 1918*. New York: National Office of the NAACP, 1919.

_____. *Forty-Sixth Annual Report 1954*. New York: National Office of the NAACP, 1955.

_____. *Twenty-First Annual Report 1930*. New York: National Office of the NAACP, 1931.

Negro Welfare Survey Committee. *The Negro in Richmond, Virginia.* Richmond: Richmond Council of Social Agencies, 1929.

Newspapers and the Race Problem. Atlanta: Commission on Interracial Cooperation, 1942.

Progress Report—Commission on Interracial Cooperation for Virginia and North Carolina 1935. Pamphlet Collection, Duke University Library, Durham, North Carolina.

Reference List of Southern Colored Schools. Trustees of the John F. Slater Fund Occasional Papers No. 20, 1918.

Richmond, Virginia. *City Directory 1923.*

Richmond, Virginia—Yesterday and Today. Richmond: The City of Richmond and the Chamber of Commerce, 1913.

Union-Hartshorn Bulletin, XXIII (Jan. 1923); XXIV (June–Nov. 1923); XXX (Nov. 1929).

U. S., Bureau of Education. *Negro Education: A Study of the Private and Higher Schools for Colored People in the United States,* Bulletin 1916, No. 30, II. Washington, D. C.: Government Printing Office, 1917.

U. S., Bureau of the Census. *Abstract of the Fourteenth Census of the United States 1920.* Washington, D. C.: Government Printing Office, 1923.

—————. *Fifteenth Census of the United States: 1930. Population,* I. Washington, D. C.: Government Printing Office, 1931.

—————. *Fourteenth Census of the United States: 1920. Population,* III. Washington, D. C.: Government Printing Office, 1923.

—————. *Negro Population in the United States 1790–1915.* Washington, D. C.: Government Printing Office, 1918.

—————. *Thirteenth Census of the United States: 1910. Agriculture,* VII. Washington, D. C.: Government Printing Office, 1913.

—————. *Twelfth Census of the United States: 1900. Population,* I. Washington, D. C.: United States Census Office, 1901.

U. S., Post Office. *Postal Route Map of South Carolina, September 1, 1944.*

Virginia Union Bulletin, Centennial Issue: "A Century of Service to Education and Religion," LXV (June 1965).

Virginia Union University. *Annual Catalogues,* 1899–1900; 1910–1911; 1920–1921.

Interviews

Brown, Dr. Emma Wesley. June 12, 1974, Richmond, Virginia.

Campbell, Rev. Gilbert C. December 13, 1974, Richmond, Virginia.

Davis, Dr. Arthur P. July 11, 1974, Washington, D. C.

Dillard, Professor Clarissa Kyles. June 27, 1974, Richmond, Virginia.

Ellison, Dr. John M. June 12, 27, 1974, Richmond, Virginia.

Garner, Mrs. Mae Hancock. June 18, 1974, Greensboro, North Carolina.
Greene, Dr. Robert. June 12, 1974, Richmond, Virginia.
Hancock, Dr. Gordon Blaine. September 25, October 21, November 15, 1968, February 5, March 7, 1969, Richmond, Virginia.
Hancock, Mrs. Marie D. September 23, 1972, August 16, 1973, Richmond, Virginia.
James, Dr. Allix B. June 12, 1974, Richmond, Virginia.
Logan, Dr. Rayford W. July 11, 1974, Washington, D. C.
McGuinn, Dr. Henry J. June 12, 26, 1974, Richmond, Virginia.
Maloney, Attorney Clarence M. September 13, 1974, Lynchburg, Virginia.
Mankins, Professor Pearl M. June 12, 1974, Richmond, Virginia.
Mays, Dr. Benjamin E. June 19, 1974, Atlanta, Georgia.
Ransome, Rev. William L. June 26, 1974, Richmond, Virginia.
Winston, Mr. George B. June 26, 1974, Richmond, Virginia.

Letters Responding to Inquiries

Brewer, Mr. William M. March 15, 1968.
Davis, Dr. Arthur P. June 24, 1974.
Ellison, Dr. John M. June 21, 1974.
Hancock, Dr. Gordon B. May 26, 1968; September 4, 1969.
Logan, Dr. Rayford W. June 28, 1974.
Mays, Dr. Benjamin E. June 20, 1974.
St. Martin, Mrs. Betty. June 26, 1974.

Individual Evaluation Forms

Bozeman, Dr. Herman H. April 1, 1976.
Dabney, Mr. Thomas L. March 6, 1976.
Daniel, Dr. Walter G. March 10, 1976
Proctor, Dr. Samuel D. April 8, 1976.
Russell, Dr. Wendell P. March 29, 1976.
Shannon, Dr. David. March 26, 1976.
Walker, Dr. Wyatt T. April 5, 1976.

Newspapers

Baltimore *Afro-American*, June 27, July 4, August 1, 27, 1942.
New York *Amsterdam News*, January 5, 1949; March 6, 1954.

Saint Louis *Argus*, March 18, 1955; November 6, 1959; February 26, April 1, 1960.

Oklahoma City *Black-Dispatch*, November 7, 1942; April 17, 1943.

Tampa *Bulletin*, July 5, 1952; April 11, 25, 1953.

Kansas City *Call*, February 14, March 21, April 18, May 9, 16, 1958; June 19, December 4, 1959; January 9, 1960.

Durham *Carolina Times*, January 22, 1938; September 23, 1939; September 14, 28, October 12, December 14, 1940; June 21, 29, July 5, November 20, December 13, 20, 1941.

Raleigh *Carolinian*, July 10, October 23, November 13, 20, 1954; February 5, 12, 19, April 2, May 7, 28, August 6, 1955.

Atlanta *Constitution*, December 18, 1942.

Pittsburgh *Courier*, May 31, July 12, 1930; September 19, 1931; February 18, 1933; September 15, 1934; March 16, 23, April 20, 1935; September 2, 9, December 2, 30, 1939; March 30, December 7, 14, 21, 1940; January 25, 1941; February 14, November 14, 1942; November 14, 1959.

Atlanta *Daily World*, December 12, 1939; August 13, September 16, 26, October 13, 20, December 29, 1940; June 29, July 25, December 12, 1941; December 5, 10, 1959.

Louisville *Defender*, August 6, September 17, December 3, 5, 1959.

Oklahoma *Eagle*, December 17, 1959.

Dallas *Express*, July 14, 1951.

West Palm Beach *Florida News*, January 24, 1953.

Houston *Informer*, April 2, 1943; July 15, 1952; February 27, 1960.

Norfolk *Journal and Guide*, July 31, 1921–August 8, 1970.

Norfolk *Ledger-Dispatch*, December 16, 1942.

Chicago *Negro Voice*, November 10, 1959; January 19, February 8, 1960.

Charleston *News and Courier*, November 11, 12, 28, 1898.

Richmond *News Leader*, March 17, 1926; August 28, 1935; November 6, 1936; December 16, 1942; January 12, 1952.

Richmond *Planet*, February 21, December 11, 1920; July 31, 1921; February 11, July 8, 1922; January 19, September 27, 1924; March 25, April 11, 18, 25, May 2, 1925; November 15, December 27, 1930; September 29, November 17, December 1, 1934; October 24, 1936.

Lima *Post*, May 28, October 2, 1954; May 13, 1955.

Westchester County *Press*, December 5, 1959; January 9, March 26, 1940.

Indianapolis *Recorder*, February 13, August 20, 1960.

Richmond *St. Luke Herald*, February 2, August 24, 1929.

Florida *Sentinel,* January 1, 1955.

Richmond *Shepherd's Voice*, December 1925; January 1926.

Florida *Star*, July 9, 1951.

Dallas *Star Post*, February 1, 15, 1958.

Shreveport *Sun*, June 21, 1952.

California *Sun Reporter*, April 18, 1953.

Columbia *State*, November 9, 1898; January 25, 1907; March 16, 1909.

Miami *Times*, January 3, 1953; December 11, 1954; April 6, October 15, 1955; October 26, December 28, 1957.

Richmond *Times-Dispatch*, June 8, February 28, 1929; June 23, 1940; January 18, 19, 1941; April 10, December 18, 1942; November 13, 21, 27, 30, 1943; November 4, 1948; February 24, 1955.

Philadelphia *Tribune*, October 19, 1957; March 21, 28, April 5, 26, May 3, 1958; November 4, 1959.

Savannah *Tribune*, November 21, 1959; March 5, 26, 1960.

Norfolk *Virginian-Pilot*, December 16, 1942.

Birmingham *World*, February 27, 1960.

Publications of Gordon Blaine Hancock

Hancock, Gordon B. "Booker T. Washington: His Defense and Vindication," *Negro Digest*, XIII (May 1964), 5–10.

_____. "The Challenge to Christianity Today," *Home Mission College Review*, I (March 1928), 25–29.

_____. "The Changing Status of Negro Labor," *Southern Workman*, LX (August 1931), 351–360.

_____. "The Color Challenge," *The Oracle*, XIX (March 1940), 5–6, 19.

_____. "The Commercial Advertisement and Social Pathology," *Social Forces*, IV (June 1926), 812–819.

_____. *Interracial Hypertension*. Atlanta: Commission on Interracial Cooperation, July 1942.

_____. "Needed . . . A Southern Charter for Race Relations," *Southern Frontier*, III (April 1942), 1, 3.

_____. "Orthodox Christianity, Does It Handicap Negro Progress?" *The Messenger*, IX (September 1927), 278–279.

_____. "Our Coming Captivity," *Southern Workman*, LIX (April 1930), 153–160.

_____. "Race Relations in the United States: A Summary," in Logan, Rayford W., ed. *What the Negro Wants*. Chapel Hill: University of North Carolina Press, 1944.

_____. "The South's Greatest Vision," *Southern Vision*, I (June 1943), 1, 4.

_____. *Supplementary Facts Pertaining to the Centennial Issue of the Virginia Union Bulletin*. Richmond: Virginia Union University, 1966.

_____. "Thinking in Ultimate Terms," *Southern Workman*, LVIII (July 1929), 291–297.

_____. "Three Elements of African Culture," *Journal of Negro History*, VIII (July 1923), 284–300.

_____. "When the Manna Faileth," *Opportunity*, VI (May 1928), 133–135.

_____. "Writing a 'New Charter of Southern Race Relations,'" *New South*, XIX (January 1964), 18–21.

Reference Tools

Fleming, G. James, and Burckel, Christian E., eds. *Who's Who in Colored America 1950*. Yonkers-on-Hudson, N. Y.: Christian E. Burckel and Associates, 1950.

The National Cyclopedia of American Biography, XXII. New York: James T. White and Co., 1932.

Work, Monroe N., ed. *Negro Year Book: An Annual Encyclopedia of the Negro 1931–1932*. Tuskegee: Negro Year Book Publishing Co., 1931.

Yenser, Thomas., ed. *Who's Who in Colored America, 1941, 1942, 1943, 1944*. New York: Who's Who in Colored America Corp., 1941–1944.

General Works

Bardolph, Richard. *The Negro Vanguard*. New York: Vintage Books, 1959.

Franklin, John Hope. *From Slavery to Freedom: A History of Negro Americans*. 4th rev. ed. New York: Alfred A. Knopf, 1974.

Gunther, John. *Inside U.S.A.* New York: Harper and Brothers, 1947.

Huggins, Nathan, Kilson, Martin, and Fox, Daniel, eds. *Key Issues in the Afro-American Experience*, II. New York: Harcourt Brace Jovanovich. 1971.

Merton, Robert K. *Social Theory and Social Structure*. New York: The Free Press, 1949.

Sinclair, William A. *The Aftermath of Slavery: A Study of the Condition and Environment of the American Negro*. Boston: Small, Maynard and Co., 1905.

Biographies and Autobiographies

Cayton, Horace R. *Long Old Road*. New York: Trident Press, 1965.

Dabney, Wendell P. *Maggie L. Walker and the Independent Order of Saint Luke: The Woman and Her Work*. Cincinnati: Dabney Publishing Co., 1927.

Du Bois, W. E. B. *The Autobiography of W. E. B. Du Bois: A Soliloquy on Viewing My Life from the Last Decade of Its First Century,* ed. Herbert Aptheker. New York: International Publishers, 1968.

_____. *Dusk of Dawn: An Essay toward an Autobiography of a Race Concept.* New York: Harcourt Brace and Co., 1940.

Dykeman, Wilma, and Stokely, James. *Seeds of Southern Change: The Life of Will Alexander.* Chicago: University of Chicago Press, 1962.

Gordon, Asa H. *Sketches of Negro Life and History in South Carolina.* Orangeburg, S. C.: Privately printed, 1929.

Harlan, Louis R. *Booker T. Washington: The Making of a Black Leader 1856–1901.* New York: Oxford University Press, 1972.

Mason, Lucy Randolph. *To Win These Rights: A Personal Story of the CIO in the South.* New York: Harper and Brothers, 1952.

Mays, Benjamin E. *Born to Rebel: An Autobiography.* New York: Charles Scribner's Sons, 1971.

Uya, Okon E. *From Slavery to Public Service: Robert Smalls, 1839–1915.* New York: Oxford University Press, 1971.

Robeson, Paul. *Here I Stand.* Boston: Beacon Press, 1971.

Special Studies

Baker, Paul E. *Negro-White Adjustment: A Study of the Interracial Movement.* New York: Association Press, 1934.

Barron, Milton L., ed. *American Minorities.* New York: Alfred A. Knopf, 1957.

Blackwell, James E., and Janowitz, Morris, eds. *Black Sociologists: Historical and Contemporary Perspectives.* Chicago: University of Chicago Press, 1974.

Bracey, John H., Meier, August, and Rudwick, Elliott, eds. *The Black Sociologists: The First Half Century.* Belmont, Calif.: Wadsworth Publishing Co., 1971.

Brisbane, Robert H. *The Black Vanguard: Origins of the Negro Social Revolution 1900–1960.* Valley Forge, Pa.: Judson Press, 1970.

Bullock, Henry A. *A History of Negro Education in the South from 1619 to the Present.* Cambridge, Mass.: Harvard University Press, 1967.

Bunche, Ralph J. *The Political Status of the Negro in the Age of FDR.* Ed. Dewey W. Grantham. Chicago: University of Chicago Press, 1973.

Buni, Andrew. *The Negro in Virginia Politics 1902–1965.* Charlottesville: University Press of Virginia, 1967.

Burrell, W. P., and Johnson, D. E., Sr. *Twenty-Five Year History of the Grand Fountain of the United Order of True Reformers 1881–1905.* Richmond: United Order of True Reformers, 1909.

Çorey, Charles H. *A History of the Richmond Theological Seminary with Reminiscences of Thirty Years' Work among the Colored People of the South*. Richmond: J. W. Randolph Co., 1895.

Crum, Mason. *Gullah: Negro Life in the Carolina Sea Islands*. Durham: Duke University Press, 1940.

Dabney, Virginius. *Below the Potomac: A Book About the New South*. New York: Appleton-Century, 1942.

——————. *Liberalism in the South*. Chapel Hill: University of North Carolina Press, 1932.

——————. *Virginia: The New Dominion*. New York: Doubleday and Co., 1971.

Dalfiume, Richard M. *Desegregation of the U. S. Armed Forces: Fighting on Two Fronts 1939–1959*. Columbia, Mo.: University of Missouri Press, 1969.

Davis, Allison. *Deep South: A Social Anthropological Study of Caste and Class*. Chicago: University of Chicago Press, 1941.

Davis, Allison, and Dollard, John. *Children of Bondage: The Personality Development of Negro Youth in the Urban South*. Washington, D. C.: American Council on Education, 1940.

Davis, Frank G. *The Economics of Black Community Development: An Analysis and Program for Autonomous Growth and Development*. Chicago: Markham Publishing Co., 1972.

Du Bois, W. E. B., ed. *The College-Bred Negro*. Atlanta University Publications No. 5. Atlanta: Atlanta University Press, 1900.

——————. *The College-Bred Negro American*. Atlanta University Publications No. 15. Atlanta: Atlanta University Press, 1910.

——————. *Efforts for Social Betterment Among Negro Americans*. Atlanta University Publications No. 14. Atlanta: Atlanta University Press, 1910.

——————. *The Negro in Business*. Atlanta University Publications No. 4. Atlanta: Atlanta University Press, 1899.

——————. *The Souls of Black Folk: Essays and Sketches*. Chicago: A. C. McClurg and Co., 1903.

Faris, Robert E. L. *Chicago Sociology 1920–1932*. San Francisco: Chandler Publishing Co., 1967.

Fisher, Miles Mark. *Negro Slave Songs in the United States*. Ithaca, N. Y.: Cornell University Press, 1953.

——————, ed. *Virginia Union and Some of Her Achievements*. Richmond: Virginia Union University, 1924.

Frazier, E. Franklin. *The Negro Family in Chicago*. Chicago: University of Chicago Press, 1932.

Garfinkel, Herbert. *When Negroes March: The March on Washington Movement in the Organizational Politics for FEPC*. Glencoe, Ill.: The Free Press, 1959.

Gill, Robert L. *The Omega Psi Phi Fraternity and the Men Who Made its History: A Concise History.* Washington, D.C.: Omega Psi Phi Fraternity, Inc., 1963.

Gossett, Thomas F. *Race: The History of an Idea in America.* Dallas: Southern Methodist University Press, 1963.

Graves, John Temple. *The Fighting South.* New York: G. P. Putnam's Sons, 1943.

Greene, Lorenzo J., and Woodson, Carter G. *The Negro Wage Earner.* Washington, D. C.: Association for the Study of Negro Life and History, 1930.

Harlan, Louis R. *Separate and Unequal: Public School Campaigns and Racism in the Southern Seaboard States 1901 –1915.* New York: Atheneum, 1968.

Harris, Abram L. *The Negro as Capitalist: A Study of Banking and Business Among American Negroes.* Philadelphia: American Academy of Political and Social Science, 1936.

Harris, Abram L. and Spero, Sterling D. *The Black Worker: The Negro and the Labor Movement.* New York: Columbia University Press, 1931.

Johnson, Charles S. *Growing Up in the Black Belt: Negro Youth in the Rural South.* Washington, D. C.: American Council on Eduction, 1941.

_____. *Into the Main Stream: A Survey of Best Practices in Race Relations in the South.* Chapel Hill: University of North Carolina Press, 1947.

_____. *The Negro College Graduate.* Chapel Hill: University of North Carolina Press, 1938.

_____. *The Negro in American Civilization: A Study of Negro Life and Race Relations in the Light of Social Research.* New York: Henry Holt and Co., 1930.

_____. *Patterns of Negro Segregation.* New York: Harper and Brothers Publishers, 1943.

_____. *Shadow of the Plantation.* Chicago: University of Chicago Press, 1934.

_____. *A Preface to Racial Understanding.* New York: Friendship Press, 1936.

_____. *To Stem This Tide: A Survey of Racial Tension Areas in the United States.* Boston: The Pilgrim Press, 1943.

Johnson, Charles S., Embree, Edwin R., and Alexander, Will W. *The Collapse of Cotton Tenancy.* Chapel Hill: University of North Carolina Press, 1935.

Johnson, James Weldon. *Negro Americans, What Now?* New York: The Viking Press, 1934.

Klineberg, Otto. *Race Differences.* New York: Harpers and Brothers Publishers, 1935.

LaFarge, John. *Interracial Justice: A Study of the Catholic Doctrine of Race Relations.* New York: America Press, 1937.

Laidler, Harry W., ed. *The Role of the Negro in Our Future Civilization*. New York: League for Industrial Democracy, 1942.

Leuchtenberg, William E. *Franklin D. Roosevelt and the New Deal 1932 – 1940*. New York: Harper and Row Publishers, 1963.

Levitan, Sar A., Johnston, William B., and Taggart, Robert. *Still a Dream: The Changing Status of Blacks Since 1960*. Cambridge, Mass.: Harvard University Press, 1975.

Logan, Rayford W., ed. *What the Negro Wants*. Chapel Hill: University of North Carolina Press, 1944.

Mays, Benjamin E., and Nicholson, Joseph W. *The Negro's Church*. New York: Institute of Social and Religious Research, 1933; reprinted New York: Russell and Russell, 1969.

Moton, Robert Russa. *What the Negro Thinks*. Garden City, N. Y.: Doubleday, Doran and Co., 1929.

Myrdal, Gunnar. *An American Dilemma: The Negro Problem and Modern Democracy*. New York: Harper and Row Publishers, 1944.

Newby, I. A. *Black Carolinians: A History of Blacks in South Carolina from 1895 to 1968*. Columbia: University of South Carolina Press, 1973.

Odum, Howard W. *Race and Rumors of Race: Challenge to American Crisis*. Chapel Hill: University of North Carolina Press, 1943.

Pickens, William. *The New Negro: His Political, Civil, and Mental Status, and Related Essays*. New York: Neale Publishing Co., 1916; reprinted New York: AMS Press, 1969.

Powdermaker, Hortense. *After Freedom: A Cultural Study in the Deep South*. New York: The Viking Press, 1939.

Powell, Adam Clayton, Jr. *Marching Blacks: An Interpretive History of the Rise of the Black Common Man*. New York: Dial Press, 1945.

Redding, J. Saunders. *On Being Negro in America*. Indianapolis: Bobbs-Merrill, 1951.

Rose, Peter I. *The Subject Is Race: Traditional Ideologies and the Teaching of Race Relations*. New York: Oxford University Press, 1968.

Rose, Willie Lee. *Rehearsal for Reconstruction: The Port Royal Experiment*. Indianapolis: Bobbs-Merrill, 1964.

Silberman, Charles E. *Crisis in Black and White*. New York: Random House, 1964.

Sternsher, Bernard, ed. *The Negro in Depression and War: Prelude to Revolution 1930 –1945*. Chicago: Quadrangle Books, 1969.

Stonequist, Everett V. *The Marginal Man: A Study in Personality and Culture Conflict*. New York: Charles Scribner's Sons, 1937.

Tindall, George B. *The Emergence of the New South 1913 –1945*. Baton Rouge: Louisiana State University Press, 1967.

_____. *South Carolina Negroes 1877 –1900*. Baton Rouge: Louisiana State University Press, 1952.

Thompson, Daniel C. *The Negro Leadership Class*. Englewood Cliffs, N. J.: Prentice-Hall, Inc., 1963.

Watson, Goodwin, ed. *Civilian Morale*. Boston: Houghton Mifflin Co., 1942.

Weare, Walter B. *Black Business in the New South: A Social History of the North Carolina Mutual Life Insurance Company*. Urbana: University of Illinois Press, 1973.

Weatherford, Willis D., and Johnson, Charles S. *Race Relations: Adjustment of Whites and Negroes in the United States*. Boston: D. C. Heath Co., 1934.

Wesley, Charles H. *History of Sigma Pi Phi: First of the Negro-American Greek-Letter Fraternities*. Washington, D. C.: Sigma Pi Phi Fraternity, 1954.

Wolseley, Roland E. *The Black Press U. S. A.* Ames: Iowa State University Press, 1971.

Wolters, Raymond. *Negroes and the Great Depression: The Problem of Economic Recovery*. Westport, Conn.: Greenwood Publishing Corp., 1970.

Woodward, C. Vann. *The Strange Career of Jim Crow*. New York: Oxford University Press, 1955.

Wright, Richard. *12 Million Black Voices: A Folk History of the American Negro*. New York: The Viking Press, 1941.

Young, James O. *Black Writers of the Thirties*. Baton Rouge: Louisiana State University Press, 1973.

Dissertations

Alexander, Ann F. "Black Protest in the New South: John Mitchell, Jr. (1863–1929) and the Richmond *Planet*." Ph.D. Dissertation, Duke University, 1972.

Brown, Emma Wesley. "A Study of the Influence of the Philosophies of Accommodation and Protest on Five Colleges Established in Virginia for Negroes, 1865–1940." Ed.D. Dissertation, Columbia University, 1967.

Burrows, Edward F. "The Commission on Interracial Cooperation, 1919–1944: A Case History of the Interracial Movement in the South." Ph.D. Dissertation, University of Wisconsin, 1954.

Gavins, Raymond. "Gordon Blaine Hancock: Southern Black Leader in a Time of Crisis, 1920–1954." Ph.D. Dissertation, University of Virginia, 1970.

Gilpin, Patrick J. "Charles S. Johnson: An Intellectual Biography." Ph.D. Dissertation, Vanderbilt University, 1973.

Hall, Jacqueline D. "Revolt against Chivalry: Jessie Daniel Ames and the Women's Campaign against Lynching." Ph.D. Dissertation, Columbia University, 1974.

Heinemann, Ronald L. "Depression and New Deal in Virginia." Ph.D. Dissertation, University of Virginia, 1968.
Matthews, Carl Stanley. "After Booker T. Washington: The Search for a New Negro Leadership, 1915–1925." Ph.D. Dissertation, University of Virginia, 1971.
Pride, Armstead S. "A Register and History of Negro Newspapers in the United States: 1827–1950." Ph.D. Dissertation, Northwestern University, 1950.

Theses

Bartle, Barbara B. "Virginius Dabney: Southern Liberal in the Era of Roosevelt." M.A. Thesis, University of Virginia, 1968.
Houser, Henry P. "The Southern Regional Council." M.A. Thesis, University of North Carolina, 1950.
Leary, William H. "Race Relations in Turmoil: Southern Liberals and World War II." M.A. Thesis, University of Virginia, 1967.
Lewis, Frank P. "A History of the Baptist General Association of Virginia, Colored." B.D. Thesis, Virginia Union University, 1937.
Neustadt, Margaret Lee. "Miss Lucy of the CIO: Lucy Randolph Mason, 1882–1959." M.A. Thesis, University of North Carolina, 1969.

Articles

Alexander, Will. "Our Conflicting Racial Policies," *Harper's Magazine*, CXCL (January 1945), 172–179.
"Biographical Sketch of Luther Porter Jackson, 1892–1950," *Negro History Bulletin*, XIII (June 1950), 195–197.
Bond, Horace Mann. "Negro Leadership since Washington," *South Atlantic Quarterly*, XXIV (April 1925), 115–130.
——————. "Should the Negro Care Who Wins the War?" *Annals*, CCXXIII (September 1942), 81–84.
"Booker T. Washington and Higher Education," *University Journal*, I (December 1901), 2–3.
"Booker T. Washington at Virginia Union University," *University Journal*, I (March 1901), 10.
Browne, Vincent J. "A Program for Negro Preparedness," *Opportunity*, XVIII (August 1940), 230–231.
"Building a Post-War South," *Southern Frontier*, V (October 1944), 30.
Bunche, Ralph J. "Education in Black and White," *Journal of Negro Education*, V (July 1936), 351–358.

_____. "The Negro in the Political Life of the United States," *Journal of Negro Education*, X (July 1941), 573–579.

"By the Sword," *Opportunity*, XVII (October 1939), 290.

Calverton, V. F. "Orthodox Religion, Does It Handicap Negro Progress?" *The Messenger*, IX (July 1927), 222, 236.

Cayton, Horace R. "Negro Morale," *Opportunity*, XIX (December 1941), 371–375.

Clark, Kenneth B. "Morale of the Negro on the Home Front: World Wars I and II," *Journal of Negro Education*, XII (Summer 1943), 417–428.

Clement, Rufus E. "Black GI Joe Comes Home," *Southern Frontier*, VI (October 1945), 3–4.

Cohn, David L. "How the South Feels," *Atlantic Monthly*, CLXXIII (January 1944), 47–51.

Dabney, Thomas L. "Local Leadership among Virginia Negroes," *Southern Workman*, LIX (January 1930), 31–35.

Dabney, Virginius. "Nearer and Nearer the Precipice," *Atlantic Monthly*, CLXXI (January 1943), 94–100.

_____. "The South Marches On," *Survey Graphic*, XXXII (November 1943), 441–443, 462–463.

Davis, Ralph N. "The Negro Newspapers and the War," *Sociology and Social Research*, XXVII (May–June 1943), 373–380.

Dorsey, Emmett. "The Negro and Social Planning," *Journal of Negro Education*, V (January 1936), 105–109.

Du Bois, W. E. B. "As the Crow Flies," *Crisis*, XL (September 1933), 197.

_____. "A Negro Nation Within the Nation," *Current History*, XLII (June 1935), 265–270.

_____. "Postscript," *Crisis*, XLI (June 1934), 182–183.

"Du Bois Literary Society," *University Journal*, III (May 1903), 11.

"Editorial," *Crisis*, XXXVII (January 1930), 11.

Eisenberg, Bernard. "Kelly Miller: The Negro Leader as a Marginal Man," *Journal of Negro History*, XLV (July 1960), 182–197.

"The Failure of the Negro Church," *The Messenger*, II (October 1919), 6.

"The Fate of Democracy," *Opportunity*, XX (January 1942), 2.

Finkle, Lee. "The Conservative Aims of Militant Rhetoric: Black Protest during World War II," *Journal of American History*, LX (December 1973), 692–713.

Foreman, Clark. "Race Tension in the South," *New Republic*, CVII (September 21, 1942), 340–342.

Frazier, E. Franklin. "The Du Bois Program in the Present Crisis," *Race*, I (Winter 1935–1936), 12–13.

_____. "The Status of the Negro in the American Social Order," *Journal of Negro Education*, V (July 1935), 293–307.

Gavins, Raymond. "Gordon Blaine Hancock: A Black Profile from the New South," *Journal of Negro History*, LIX (July 1974), 207–227.

_____. "Gordon Hancock: An Appraisal," *New South*, XXV (Fall 1970), 36–43.

Graves, John Temple. "The Chance Taking South," *Virginia Quarterly Review*, XXI (Spring 1945), 161–173.

_____. "The Fighting South," *Virginia Quarterly Review*, XVIII (Winter 1942), 60—71.

_____. "The Southern Negro and the War Crisis," *Virginia Quarterly Review*, XVIII (Autumn 1942), 500–517.

Gross, H. B. "The Essential Factors of Race Education," *University Journal*, I (January 1901), 5–7.

Hamlin, Wilhelmina E. "Luther Porter Jackson—Historian," *Negro History Bulletin*, VI (November 1942), 34–35.

Hill, T. Arnold. "Open Letter to Mr. William Green, President, American Federation of Labor," *Opportunity*, VIII (February 1930), 56–57.

_____. "The Plight of the Negro Industrial Worker," *Journal of Negro Education*, V (January 1936), 40–47.

"Historical News," *Journal of Negro History*, XLVIII (January 1963), 68.

Holtzclaw, William H. "Present Status of the Negro Farmer in Mississippi," *Southern Workman*, LIX (August 1930), 339–344.

Jackson, Luther P. "The Call for the Highly Educated," *Virginia State College Gazette*, XLV (December 1939), 34–40.

_____. "Citizenship and Government Participation," *Virginia State College Gazette*, XLIII (November 1937), 10–15.

_____. "Citizenship Training—A Neglected Area in Adult Education," *Journal of Negro Education*, XIV (Summer 1945), 477–487.

_____. "The Early Strivings of the Negro in Virginia," *Journal of Negro History*, XXV (January 1940), 25–34.

_____. "Improving the Economic Status of the Negro through Governmental Participation," *Virginia Teachers Bulletin*, XVI (January 1939), 15, 42.

_____. "The Petersburg Negro Business Association," *Virginia State College Gazette*, XLIV (November 1938), 19–20.

_____. "Race and Suffrage in the South since 1940," *New South*, III (June–July 1948), 1–26.

_____. "Unexplored Fields in the History of the Negro in the United States," *Negro History Bulletin*, VIII (December 1944), 57–58, 65–67.

_____. "The Work of the Association and the People," *Journal of Negro History*, XX (October 1935), 385–396.

"The Job," *Southern Workman*, LXI (January 1932), 4.

Johnson, Charles S. "The Negro and the Present Crisis," *Journal of Negro Education*," X (July 1941), 585–595.

_____. "The Present Status of Race Relations in the South," *Social Forces*, XXIII (October 1944), 27–32.

_____. "Social Changes and Their Effects on Race Relations in the South, " *Social Forces*, XXIII (March 1945), 343–348.

_____. "The Will and the Way," *New South*, II (May 1947), 1–5, 8.

Johnson, Guy B. "Southern Offensive," *Common Ground*, IV (Summer 1944), 87–93.

Johnston, James H. "Luther Porter Jackson, 1892–1950," *Negro History Bulletin*, XIII (June 1950), 195–197.

Jones, Lester M. "The Editorial Policy of Negro Newspapers of 1917–18 as Compared with That of 1941–42," *Journal of Negro History*, XXIX (January 1944), 24–31.

Leap, W. L. "The Standard of Living of Negro Farm Families in Albemarle County, Virginia," *Social Forces*, XI (October 1932), 258–262.

Logan, Rayford W. "Negro Status Under the New Deal," *Sphinx*, I (May 1937), 38–39.

"Lynching and Liberty," *Crisis*, XLVII (July 1940), 209.

Matney, W. C. "Exploitation or Cooperation?" *Crisis*, XXXVII (January 1930), 11–12.

Mays, Benjamin E. "We Are Unnecessarily Excited," *New South*, IX (February 1954), 1–3.

Miller, Kelly. "The Farm—The Negro's Best Chance," *Opportunity*, XIII (January 1935), 21–25.

_____. "Orthodox Christianity, Does It Handicap Negro Progress?" *The Messenger*, IX (August 1927), 254–255.

Morgan, T. J. "Virginia Union University: What It Signifies," *Virginia Union Bulletin*, LXX (October 1969), 6–16.

"Now Is the Time Not to Be Silent," *Crisis*, XLIX (January 1942), 7.

Odum, Howard W. "The Position of the Negro in the American Social Order in 1950," *Journal of Negro Education*, VII (July 1939), 587–594.

"On the Southern Scene," *New South*, VII (May 1952), 5–7.

Ottley, Roi. "A White Folk's War?" *Common Ground*, II (Spring 1942), 28–31.

"Our Place and Work in the 20th Century," *University Journal*, I (January 1901), 8.

Padmore, George. "The Second World War and the Darker Races, *Crisis*, XLVI (November 1939), 327–328.

Palmer, L. F. "He Left a Lonesome Place," *Negro History Bulletin*, XIII (June 1950), 198, 214.

"Personal," *Journal of Negro History*, XLII (January 1957), 86.

"Phi Beta Kappa Members Debate Action on Segregated Schools," *Southern Frontier*, VI (October 1945), 2.

Porter, Dorothy B. "Luther P. Jackson: Bibliographical Notes," *Negro History Bulletin*, XIII (June 1950), 213–215.

Powell, Adam Clayton, Jr. "Is This a 'White Man's War'?" *Common Sense*, XI (April 1942), 111–113.

"Program for 1945," *Southern Frontier*, V (December 1944), 1–2.

Randolph, A. Philip. "The Economic Crisis of the Negro," *Opportunity*, IX (May 1931), 145–149.

"A Recommendation for Action by the Southern Governors," *New South*, IV (May–June 1949), 1–2.

Redding, J. Saunders. "A Negro Speaks for His People," *Atlantic Monthly*, CLXXI (March 1943), 58–63.

_____. "Southern Defensive I," *Common Ground*, IV (Spring 1944), 35–42.

Reid, Ira DeA. "Some Aspects of the Negro Community," *Opportunity*, X (January 1932), 19–20.

_____. "The White Primary Problem Must Be Solved to Strengthen Democracy," *New South*, I (January 1946), 7.

"Resolution Launching the Southern Regional Council," *Southern Frontier*, IV (August 1943), 1.

Schuyler, George S. "A Long War Will Aid the Negro," *Crisis*, L (November 1943), 328–329, 344.

Simpson, Josephus. "Are Colored People in Virginia a Helpless Minority?" *Opportunity*, XII (December 1934), 373–375.

Sitkoff, Harvard. "Racial Militancy and Interracial Violence in the Second World War," *Journal of American History*, LVIII (December 1971), 661–681.

Smith, Lillian E. "Addressed to White Liberals," *New Republic*, CXI (September 18, 1944), 331–333.

_____. "Growing Up into Freedom," *Common Ground*, IV (Autumn 1943), 47–52.

_____. "Southern Defensive II," *Common Ground*, IV (Spring 1944), 43–45.

"The Southern Regional Council," *Southern Frontier*, V (March 1944), 1, 4.

Streator, George. "In Search of Leadership," *Race*, I (Winter 1935–1936), 19–20.

"The Supreme Court Considers Segregation," *New South*, IV (November–December 1949), 4–6.

"Supreme Court Considers Segregation," *New South*, VII (December 1952), 1–5.

Thompson, Charles H. "Mr. Dabney and the 'Precipice,'" *Journal of Negro Education*, XII (Spring 1943), 141–143.

_____. "The American Negro and the National Defense," *Journal of Negro Education*, IX (October 1940), 547–552.

"Toward the South of the Future: A Statement of Policy and Aims of the Southern Regional Council," *New South*, VI (December 1951), 1–2.

Trigg, Harold L. "SRC and Southern Progress," *New South*, I (November 1947), 7–8.

"Two Opinions on School Segregation," *New South*, VI (July 1951), 7–11.

"Virginia Conference on Race Relations," *Southern Workman*, LX (January 1931), 6.

"White House Blesses Jim Crow," *Crisis*, XLVII (November 1940), 350–351, 357.

Wilkins, Josephine. "An Answer When Negro Southerners Spoke," *New South*, XIX (January 1964), 22–26.

"Will Missouri University Admit Negro Students?" *Southern Frontier*, V (February 1944), 3.

Woodson, Carter G. "Negroes Not United for Democracy," *Negro History Bulletin*, VI (May 1943), 170, 177–178.

Wynes, Charles E. "The Evolution of Jim Crow Laws in Twentieth Century Virginia," *Phylon*, XXVIII (Winter 1967), 416–425.

Young, P. B. "Civics and Citizenship," *Virginia Teachers Bulletin*, XII (January 1935), 4–6.

—————. "Diminishing Distances," *Southern Workman*, LXII (October 1933), 392–397.

—————. "The Extent and Quality of the Negro Press," *Southern Workman*, LXII (August 1937), 323–329.

—————. "The Negro Press—Today and Tomorrow," *Opportunity*, XVII (October 1939), 204–205.

Index

at Virginia Union, 31–33; becomes minister of Moore Street Baptist Church, 33–35; discusses role of Negro church, 37–38; advocates interracial cooperation, 51–52; warns of Negro job-displacement, 54–55; analyzes Negro labor, 55–56; preaches hold your job, back to the farm, and double duty dollar ideas, 59–69; takes pragmatic stand on segregation, 69–71; encourages blacks to vote for Roosevelt, 71; criticizes New Deal, 72–75; promotes black self-help, 76–97; experiences disappointment, 97–98; becomes militant in pronouncements, 98–99; defines issues during World War II, 115–117; meets with Jessie Daniel Ames, 117–118; hosts meeting of black leaders, 119–121; attacked, 121–122; central figure in the Durham conference, 124–125, 127; prominent in founding of Southern Regional Council, 140–146; involved in postwar debate on segregation 148–159; discusses race issues during 1950's and 1960's, 168–177; evaluated, 180–190.

Hancock, Marie D.: background of and marriage to Gordon B. Hancock, 13–14; persuades husband to relocate, 16; assists her husband at Colgate University, 17; recalls interracial experiences in Hamilton, New York, 18; arrives in Richmond, 22; sustains her husband through troubles at Virginia Union, 82; attends her husband at his death, 179

Hancock, Robert Wiley: birth, marriage, and family of, 7–8; ministry and influence on Gordon B. Hancock, and death of, 8–9

Harding, Warren G., 22

Harris, Abram L., 89, 185; distinguished Virginia Union graduate, 26; student of Gordon B. Hancock and Clarence M. Maloney, 30; rejects Moton's optimism, 51; examines Negro's relations with labor movement, 56–57, 58; objects to doctrine of black support for black business, 67–68;

Hartshorn Memorial College, 23

Harvard University, 3, 63, 78, 98, 121, 186; influences Hancock's sociological perspectives, 18–19

Hastie, William H., hails Durham manifesto, 130

Hatcher, James S., argues with McKinney and Hancock about John Jasper, 36–37

Hayes, Gregory W., refuses to accept American Baptist Home Mission Society control of Virginia Seminary and College, 25

Hayes, Roland, 76

Haynes, George E.: black sociologist, 19; studies Negro life, 27; influences Luther P. Jackson, 109

Henderson, J. Raymond, 26

Henderson, Thomas H.: graduates from Virginia Union, 26; advises Hancock, 165–166; warns students, 176

Hill, T. Arnold, 26; denounces organized labor's narrowness, 53; says New Deal discriminates against Negroes, 73

Hitler, Adolph, 98

"Hold Your Job," 59

Homestead Project, 72

Hoover, Herbert, 64, 71, 114

Hope, John, 93

Houston, Charles, warns Democrats about black vote, 74

Houston *Informer*, 93, 119, 129

Houston, Texas, Riot of 1917, 16

Howard University, 12, 21, 22, 30, 62, 82, 83, 89, 107, 130, 135, 163, 188

Hubert, Benjamin F., 63; urges Negroes to leave urban centers, 65–66

Hucles, Henry B., 48

Huntington High School, 120

Independent Order of Odd Fellows, 6

Independent Order of St. Luke, 44

Industrial History of the Negro Race, The, 45

Interracial cooperation, 178–179, 181, 185, 186, 187, 190; Hancock's first steps toward, 15; nature of Hancock's commitment to, 18, 28; Moton is hopeful of, 51; advocated by Hancock, 52; annual conference hears report on Richmond Negroes, 54; necessity of, 58; Hancock works for, 77; through scientific information, 79; involves closing cultural gap, 81; nuances of 84–85; through assimilation and cultural pluralism, 91; Hancock participates in continuing dialogue on, 91–92; is strained by black-white tensions, 93–97; theme is criticized by Richard H. Bowling, 97; seen as solution to wartime racial tensions, 114, 117–119; sought by black